INSIDE THE SOVIET MILITARY

INSIDE THE SOVIET MILITARY
CAREY SCHOFIELD
WITH PHOTOGRAPHS BY LEONID YAKUTIN

Preface by Marshal Dmitri Yazov, Minister of Defense of the Soviet Union
Foreword by Christopher Donnelly, Sovietologist in Residence, NATO

Abbeville Press · Publishers
New York · London · Paris

Acknowledgments

The author and photographer would like to express their gratitude to all the officers and men of the Soviet Army who helped in the preparation of this book. First and foremost we would like to thank Army General Mikhail Moiseev, Army General Dmitri Lizichev, Colonel General Gennadi Stefanowski, and Major General Valery Manilov, all of whom lent us their unfailing support and showed us endless kindness and tolerance throughout our research. A great debt of gratitude is owed to Army General Varennikov, Army General Mikhailov, Colonel General Achalov and Colonel General Deinikin for the practical help and advice that they have given.

Thanks are also due to Admiral Khronopolou, Admiral Kvatov, Lt General Petrov, Major General Lebyed, Colonel Solyuyanov, Colonel Bashkirov, Colonel Yakunov, Colonel Kashin, Lt Colonel Bolyenko and Lt Colonel Dementiev for their kindness and hospitality. We would also like to thank Sergei Klokov, Vladlen Klokov, Marina Kuznetsova, Viktor Likhachev, Lt Colonel Sosnitsky, Colonel Globenko, and Alexander Vorobiov of the USSR Commission for UNESCO.

Carey Schofield and Leonid Yakutin would also like to thank Igor Melekh (for his advice and assistance with linguistic and technical matters), Boris Chernov, our kind and infinitely knowledgeable driver, and Aleksei Paladin, who provided useful insights into life in the barracks. But above all we would like to record our gratitude to Sergei Lavrov, the official interpreter. The Ministry's decision to allocate Major Lavrov to our project was the greatest stroke of luck to befall us in the course of our work. Throughout the two years he worked with us, he was singleminded and goodnatured, and, although he was working absurdly long hours, he never asked for any personal reward. Igor Azarionok was very helpful during the early stages of our work.

Laurence King of John Calmann & King Ltd supported us morally and financially. Without his commitment to the project and his encouragement it would have been impossible to produce this book. We would also like to thank our resourceful and untiring editor, Elizabeth Thussu, her henchman Kevin Childs, Judy Rasmussen, Robert Updegraff, Amelia Bowden and Lorna Damms, who displayed patience and skill above and beyond the call of duty in knocking our material into shape.

The author would also like to thank Alexandra Murdoch for advice on military discipline, and Paul Williams and Kieran Walsh for help with questions of supply and support. Like most Londoners with an interest in Russian history, Carey Schofield owes to Johnny Stuart a debt that can never be repaid.

First edition

This book was designed and produced by John Calmann and King Ltd, London
Designer: Robert Updegraff

Quality Printing and Binding by
Toppan Printing (Singapore) PTE., Ltd
38 Liu Fang Road
Jurong Town, Singapore 2262

Library of Congress Cataloging-in-Publication Data

Schofield, Carey.
  Inside the Soviet military / text by Carey Schofield: photographs by Leonid Yakutin; preface by Dmitri Yazov; foreword by Christopher Donnelly.
    p.   cm.
  Includes index.
  ISBN 1–55859–160–5
  1. Soviet Union—Armed Forces.   2. Soviet Union—Armed Forces—Pictorial works.   I. Title.
UA770.S329   1991
335'.00947—dc20   90–14436
                                                            CIP

CONTENTS

Preface

Marshal Dmitri Yazov
MINISTER OF DEFENSE OF THE SOVIET UNION

When diplomats talk about peace it is what one expects. When generals start to talk about peace, then something extraordinary is happening, something demanding radical action. As professionals, soldiers know better than anyone the capabilities of modern weapons, the ecological, demographic, and socio-economic consequences of their application. More clearly than anyone else they understand the irrationality of war in which such weapons are deployed. War, whether nuclear or conventional, has ceased to be an acceptable form of politics, because it is no longer possible for there to be a winner. Everyone becomes a loser, condemned to degeneration and death – the aggressor, the victims of aggression, even peoples living on other continents. Which is why the avoidance of war is a task demanding the active and constructive participation of all peoples and states, without exception. Mankind must, using all its combined strengths, break out of the rut of confrontation, military rivalry, and the arms race, which have brought it to the very brink of the global abyss.

The paradox of the age lies in the fact that the mastery of nuclear energy and the breakthrough into space have shown not only the greatness of the human mind but the frailty of human civilization. It has become clear that we are, all of us living on this planet, very different, but nonetheless indivisible parts of one civilization, of one single, interlinked and mutually dependent world. The path to this understanding was far from simple, and was by no means strewn with roses. The peoples of this world, both in the past and those alive today, have passed through great tragedies, bloody civil strife, conflicts, fratricidal struggles, and the traumas and many millions of victims of two world wars, to the realization, at last, that men were indeed created to work together. And this has found expression in the form of a new political thinking, which focuses attention not on what divides states and peoples but on what unites them – on universal values. If in the past a neglect of these values led, in the very worst cases, to the destruction of states and peoples, then nowadays it could lead to a global catastrophe, which is why the most important of these values is peace. To maintain it is to guarantee the survival of the human race.

It is significant that disarmament started with nuclear weapons, as they pose the greatest threat to peace. But this threat does not disappear with nuclear weapons, and that is why we consider it important to extend the disarmament process to other types of weaponry. To this end, the Soviet Union has embarked on a large-scale, unilateral reduction of its armed forces by 500,000 men, 10,000 tanks, 8,500 artillery systems, more than 820 combat planes, and significant quantities of other hardware. This decision of ours has been consistently carried out, and will be implemented in full, as planned, by the end of 1991, under conditions of *glasnost* and openness. So the world at large has every opportunity to see for itself the goodwill of the Soviet Union and that our word is our bond.

Echo II (two) cruise missile submarines at the beginning of the working day. These boats are 390 feet long with a displacement of 5,800 tons (dived). While they are in harbor routine maintenance work will be carried out and the officers and men will catch up on their sleep. No submariner ever has enough uninterrupted sleep at sea.

There are three cornerstones without which all the structures of modern security would be insecure and unstable. The first of these is a clear understanding that force, including military force and the threat to use it, must be excluded from the range of options available in international politics. The second is the fact that national, as well as global security can and must be achieved by giving unquestioned preeminence to political means. The third is that peoples must have the unconditional right to choose what course their society will follow. In such conditions, in our opinion, the main hope and the main guarantor of success in building a new model for security lie in the transition from a situation of mistrust and suspicion between opposing states and their allies to one of mutual understanding and cooperation, from overkill to a level just sufficient for defense, from confrontation to dialogue.

This argument for the construction of a stable system of peace, security, and cooperation corresponds exactly to the defense policy of the Soviet Union. It is embodied in the new Soviet military doctrine, as formulated in 1987, which is exclusively defensive in character, and entirely devoted to the task of preventing war. This, by the way, is the first time in history that such a task has been put into such a doctrine. According to the doctrine, the Soviet Union undertakes that it will under no circumstances instigate military action against any state or alliance of states, unless it finds itself the object of military attack; it will never use nuclear weapons in a first strike; it has no territorial ambitions, and regards no state as its enemy. Practical evidence of the defensive nature of our doctrine is the liquidation of short- and medium-range missiles. At the time of writing, all Soviet and American short-range missiles have been liquidated under strict reciprocal controls, as have more than 80 per cent of Soviet and over 50 per cent of American medium-range missiles.

We have withdrawn our forces from Afghanistan, thereby confirming our adherence to the resolution of regional problems and conflicts by political means. In 1989 we unilaterally withdrew 500 nuclear warheads from the territory of our European allies. In bilateral agreements with Czechoslovakia, Hungary, and Mongolia we are withdrawing our forces from these countries and will complete the withdrawal in 1991.

All these, and many other practical measures, taken together constitute a fundamental reform of the Soviet military which has been underway for over three years, from the moment the defensive military doctrine was passed. The essence of the reform lies in organizing the personnel, structure, and equipment of the Soviet Armed Forces, taking into consideration the achievements of the negotiated disarmament process and the real actions of the West, in accordance with the defensive military doctrine and the principle of 'adequacy.' The most important goals of the reform are replacing quantity with quality; optimizing personnel; updating equipment; reorganizing the structure of the armed forces; improving the training and education of serving soldiers to guarantee the implementation of duties with the minimum expenditure of means and resources; organizing cadres made up of volunteers and conscripts with general military duties; unity of command organized on a democratic, legal basis; and internationalizing the way of life and training of the troops by extra-territorial postings.

The military reform being undertaken in the Soviet defense mechanism is an all-state task. It is being carried out in tandem with *perestroika*, the renovation of our society, organically linked to the practical resolution of problems of political and economic reform, the creation of a socialist, legal state, including radical changes in military legislation. The goals and scope of the military reform are such that, as estimates show, they will take a long time to implement.

At the heart of all the military reforms lies the reorganization of the armed forces of the USSR. In tackling the problems of the reorganization we are working from the basis of 'adequate defense' and 'defensive strategy.' Naturally, it must be said, that is as we understand these concepts. The idea of 'adequate defense' is based on the gradual reduction, on a reciprocal basis, of the levels of military confrontation to the point where they fulfill a purely defensive purpose. The realization of the concept of 'adequate defense' presupposes military and strategic parity while simultaneously reducing troop levels, and the step-by-step reduction and eventual elimination of nuclear weapons. According to the 'defensive strategy,' any warning strike is ruled out. In the event of any aggression against the Soviet Union the basis of any action by our forces will be defense.

Guided by the principle of defensive strategy, we are not only carrying out large reductions in our troop levels and weaponry, as I have already discussed, but we are radically altering the organizational structure of our armed forces. Recently we saw the abolition of two military districts as a result of mergers between Central Asia and Turkestan, and the Volga and Ural commands. The administration of one missile and 2 combined arms armies, and of 5 army corps has been disbanded. Six missile and 21 combined arms divisions (13 motorized rifle, 8 tank) have been removed from the armed forces, as well as a series of formations and units of other types of troops. The structure of combined arms forces is being reformed in a defensive manner. The number of tanks is being reduced by 20 to 40 per cent, and landing craft and other 'attack' vehicles are being withdrawn, while 40 warships are being decommissioned from the Soviet Navy.

As a result of carrying out the whole complex of changes, the armed forces of the USSR have taken on a qualitatively new look. By means of reductions in troops and weapons on both sides, closer to the bounds of 'adequacy,' a point will be reached at which it will be possible to carry out effectively all the tasks of defense, whether strategic, operational, or tactical, with only minimal expenditure. It is planned to remove civil defense forces and road-building units from the armed forces. As a result of the amalgamation of units with similar military tasks, the types of forces and soldiers are changing fundamentally. The number and make-up of formations and units in the strategic rocket forces is being reduced. The number of military districts, armies, and divisions of the ground forces will be reduced. Radical changes are planned in the staffing, structure, and principles of the military application of air defense forces. In the air force it is planned to change aviation units, to radically reduce the types of technology employed, and to improve the system of bases. Major changes are planned for the personnel, structure, equipment, and deployment of the navy. It is intended to considerably improve the reliability and effectiveness of the weaponry and military technology of all branches of the armed forces.

Today approximately one third of our army and navy are volunteers who have chosen military service as their profession – officers, ensigns, warrant officers, and several other categories of servicemen. They hold crucial positions from the point of view of war readiness. The rest of the ranks are made up of conscripts. We plan to raise the level of professionalism in our armed forces and to maintain conscript and contract volunteer systems with a gradually increasing emphasis on various categories of soldiers serving on a contract basis. With this in mind, the system of training military cadres will be reformed. Alongside the reduction in the number of military colleges and academies it is intended to reduce their intake by 15 to 20 per cent. At the same time the educational element in the training at military colleges and institutes will be greatly increased. During the course of the administrative reforms of the armed forces we intend to reduce the administrative staff of central, district, and army branches by 15 to 20 per cent.

One of the priorities for reforming the armed forces is the further democratization of military life. This process is part of the socialist renewal of society. A special state-wide program of social welfare for serving soldiers and their families has been worked out, which includes those discharged from service. This constitutes a vast improvement in the standard of living of the serving soldier, the provision of housing, and legal rights. In short, by the end of the twentieth century the Soviet Armed Forces will have a different image, equipped with the most up-to-date hardware, showing a high degree of professionalism, and true to the military duties and the heroic traditions of service to the Fatherland. These are real, practical steps that illustrate the new Soviet policy on defense and security, our defensive military doctrine. In parallel with these steps we are actively working to ratify the reciprocal measures taken thus far to produce equal and identical security for both sides.

The problem of building up mutual trust overshadows all others. In general, military openness should become the universal norm of international life. It seems natural to us that measures for strengthening trust, a guarantee of predictability of military activity, should encompass the whole spectrum – not just ground forces, but air and sea forces, and should include a policy of 'open skies,' 'open seas,' 'open land,' and an 'open cosmos.' All these form the elements of a new, comprehensive system of security, the particular core of which, in our view, must be a structure free of opposing blocs, with a supportive construction, a common European home built by our combined efforts. Such a system is capable of guaranteeing an end to war for mankind, and the establishment of a genuinely safe, democratic, nuclear-free, non-violent world on this planet.

Such, in the most general outline, is the political background to the Soviet defensive reassessment, the raising of the armed forces of the USSR onto a modern level. This is also the context in which it has become possible to write this book, which is also in its own way a breakthrough – overcoming ideological and psychological obstacles and barriers, through a tissue of prejudices, conjecture, and fears based on untruths, through to the task of erasing the image, ossified over many decades of the 'cold war,' of the enemy in the form of the Soviet Armed Forces. I suggest that the role of 'discoverer' in the journalistic and authorial sense belongs by right to the prime mover behind this book – Carey Schofield. She visited many military posts, units, and warships, which for a long time had been by tradition considered 'closed' to foreigners, and not only to them. She met and talked with Soviet servicemen – from the ranks to the Minister of Defense. Her interest, and, I hope, sufficiently objective view of the armed forces of the USSR, not just from the outside, but from within, will enable a wider readership in the West to see the Soviet army and navy, the Soviet soldier and officer as they really are – living people with their own merits and shortcomings, problems and worries, traditions and hopes, devotion to their people and homeland, with a desire to be on good terms with all countries and for a safe, lasting peace.

With sincere and deep respect

Dmitri Yazov
MARSHAL OF THE SOVIET UNION

Foreword

Christopher Donnelly, Sovietologist in Residence, NATO

The East–West confrontation as we know it after 1945 was not a confrontation of weapons but of men. It is men who make wars, weapons are merely their tools. The *cause* of conflict is in our hearts and minds, not in our hands. In seeking to defuse tension and replace confrontation with cooperation, the reduction of armaments plays, to be sure, a most important role, particularly in the building of confidence. But what *causes* peace is a change in attitude, a change in relations between men and between peoples.

It is this which makes Carey Schofield's book so very important. Indeed, it is a landmark in the process of the changes now underway in East–West relations for two important reasons. First, never before has a Western observer been allowed to see and report on the Soviet Armed Forces from the inside, never has such unrestricted access to military facilities and personnel been granted. That it was granted at all is amazing. That it has been granted so completely and free from official restraint is one of the most heartening signs for the development of that dialogue essential to a permanent improvement of relations between the USSR and the West.

Second, the book is important because it lays bare, as does no other book, the human side of the Soviet military machine. To be sure, other excellent books have addressed the Soviet soldier, his way of life and training. Former Soviet soldiers have described their experiences. But this book does more than that. It looks with a sharp eye, both critical and compassionate, at the soldiers' way of life, both as the Soviet soldiers themselves see it and as it appears to a Western eye. It is this combination of views – the Soviet point of view contrasted with the unclouded view of an outsider with a Western perspective – which provides for the first time a credible, three-dimensional image of the Soviet fighting man.

Miss Schofield accomplishes her task in a most readable way. She illustrates and illuminates her facts and comments with personal anecdotes and observations that do more than anything else to explain to us the human face of the Soviet Armed Forces. Her insight will help Western readers to understand the apparent contradictions and anomalies that so often spring up to confuse us when we attempt to understand the Soviet military system.

It is particularly important today that we *do* understand how the Soviet military system works, thinks, and acts, because our attitude toward the Soviet military will be the single most important factor in our developing relations between the West and the USSR. The events in Eastern and Central Europe over the last two years have destroyed the security architecture that characterized European and transatlantic politics for forty years. In its place, the nations of Europe and North America are faced with the need to develop new security structures, retaining and building on those institutions that have been successful and that inspire confidence in all, amending and altering those that are no longer totally appropriate, and discarding those institutions that have failed. This will be a difficult and possibly painful process, and it will only be possible at all if there is frankness, flexibility, and understanding on both sides.

For the Westerner – European or North American, soldier or civilian, politician or voter – the problems of coming to grips with the Soviet military system and its part in a future European and world order are formidable. It is difficult enough for citizens of any country to understand their own armed forces if they have never seen service. It is very hard for citizens of one country to understand and empathize with the people of another. It is harder still for those brought up in one ideological framework to understand and see eye-to-eye with those raised in another. But in trying to understand the Soviet Armed Forces all three dimensions are inextricably interlinked. It is in disentangling these strands that this book is so useful, because it helps us to distinguish, in the actions, reactions, and attitudes of the Soviet military, what is a *military* viewpoint, what is based on *ideological* concepts, and what is the essence of national *Russian* interest.

The Soviet Army that the author describes is not only the military machine of a state in turmoil, it is itself in turmoil, and it is the key player in the rethinking of a strategic position that has been accepted unthinkingly for over forty years. It is of great importance to us to be able to assess how the process of political change in the Soviet Union will affect the armed forces, now that the Communist Party no longer plays the leading role in Soviet political life. We no longer know how the armed forces are controlled and how military policy is formulated. As the Soviet Union moves toward a much looser kind of federation, without the overriding faith in the communist ideology that has in the past provided the rationale for both state and military, the question must arise as to how the Soviet Armed Forces can survive in their present form. What will become the focus of loyalty? Why should an Uzbek soldier continue to obey a Russian officer? Will we see the Soviet Army become the Russian Army and, if so, what will be the basis of relations with non-Russian troops in the army? We must expect to see fundamental changes in the organizational basis, structure, composition, and manning of the armed forces in the very near future.

However, as democratization becomes more and more a feature of Soviet life, the role the armed forces play in the political transformation of the country is bound to increase. The military, as it decommunizes, has begun to be involved in the parliamentary system and influence the political process as never before. Mid-level officers are very vocal in support of radical change, whereas officers of the General Staff largely support the nationalist conservative cause.

The impact of the armed forces on political change; the means by which they might be brought under some kind of parliamentary control; the potential for a coup or for giving undemocratic support for a 'military candidate' to lead the country; all these are considerations that are not just important to Soviet citizens but are of absolutely fundamental importance to us, as we plan the development of our relationship with the Soviet Union. If we hope to establish a stable security system that involves not only Europe and North America, but also enfolds in its cloak the Soviet Union, however that country might develop, we need to know for certain what the position of the armed forces will be in that society.

At a more mundane, though more immediate level, the current East–West negotiations on arms control and confidence building require that we understand the fears of the Soviet military for the security of their country. These are fears based not just on a perception of the West's military power and political intentions, but also on the effects of current political and nationalist turmoil in the Soviet Union on the viability of the Soviet Armed Forces and their performance in war. There are well-founded military concerns arising from the effective collapse of the Warsaw Pact as a military alliance, the unification of Germany, the need to withdraw from East and Central Europe, and the consequent need, from the soldiers' point of view, to rethink completely the strategy, operation, and tactics by which the Soviet Armed Forces might have to defend the country. For whatever happens in East–West relations, certain military realities will not change. Defensive doctrines may be adopted, but offensive operations will remain essential to their implementation. Tanks are as essential today to the defender as to the attacker. It will remain the duty of the Soviet General Staff to plan for victory in war, should it break out. We must appreciate these military realities and not base our attitude toward future East–West relations on wishful thinking born out of military ignorance.

This is the final, and perhaps the most useful, message of the book. That, despite its problems and the problems of the Soviet society, the Soviet Army, with its roots firmly in the Russian military tradition, is, and is likely to remain, a good army, an effective army. It will face tremendous problems in the coming years and can be expected to undergo profound changes. But it has immense institutional strength and flexibility, and is highly unlikely to lose its military capabilities. The better we know its human element the better we will be able to understand the changes we perceive in it, the role it will play in society, and the impact it will have on the future relationship that develops between the Soviet Union, or Russia, and the rest of Europe and the world.

1 INTRODUCTION

The Soviet Army is unlike any other that the world has ever seen. It wields such colossal power that, for nearly half a century, its specter has dominated Western foreign policy and defense spending. Its assets include 4 million men, one hundred and forty motorized rifle and tank divisions, and the world's largest nuclear arsenal. It can also draw on trained reserves of 55 million former soldiers and officers. It exists in order to defend the largest country on earth, stretching almost halfway around the globe and covering one sixth of the inhabited surface of the world. From the Baltic Sea to the Pacific, the distance is 6,000 miles; Leningrad is nearer to New York than it is to Vladivostok. Although, in principle, every young male Soviet citizen is called up to serve for two years in the army, it remains something of a mystery, even to many Russians. Civilian intellectuals, especially, have little contact with the officer corps. The army is a separate world, with its own traditions, its own morality, its own arcane mysteries and esoteric knowledge.

I lived with the Soviet Army throughout 1989 and a large part of 1990. During that time revolution spread across Eastern Europe, sweeping away the communist regimes that had provided the 'buffer zone' between the Soviet Union and Western Europe for so long. The Warsaw Pact appeared to be disintegrating before our very eyes, threatening the very existence of NATO. But inside the armed forces it seemed that these events passed almost unnoticed. Each revolution came so suddenly that it had been accepted before anyone had foreseen it. For no sooner had these momentous changes gathered pace in Eastern Europe than the Soviet Union itself seemed to be seriously threatened from within. Political ferment, separatist movements in the Republics, and the social upheavals caused by Gorbachev's reforms seemed to assault the very fabric of the state. These tensions within the country were so alarming that they distracted ordinary officers from affairs abroad. They could live without the satellite states, if necessary, but the idea that the Union itself was breaking up really distressed them. Only the discussions concerning the reunification of Germany seemed to stir any interest in the average officers' mess — no Russian soldier could hear that sort of talk without feeling some alarm. But the problems at home were so great that they even overshadowed what would previously have been unthinkable. There were not only the crises facing the country as a whole. The army had its own problems, which, as we shall see, were coming to a head at precisely this moment.

Surface-to-air missiles (S-125, *Pechora*) at the air defense base at Kotlas. These are two-stage, solid fuel missiles, fired from twin quadruple launchers (launch weight 2,000 pounds). From the moment the transporter arrives at the site, it will take 20–25 minutes to prepare the missiles. The NATO name for them is SA-3.

I was keen to study the lives of the people who make up the Soviet Armed Forces. Originally, it was going to be an objective study, with no first-person intrusion into the text. It seemed important not to trivialize the subject matter with comments and opinions, or to allow it to degenerate into a travelogue. But, while working with the army, I realized that I could only write the book from a personal point of view. The last few years have seen such phenomenal change in the Soviet Union, that there are no longer many matters about which it is possible to make unqualified statements with any degree of confidence. Everything has been in flux. No one, it seems, has known what is really going on, from one republic to another, from day to day, at some times even from hour to hour. In these circumstances only the bravest, or those with the least direct personal experience of the situation would claim to be fully aware of what is happening. In the end, I can only report on what I saw, and what the people to whom I spoke told me. This is what I have set out to do. I am not attempting, here, the sort of analysis that is so competently carried out by Western military commentators, nor am I concerned to compare the Soviet Armed Forces with those of any other country: that would be a different book.

In 1988 I asked the Soviet Ministry of Defense to let me write this book. I argued that a greater understanding of the people who make up the Soviet military might help to reduce the level of fear with which we in the West view it. After much discussion, I was finally given permission. The agreement was that the Army would provide an interpreter, who would travel with me to the units. I had permission to work with a Western photographer, but it soon became clear that this was an unnecessary complication. I had met Naval Captain First Rank Yakutin some time before, in Moscow, and had realized at once that he would be the perfect partner for an undertaking such as this, requiring patience and endurance. His firsthand knowledge of the workings of the armed forces was also, of course, invaluable.

We began our work during the final stage of the Soviet withdrawal from Afghanistan. Most of the next eighteen months was spent traveling to different parts of the Soviet Union. We crossed the country from Leningrad in the west to Kamchatka in the east, from Murmansk in the north to Termez in the south. We traveled by train, ferry, aircraft (military and civilian), and by jeep. We became experts on the different types of desert to be found in the Soviet Union, and connoisseurs of the varieties of melon grown in Central Asia. I learned to shoot with a rifle, a machine gun, and a pistol. I practiced *rukopashni boi* with a general, rode with the cavalry, and drove a tank. I climbed mountains, and was even given permission to make a parachute jump.

Over this period I had contact with hundreds of soldiers, sailors, and officers. I spoke to the Minister of Defense, Marshal Yazov. I met Army General Lizichev, then head of the Main Political Directorate of the Army, and Army General Moisev, the Chief of the General Staff, several times. I interviewed the chiefs of all five armed services and other senior military figures, including the head of Soviet Military Intelligence (GRU), in the first interview that any occupant of the post had ever given. Apart from my formal meetings with these people, I began, after a while, to run into them informally at the military gatherings that I tried to frequent. For example, there was a very good turnout of the top brass for the annual military academies' graduation ceremony at the Kremlin in June. At the Navy Day celebrations in Sevastopol we met, by chance, Army

General Lizichev, who happened to be on holiday nearby. I became steeped in the culture of the army. I began to understand the implications of remarks made by soldiers and officers and to recognize the different character types that we met. I heard the favorite army jokes over and over again. I became bored with the clichés of military life and fascinated by the variations between one unit and another. Slowly, I started to feel that I understood something of the spirit of the army.

Our work was coordinated by the Main Political Directorate of the army (GlavPU), since they were then responsible for all press work within the army. Initially, I was given permission to visit about half the sites listed in my original application, but, in order to acquire a broader-based view of the armed forces I was concerned to increase the number of units that I was allowed to visit. This was not always easy. Every army in the world worries about security and is therefore more than apprehensive about allowing access to foreign journalists. This exacerbated the usual difficulties that foreigners encounter when trying to make arrangements in the Soviet Union. The book was a major exercise in determining the limits of *glasnost* in the Soviet Army, and those limits were changing all the time. Eventually I was allowed to visit nearly all the places on my original list, although my only contact with the Strategic Rocket Forces was in connection with the elimination of missiles. I was not able to secure permission to visit a strategic rocket base with modern missiles. But this was the only major disappointment. Frankly, I was given much greater access than I had expected. It is worth pointing out that, in the end, the Soviet Ministry of Defense gave me more wide-ranging opportunities than most of its Western counterparts would have been likely to.

Of course there were difficulties, usually at the local level, and over the months I developed ways of coping with them. I quickly learned that each morning I should inquire carefully what I was going to be shown that day. If it was less than the agreed program, I would refuse to leave my room. In this way, the local officers responsible for the visit would be unable to report to Moscow that it had been a success. I would agree to leave my room only once we had ascertained that we really were going to be shown what we had been promised. Sometimes it emerged that the difficulty was with local security people, who seemed to feel that the arrival of a foreigner was the chance of a lifetime. My visit was the justification for years of vigilance in remote garrisons. Finally, they had the chance to prevent somebody from doing something, and they were not going to miss it. At other times, after long arguments, the officer in charge would confess, for example, that he could not show me any tanks moving because there was a shortage of fuel. In any case, it is not easy to write about an army. The worst people hover around, making sure that one has the correct spelling of their names. The best of them dislike journalists on principle. They do not want to be written about and, invariably, the best stories are prefaced by 'this is not for publication, but . . .' Despite this, I have written about certain individuals who interest me. I have attempted to do this without betraying confidences. Occasionally, I have omitted specific details and in one or two cases I have altered some element so that the characters cannot be identified. I do not wish to imply that I found the officers unhelpful, or the army as a whole unsympathetic. Nothing could be further from the truth. Almost everyone I spoke to, from the highest reaches of the General Staff to the youngest conscript, seemed anxious to help Captain Yakutin and me in our work.

The author undergoing small-arms training in the airborne regiment in Fergana, under the tuition of the commander, Hero of the Soviet Union Colonel Aleksandr Solyuyanov. Pistol-shooting is all in the mind, he says. Don't spend time staring at the target, worrying about it. Just relax your whole body and stand with your arms by your side. Then with confidence – look at the target, raise your arm and shoot. It works when he does it.

Working in the rain at the Vladivostok marine base, autumn 1989. Standing behind the author is Major Sergei Lavrov, the Ministry of Defense interpreter.

The place of the army in the Soviet Union

From World War II until the accession of Mikhail Gorbachev, the Army benefited from a constant barrage of propaganda intended to maintain its public prestige. You could not escape the glory of the Soviet Army in those years; everywhere in the Union you would be bombarded with reminders of it, disseminated by all possible means. Most of it was uninformative and fatuously uncritical, feeble litanies of praise and wan hagiographies of heroes living and dead. However, the reason for the unceasing promulgation of all this material is not hard to find. The Great Patriotic War was, for the Soviet Union, a trauma that is still difficult for Westerners to understand. One adult male in four was killed or seriously injured during the war. Well over a million people are estimated to have died in Leningrad alone between 1941 and 1945 (the number of dead at Hiroshima and Nagasaki combined is usually reckoned to be 130,000). Fifty years is not a long period of rehabilitation for a country that has suffered such horror. The constant replaying of the victories, the construction of vast and theatrical war memorials all over the country, and the oversimplified history really struck a chord in the hearts of Russians. Every family that survived the war had lost members. Forty years after the Nazis had been vanquished, Soviet war veterans were still accorded privileges and respect that had never been enjoyed by those of Britain or America. But the men and women who came back from the war could reasonably be seen as the representatives of those who did not. It is easy to sneer now at the crude official attempts to keep alive the memory of the war; those who were there tend not to do so.

The horrors of World War II have not been forgotten in the Soviet Union; far more respect is shown for war veterans than in any of the other allied countries.

The continual reminders of the war were not necessary only as a mark of piety toward the dead. They were also needed to unite the population behind the government. Successive Soviet governments wanted to concentrate attention on the victory because it was the one uncontroversial achievement of the country, the one of which the entire country could be proud. The Germans treated everyone with appalling brutality, even those who had been prepared to collaborate, on the grounds that nobody could be worse than Stalin. Communists, Christians, and Jews, peasants, and workers all had reason to identify with the army and its eventual triumph. Each republic played its part, contributing to the war effort and sharing in the vicissitudes of the war. Against all the odds, despite Stalin having systematically undermined the armed forces, the people of the Soviet Union beat back the Germans by sheer force of will. You could say what you liked about any other aspect of the country, but you could not take away or belittle that achievement. So, for reasons that are easy to understand, the army played a large role in the country's official self-portrait for many years.

With the arrival of Mr. Gorbachev things started to change. Gorbachev realized that the country's economic machinery needed to be speeded up and one of the first buzz words of his rule, *uskoreniye* (acceleration), reflected this. It soon became clear, however, that the economic failures were only symptoms, caused by an underlying decay and that the machinery would have to be 'rebuilt' – hence *perestroika*. But the difficulty was that during the Brezhnev period – the so-called 'stagnation period' – all instability had been written out of the political system. *Glasnost* was Gorbachev's campaign to create the conditions that were necessary for any reforms to succeed.

After the withdrawal from Afghanistan, many tanks, such as these T-62s, were transported to their ultimate destinations by rail.

Although it is often translated as 'openness,' the word *glasnost* in fact derives from the Russian *golos* (voice), and really means to stand up and shout, to voice one's complaints. Gorbachev wanted to bring the country's problems out into the open, and to encourage people to complain. It was not until around the beginning of 1989 that ordinary people really began to take him at his word. But once they did, there was no stopping them. It suited Gorbachev that the army should come in for a generous share of the criticism. First, he thought it economically necessary to switch resources from the military to the civilian sector. Second, he simply had no affection for the army — he had never been a soldier himself. Third, he owed too much to the other pillars of the state — the KGB and the Communist Party — to confront them openly at that time. The army, at this stage, appears to have been unable to reach any real understanding with Gorbachev. Officers of every rank were taken by surprise by the ferocity with which they were suddenly being attacked. They resisted most of the changes that were being suggested, partly because (like all professional soldiers) they tend to be conservative, and partly because many of the far-reaching reforms that were being put forward were, to the military, patently ridiculous.

The public, and especially the media, however, were happy to go along with the criticism of the army. There were several reasons for this. The first was the simple and healthy instinct of reaction. Throughout the years of stagnation the armed forces had been sacrosanct, and people had been told endlessly that they embodied all that was noblest and best in the country. They were, perhaps, not really concerned to assess the behavior of the army and its impact on society, nor to compare it with the other organs of power. They were content to see the army undermined because they were sick of the dreariness of Brezhnevite propaganda. But some of the subsequent revelations were so truly startling that they shocked even those who would by nature have supported the military. The crucial matter that was brought out into the open was *dedovshchina*, the systematic bullying of new conscripts by those who have served longer. Everybody's son was meant to do military service, so if the conditions of this service were intolerable it was a matter of national concern and not merely an internal army affair. In the autumn of 1987 the novel *One Hundred Days Until Demobilization* by Yuri Polyakov was published, which described the bullying in the army from a soldier's point of view. The effect of this novel was 'like an earthquake,' according to soldiers and officers. Any complacency that the army might have enjoyed was shattered as more and more *dedovshchina* stories were made public in the months that followed. The most appalling episode that came to light concerned a conscript called Sokolauskus from one of the Baltic states who, driven to insanity by the brutality of older soldiers, opened fire, killing people as they slept. In fact, the army itself was already aware of the problem and had been taking steps to improve things. Nevertheless, the public discussion of *dedovshchina* seriously damaged its status.

The other key factor determining attitudes to the army was the war in Afghanistan. The last troops were withdrawn in February 1989, at precisely the moment when the public was finding its voice and the trickle of complaints about the difficulties of the Soviet period was turning into a flood. Although nearly 15,000 officers and men had come home in coffins during the ten-year campaign, there had not been extensive public criticism of the war. After the withdrawal the criticism of the Soviet role in

At a collection center just outside Termez a conscript unwinds after the difficulties of the war.

Near the 'Three Brothers' landmark rocks in the harbor at Petropavlovsk-Kamchatka, two Mi-14 search and rescue helicopters take part in a small exercise in the middle of winter.

Afghanistan gained momentum. The army itself was blamed for the political decision to invade, and therefore for the cost in human life. Soon, by some bizarre extension, the army seemed to be being blamed for all the ills of the Stalin and Brezhnev years. At the first session of the newly elected Congress of People's Deputies in 1989 the armed forces came under direct attack, from serving officers as well as from civilians. It was clear by the end of that year that the military had suffered a massive reversal of status. Almost daily, the Soviet press ran stories criticizing the army in one way or another.

At the same time, the military press began to air the grievances of officers themselves. Just as the people of the Soviet Union had found their voice and begun to criticize many aspects of their society, so members of the armed forces were heard to complain about the conditions in which they had to live and work and about the policies of their superiors. Scraps of information picked up from army publications were then used by the media to support their case against the military. Rumor, isolated incidents, lies, misapprehensions, and truth tended to be mixed up in breathless catalogs of supposed abuses. Anyone whose impression of army life was based on these sources would suppose that the armed forces were on the verge of an absolute collapse into disorder, with garrisons breaking down entirely and licentious soldiery running amok. Certain commentators in the West, relying on these sources, drew precisely these conclusions and even in Moscow there were those who would not disagree with them. But what I found while I was with the army during that time did not quite accord with this.

I found an army that was in a state of shock. Not only was the army suddenly subject to widespread criticism, but drastic cuts were being implemented which meant that up to one officer in five might have to go. Therefore, a great many of them were looking over their shoulders, worrying about their jobs. The military community as a whole was having to cope with the fact that the men whose jobs were axed faced an uncertain future, with poor prospects for jobs or housing. I found an army having to cope with conscripting young men at a time when strong antimilitary and even anti-Soviet sentiments were being aired all over the country. Society was being almost torn apart by struggles between interest groups and nationalities, and yet the army was having to weld boys from warring communities into a single fighting force. As civil disorder spread across the country the army was faced with all the inevitable horrors attendant upon such strife. For the first time, on such a large scale, they had to take up the thankless task of policing hostile communities within the Soviet Union. There was an ever-increasing number of thefts of weapons and ammunitions from military bases (250,000 in the first nine months of 1989). There were desertions by soldiers from the minority communities concerned. Even more serious were the outbreaks of fighting among armed civilians who had recently served in the army and therefore knew how to use any piece of equipment that they managed to steal. Numbers of soldiers were killed or wounded in Azerbaijan by former Soviet soldiers using stolen equipment.

Despite all these difficulties, I found an army that was doing its job. I found officers battling to maintain the combat readiness of their units despite the cuts in manpower and material resources and, it appeared, succeeding. They were succeeding by making do and mending, and by working themselves and their men until they dropped. They were succeeding because it did not occur to them that they might fail. Both in the units

A pilot in the cockpit of his aircraft. The air force has not escaped the difficulties with which the armed forces as a whole have had to contend.

threatened by cuts and in those that were not I found officers with an ingrained acceptance of the demands of service life. They were tough, resilient, often kind, sometimes suspicious, and always humorous. I found a system that is, despite all its shortcomings, far more solid than its critics admit. New weapons systems are developed along the lines demanded by the army rather than to suit the convenience of industry, with maintenance schedules sensibly planned for the realities of war. Soviet aircraft, for example, have to be serviced more frequently than their Western counterparts. But, taking into account how brief their expected combat lifetimes are, it is not clear that this puts them at a disadvantage. Much of the army's equipment is sturdy and serviceable, and some creations such as the Kalashnikov automatic, are all-time design classics. This could not be said of many other Soviet products. (The utilitarian chic of the army is recognized by European and American importers of Soviet Army watches and sunglasses, greatly sought after in the West in recent years.)

I approached the officers and men of the Soviet Army in a mood of proper cynicism. I assumed that they would speak to foreigners in pious falsehoods. My instincts were always to believe whatever they told me that reflected badly on the army or that appeared to reveal their negative attitudes toward it. I discounted entirely anything they said that seemed too perfect, too positive, too much part of the machinery of propaganda. I designed a working method that was intended to weed out, as far as possible, the establishment running-dogs who would have wasted my time. I asked to be allowed to speak to soldiers without any officers present, and to choose for myself the soldiers to whom I would talk. I tried to speak to officers I liked at home in the evenings, often over several drinks.

Having taken all these precautions, I came to the conclusion that there is, among the ordinary Russian people, a simple patriotism that hardly exists any more in the West. The strength of the Soviet Army, in the end, is the sense of duty that exists among the officers. Despite all the difficulties the soldiers face, I believe that many of them, too, take pride in serving their motherland. It is extremely hard for many Westerners to appreciate this, but it seems to me that this feeling exists very strongly. It was demonstrated by a silly conscript who cheerfully admitted to disliking army life and to having committed almost every crime in the book, but who took offense when I implied that he was a bad soldier. He insisted that he was just bad at keeping the rules. I shall deal with all these matters in greater detail later, but I should emphasize now that if you cannot admit the possibility of old-fashioned patriotism you will not, in the end, understand the Soviet Army. Ultimately, implacable cynicism is no better a guarantee of arriving at the truth than wide-eyed credulity.

It is important to stress these points because it seems to me that the position of the army has been misrepresented, in both the Soviet Union and the West. When I was living with the army the units we visited were not on the point of collapse, and to suggest that they were would be to underestimate grossly the skills and the character of their officers, and the stability of the army. If my affection for many of the officers and men of the Soviet Army urges me to speak up on their behalf, other, vaguer instincts prompt me to say that I think it would be imprudent for any interested planners, wherever they might be, to underestimate the power and the resolve of this extraordinary fighting force.

A paratrooper wearing the famous blue beret of the airborne forces. It is of no special significance that it does not have the usual red flash – the beret was newly issued and there had not been time to sew it on.

2 THE MILITARY ESTABLISHMENT

Anyone who goes to Moscow, even for the shortest tourist visit, will notice that there seem to be a lot of soldiers about. Despite the fact that a great many jobs in the armed forces have been cut, the military is still far more visible in the Soviet Union than in any Western country. Not only are there soldiers performing the sort of state ceremonial that you might see anywhere (such as guarding the Kremlin), but along almost every street in the center of the city there will be a few officers walking purposefully, clutching their service-issue briefcases. It is also quite likely that there will be a few national servicemen around, making the most of some task that has brought them into town.

The newcomer's impression that this is a country teeming with soldiers is perhaps reinforced because the uniform of the *militsia* (the ordinary, civilian police) has a strong military appearance. Even more significant, for the cityscape of Moscow, is the fact that the Western-style Ministry of Defense civil servant is virtually nonexistent in the Soviet Union. Part of the responsibility for policy-making, which in the West would rest with the minister of defense, has, in the Soviet Union, been vested in the general secretary of the Communist Party and latterly in the president. The Soviet Ministry of Defense is, in effect, the administrative body of the army and the minister is an army officer, as is almost everyone who works under him. The main planning and executive organ of the Ministry of Defense is the General Staff, manned entirely by officers. Almost all the administrators who are needed to run the vast Soviet military machine (and Russians don't skimp on pen-pushers) wear uniform. Consequently, the presence in Moscow of thousands of people who do, in effect, the jobs of civil servants in the General Staff but who look like career soldiers inevitably contributes to the impression of a highly militarized society. However, the basic reason why there seem to be so many soldiers is the fact that the Soviet Army is, simply, very large. Even now, after the loss of 500,000 jobs, it remains the single most formidable fighting force in the world.

Very few countries have such a high percentage of their military establishments in the capital. But in the Soviet Army, there is a very high degree of centralization. The nerve center is the main Ministry of Defense building between Ulitsa Frunze and

An officer cadet (*kursant*) on parade.

The heads of the five armed services on the Mausoleum during the November 1989 Red Square Parade. *Left to right:* Army General Tretyak (Air Defense Forces), Army General Varennikov (Ground Forces), Air Marshal Yefimov (since retired, then the much-loved head of the Air Forces), Army General Maksimov (Strategic Rockets) and Admiral Chernavin (Navy).

Paratroopers marching in Red Square. The official army measurement of Red Square is 350 steps – to be taken at 120 steps a minute. The first in each line should stare straight ahead. The others should keep their eyes fixed on the chest of the fourth man along the row to keep the line straight.

Kalinin Prospekt in the heart of Moscow. The Minister of Defense and the chief of the General Staff have their offices in this building, usually referred to as 'the new General Staff building.' This is to differentiate it from 'the old General Staff building' situated nearby in Gogolovsky Boulevard, from where the rest of the General Staff and the Main Political Directorate work. These two buildings together are officially called 'House Number One' of the Ministry of Defense. 'House Number Two' is in Ulitsa Razina, just off Red Square, with one whole wall overlooking the Kremlin. From this building most of the supply and support work of the army is administered. There is nothing secret about its location. Most officers serving in Moscow know the place, and its function is not considered to be any more sensitive than that of the other main Ministry of Defense buildings, which are public landmarks in the same way that major ministries are in most capital cities. But a surprising number of civilian Muscovites are completely unaware that one of the biggest buildings in Red Square is occupied by the army. 'House Number Three,' on the Frunzenskaya Embankment, is occupied by the administration of the ground forces.

There are many other military buildings dotted around the city such as the Naval Staff in Bolshoi Kozlovsky Pereulok, and the Air Force at Bolshaya Peragovskaya Ulitsa 23. Of the five arms of service only the Strategic Rocket Forces have their headquarters outside central Moscow. Their staff is located at Perkhushkovo, half an hour's drive from Moscow. Then there are the many military colleges and academies in and around the city.

The administration of the army

Control of the armed forces lies with the Minister of Defense and the Main Military Council. This consists of the minister, the head of the Main Political Directorate, the chief of the General Staff, the heads of the five armed services, and all other deputy ministers of defense, including the heads of the Military Inspectorate, Rear Service, and Civil Defense. The Main Military Council is responsible for providing the minister with collective advice on matters of policy, but it is the General Staff that actually implements every decision that is taken. The chief of the General Staff reports directly to the Minister of Defense.

The heads of all the armed services and branches of service are subordinate to the chief of the General Staff. So too is the head of the Main Intelligence Directorate (GRU), whose staff provides much of the information upon which the General Staff depends in its planning. Then again, the Voroshilov Academy of the General Staff is a vitally important center for research and discussion on all operational and strategic matters, and it too comes under the control of the chief of the General Staff. Consequently, the General Staff is more than just the executive organ of the Ministry of Defense. It is also the driving force behind the most important developments in Soviet military thought and probably generates in the first place nearly all of the ideas that it is subsequently asked to put into practice. The Soviet General Staff provides a degree of centralized command over the armed forces unparalleled in today's NATO armies. The strength of the General Staff helps to reduce the interservice rivalries that often bedevil Western armed forces.

Flags of the navy, air and ground forces.

It is fashionable in certain circles in the West to say that the traditional role of the General Staff, in formulating Soviet defense policy, has been largely superseded by Moscow's civilian defense institutes, such as the Institute for Europe, the United States–Canada Institute (often called the Arbatov Institute), and the World Institute of Economic Affairs (IMEMO). The *institutchiks*, as these people are called (not entirely affectionately), have undoubtedly wielded great, if fluctuating, influence over the past few years. They travel to the West, have access to all foreign publications, and meet military experts and opinion-makers wherever they go. They understand public relations and they are masters of the clever and flexible approach to new developments. On the whole they come from the same radical Party/KGB background as the President. They speak Gorbachev's language and therefore have his ear. They are not hidebound by the military obsession with security, so they glean and distribute information freely. But although their presentation is smooth and although they are slick and quick with their advice, some of it is not very good. During the past couple of years they have advocated courses of action that were, in the view of both Western and Soviet military thinkers, military stupidity. The army has had to struggle to ensure that the voice of professional common sense is heard amid the rhetoric. The prominence of the *institutchiks* and their deployment as spokesmen on military matters has made a significant contribution to the decline in the army's prestige during the past couple of years. But it seems to me that their importance, in relation to the General Staff, has been overrated. They are good 'rent-a-quote' performers, but they cannot, in the end, compete with the sheer professionalism of the General Staff. After all, no organization in the world has devoted more energy to studying the art and science of war: in the end its voice will be heard, simply because it has so much more to say.

Perhaps the most important dilemma facing the Soviet Army, and the one that will most influence its future shape and character, is the tricky question of that the next threat will be. It is the traditional job of the General Staff to prepare, in every way, to defend the Soviet Union against any threat. In the past it was as clear in Moscow as it was in Washington and London what this threat would be. But the Russians now have to address the same difficulty as NATO, that is, developing a strategy for an unpredictable future war. The resources are not available for them to anticipate all possible types of war. But without being able to identify the future enemy and the character of the conflict to come, it is difficult for the Soviet Armed Forces to be ready for it without fundamentally altering their approach. The old emphasis on the academic study of future war will have to give way to a more flexible approach.

The importance of the General Staff may be increasing with the current uncertainty about where power really lies in the Soviet Union. During 1990, responsibility for all military matters in the Soviet Union lay with the Presidential Council, and with the President himself, as the commander-in-chief of the armed forces. It was in the Presidential Council, we were told, that major decisions on defense policy would ultimately be taken, including those on resource allocation. But the office of the President and the Presidential Council were only established at the beginning of 1990 and the Council was abolished before the end of the year. The system still appears to be in a state of flux. Nobody really seems to know where power lies, at present. The General Staff, with its inherent stability and expertise, therefore appears all the more authoritative as other structures crumble.

Structure of the USSR Armed Forces

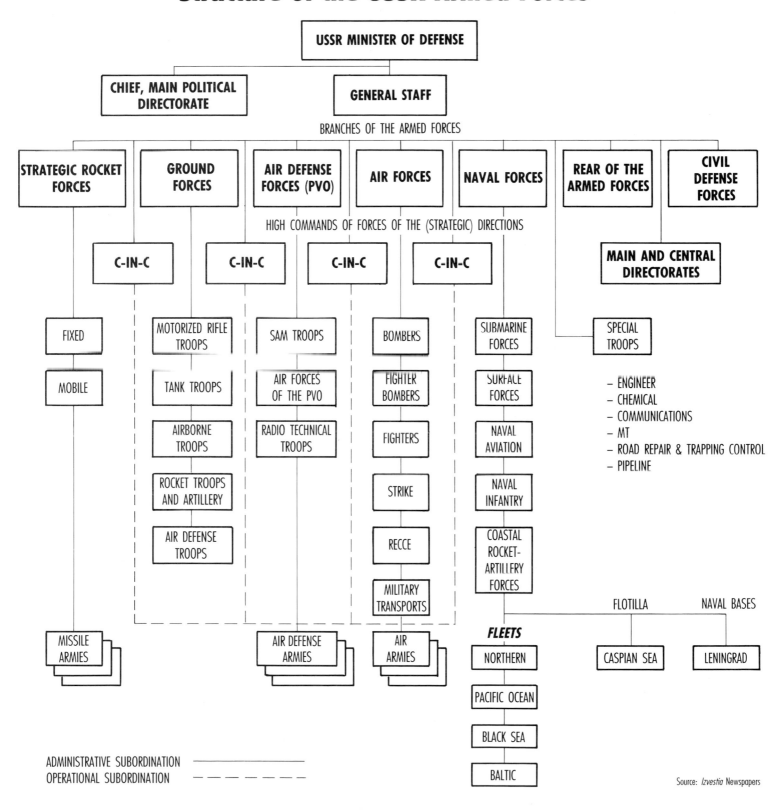

USSR MINISTER OF DEFENSE

CHIEF, MAIN POLITICAL DIRECTORATE

GENERAL STAFF

BRANCHES OF THE ARMED FORCES

STRATEGIC ROCKET FORCES

GROUND FORCES

AIR DEFENSE FORCES (PVO)

AIR FORCES

NAVAL FORCES

REAR OF THE ARMED FORCES

CIVIL DEFENSE FORCES

HIGH COMMANDS OF FORCES OF THE (STRATEGIC) DIRECTIONS

C-IN-C

C-IN-C

C-IN-C

C-IN-C

MAIN AND CENTRAL DIRECTORATES

FIXED

MOBILE

MOTORIZED RIFLE TROOPS

TANK TROOPS

AIRBORNE TROOPS

ROCKET TROOPS AND ARTILLERY

AIR DEFENSE TROOPS

SAM TROOPS

AIR FORCES OF THE PVO

RADIO TECHNICAL TROOPS

BOMBERS

FIGHTER BOMBERS

FIGHTERS

STRIKE

RECCE

MILITARY TRANSPORTS

SUBMARINE FORCES

SURFACE FORCES

NAVAL AVIATION

NAVAL INFANTRY

COASTAL ROCKET-ARTILLERY FORCES

SPECIAL TROOPS

- ENGINEER
- CHEMICAL
- COMMUNICATIONS
- MT
- ROAD REPAIR & TRAPPING CONTROL
- PIPELINE

MISSILE ARMIES

AIR DEFENSE ARMIES

AIR ARMIES

FLEETS

NORTHERN

PACIFIC OCEAN

BLACK SEA

BALTIC

FLOTILLA

CASPIAN SEA

NAVAL BASES

LENINGRAD

ADMINISTRATIVE SUBORDINATION ——————
OPERATIONAL SUBORDINATION — — — — —

Source: *Izvestia* Newspapers

The armed forces

Unlike most Western armies, which consist of an army, a navy and an air force, the Soviet Armed Forces consist of five arms of service (ground forces, navy, air forces, air defense forces, and strategic rocket forces). The first four services are often referred to as 'the army' in informal conversation.

1 The Strategic Rocket Forces (*Raketniye Voiska Strategicheskovo Naznacheniya*) are considered to be the senior service, responsible for all land-based intercontinental and medium-range ballistic missiles.

2 The Ground Forces (*Sukhoputniye Voiska*), easily the largest of the services, consist of about one hundred and forty divisions (maintained at different levels of readiness). The main branches of the ground forces are the motorized rifle troops, tank troops, rocket and artillery troops, army air defense troops, and the airborne forces. The airborne troops (*Vozdushno-Desantniye Voiska*) are, without any question, the most prestigious in the popular Soviet imagination. They have their own commander who is subordinate to the chief of the Ground Forces in peacetime, but during a war would be allocated by the General Staff to frontal or theaters of operation command for specific airborne tasks.

3 The Air Forces (*Voyenno-Vozdushniye Sily*) comprise four main elements — long-range aviation (strategic nuclear bombers), frontal aviation (all tactical aircraft), a number of air armies under central control (light and medium bombers), and transport aviation.

4 The Air Defense Forces (*Voiska Protivovozdushnoy Oboroni*) consist of fighter aviation (aviation regiments with interceptors) and missile forces (surface-to-air missiles), and also a radio-technical branch (radar and other electronic systems) and an antiballistic missile branch. The Soviet Union is divided into air defense districts, but it is worth noting here that air defense is taken so seriously that Moscow is encircled by a double ring of air defense and space missile sites, and Leningrad by a single ring of conventional air defense sites.

The Navy (*Voyenno-Morskoy Flot*), including surface ships and submarines, naval infantry (marines), coastal missiles and artillery and naval aviation, is divided into four fleets: the Northern, the Pacific, the Baltic, and the Black Sea; and one flotilla, the Caspian.

Other branches of the armed forces include engineering troops, chemical defense troops, rear services, and signals and communications troops, each of them coming under the General Staff. There are also construction troops, who participate in both civilian and military building projects, and civil defense troops. These are integrated into the vast Civil Defense network, which has civilian representatives in every farm or factory in the country.

Parallel to these sections of the armed forces there is a peacetime administrative command structure that is simply geographical and, in fact, more important. At present the country is divided into 13 military districts, although the system is being reviewed and may well change. Before the withdrawal from Eastern Europe, the troops there were divided into four groups of forces. The commanders of the military districts come under the chief of the General Staff.

The importance of these military districts lies in the fact that they have to be capable of maintaining themselves and rapidly transforming their forces for wartime operations with very little support from Moscow if hostilities should break out. In peacetime they are responsible for conscription, mobilization, garrisoning, training, and the rear supply of their forces.

The role of the political deputies

The Main Political Directorate of the Soviet Army and Navy (GlavPU) is, to the Western mind, the most bizarre element in the Soviet military system. Throughout the armed forces the commander of every unit, down to company level, had, until recently, a deputy responsible for political affairs, a zampolit. The work of these deputies was coordinated by the Main Political Directorate.

For 70 years the Party considered that it had a duty to oversee the molding of young minds and their subsequent development into ideologically correctly-thinking adults: hence the city streets and schools and workplaces plastered with propaganda posters. The Party's automatic right to the leading place in society has now been challenged, but today's adults grew up in a world where it was taken for granted. This obsession with ideological purity did not originate in Russia with the Bolsheviks. There has always been a debate between orthodoxy and heresy, between, as many Russians would see it, order and chaos. So the idea of an officially appointed propagator of truth, which is completely intolerable to many Westerners, has never been anathema to many Russian minds for very long. However, in the late 1980s, the traditional role of the Main Political Directorate — exercising Communist Party control of the military — was no longer considered acceptable.

After a great deal of argument, it was finally decided in 1990 that GlavPU should be divided into two sections. The larger section is concerned with training and welfare and a separate, much smaller organization deals with Party matters. Most of the zampolits in the army were relieved when these changes were announced. For some time they had, in any case, been devoting most of their time to welfare work, so from their point of view the changes simply ratified the existing situation. In fact, they are still usually referred to as zampolits but they are now free to concentrate on the time-consuming practical problems of the officers and men, especially the hardships faced by officers who are losing their jobs. It is they who are supposed to do whatever is possible to prevent army families from breaking up under the strain of trying to survive in remote and unhealthy outposts of the Union. All that they can do, of course, is to juggle the resources available, in an attempt to alleviate the difficulties of whichever family seems to be in the worst shape at any given moment.

In many units where the conditions are hard, the zampolits themselves are under considerable stress as they shoulder the burdens of other men's misery. A political deputy in an air force unit told us that he holds a weekly surgery, when any of the

The political deputy (zampolit) of the commander of a nuclear submarine belonging to the Pacific Fleet.

A tank company and a motorized rifle company equipped with BMP-1s and BMP-2s formed up during maneuvers in the Byelorussian Military District. The vehicle center left, marked with the number 210 is a BMP-1, those with the thinner cannon, instead of a gun, are BMP-2s.

officers can come to him to discuss personal problems. Week after week, the problems are all the same: housing. He listens to what they have to say, encouraging them to unload their problems. Then he tells them lies. He invents stories about new apartments that are being built, or good, cheap accommodation that will soon be available in the village. He says that to him it seems better to send them back to their wives with some hope rather than with none. Then he goes home, feeling disgusted with himself.

The zampolits are also responsible for every aspect of the conscripts' well-being, for any problems there may be concerning their families back home and also for any difficulties that they may experience in the army. In an army in which there is no significant NCO class, it is necessary to ensure that somebody knows what is going on in the barracks. Furthermore, with conscripts from so many different nationalities and backgrounds, civic education is clearly a vital function of the army. It is not unreasonable to combine the responsibility for both welfare and general education.

In practice, the way the system works depends entirely on the people concerned. It is impossible to generalize about the relationships between commanders and their political deputies, or about the caliber of the deputies themselves. Some of the ablest, most forthright and progressive people I met in the armed forces were zampolits. The best of them were invariably the people who were not instantly recognizable as political workers. The old image of the zampolit, partly a joke, partly deadly serious, was of a sanctimonious bore drearily spouting Party dogma, socially kill-joy and professionally second-rate. These still exist, and their capacity for damaging the Party, the army, and the *esprit de corps* of their units is considerable. In my experience the sure sign of a bad zampolit is the way he tells you, starry-eyed with desperate yearning, that he is expecting to be posted to Moscow soon, to a very important job. A good zampolit is a good commander and a skilled professional, and therefore he will have mixed feelings about a job in which he will be deprived of the opportunity to fly or to go to sea or whatever. Judging by the units I visited, however, the bad zampolits are not in the majority. Working relationships between commanders and their political deputies seemed, in general, to be close and successful, with the commanders relying on the zampolits on a wide range of issues, not merely on political matters.

Evidently the real test of the zampolits is the effect they have on their units in combat. A majority of the officers we met who had served in Afghanistan said that, on balance, they would retain the system (I should point out here that the veterans of Afghanistan speak their minds – if they thought that the zampolits should go, they would say so). Under the new system, the zampolits will continue to be responsible for the morale of the men during combat.

The political deputies were never the only means of exercising political influence and control in the armed forces. There are also independent Party cells in every unit, which traditionally carried considerable weight in enforcing standards of discipline and political orthodoxy within the army. But the authority of the Party itself has, of course, been shattered in the recent past, and it remains to be seen in what form it will survive inside the armed forces in the years to come.

Control of the military is ensured by the attention of the KGB. The counter-intelligence 'Special Department' (*Osobii Otdel*) exists throughout the armed forces, down to regimental level. At divisional level the '00' Department (as it is always

A field hospital during maneuvers, labelled 'laboratory,' because diagnostic tests are carried out here.

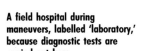

called) consists of about five people, and at regimental level there is usually one officer. Whereas the political workers are unquestionably soldiers and an integral part of the army, the *Osobists*, equally unquestionably, are not. The Ministry of Defense army generally expresses respect for the KGB's border guards and its other armed units. But the *Osobists*, with their somewhat broad interpretation of counter-intelligence, are another matter. However necessary their function might be known to be, at the local level there is clearly no love lost between them and the commanders. The army's nickname for these people, *molchi-molchi* (roughly, 'keep your mouth shut'), says it all.

The other armies

This book deals primarily with the forces of the Ministry of Defense; but there are two other organizations that have their own 'armies.' The first of these is the Ministry of the Interior (MVD), which has at its disposal 360,000 internal troops that have a number of roles. These include the provision of prison guards and fire-fighting services throughout the Soviet Union. MVD troops also have an internal security role and for this reason are usually stationed in large towns. They now have a recently expanded force, some 72,000 strong, that acts as a central reserve to be deployed in trouble spots when there is civil unrest. This army has its own helicopters, armored personnel carriers, and tanks. Ministry of the Interior forces are usually of lower caliber than those of the Ministry of Defense, except when they are part of one of the MVD's élite units, such as the crack Dzerzhinsky Division.

A lieutenant (looking hardly older than a conscript) instructing a tank crew at Kazandhik in the Turkestan desert.

The Committee for State Security (KGB) has about 220,000 uniformed men, including border guards, the Kremlin Guard, VIP protection troops, and some signals units, all of which are concerned with matters of state security. The KGB's soldiers — conscripts and officers — are well trained and equipped. Both the KGB and the Ministry of the Interior have their own Spetsnaz ('special purpose') units, consisting of highly skilled men able to cope with particularly difficult or specialized missions.

The division of responsibility between these forces is, in theory, quite clear, but in practice their deployment has been more complicated. For example, border guards took part in the war in Afghanistan. Similarly, when the situation in Azerbaijan ran completely out of control, the government sent in Ministry of Defense troops. So in practice, despite their different orientations, any of the different 'armies' might be employed by the government for any operation needing military force.

3 THE OFFICER CORPS

The Soviet Armed Forces depend entirely on the officers corps. These are the professionals who run the army, who set the standards for everybody else and who determine the nature of the military. Officers have, of course, many common characteristics and problems, but it is important to remember that each armed service produces a different type of officer, since each demands a different kind of bravery. In the Ground Forces, everyone up to the level of battalion commander faces the enemy within rifle range. Sailors, on the other hand (with the possible exception of the captain), never see the enemy, but they live and work in the knowledge that they may die sealed into a metal compartment below sea level. Pilots know that in war they would face colossal risks, but that they might have the opportunity to shirk that duty; their courage involves great personal integrity. These are not specifically Soviet military characteristics. They apply to all armies, and underlie any specifically national features. But in many other respects the Soviet officer corps is unusual, largely because of the historical position of the army in the country.

A career in the army has always had its attractions for Soviet men. In the past, one of the most important of these must have been the popular prestige that the army enjoyed. And, naturally, there are many people to whom the rugged adventure of army life appeals. But for much of the Soviet period there was a further consideration in favor of an army career: the demands made of an officer were ethically less complicated than those that might be made of him elsewhere. Working for either of those other pillars of the state (and mass employers) – the Party or the KGB – he might at some stage be asked to take part in activities that were, at the worst, appalling and, at the least, absurd. Admittedly, he could hope to enjoy great privileges, but even while he possessed these he might attract some contempt. As an army officer, he would share some of the privileges of Party or Secret Police employees, but he would be part of an organization that generally managed to avoid the excesses to which the other organs of the state were prone.

Some of the men who become officers in the Soviet Army would, in Western Europe, probably have become civil servants, industrialists, or academics. But the Soviet bureaucracy has, in general, lacked the dignity of the civil service in most Western countries, and the central planning system did not create many opportunities for able and ambitious men to fulfil their potential in industry. Academic life in the Soviet

The graduation ceremony outside the Zhukovsky Military Air Force Engineering Academy in Moscow. From this late eighteenth-century building, formerly the Petrovsky Palace, Napoleon watched Moscow burning.

A junior sergeant issuing the crew of an anti-aircraft gun with their instructions during a training session.

Union could become very complicated with the unpredictable changes in current policy and past events. It was all too easy to stray into hazardous ideological heresy, and, in any case, the pursuit of contemporary knowledge was difficult without access to foreign scholars and publications. The army offered almost the only environment in which men could pursue historical and scientific ideas without running the risk of being told that they were unpatriotic. Not only was it safe to be heard arguing about Clausewitz or Chobham Armor, such discussion was officially encouraged. So the army offered a dignified and an honorable profession, and there were not many of these in the Soviet Union of Stalin and Brezhnev. Since *glasnost* began, there are far more career opportunities than there used to be, and certain professions such as the law and psychiatry are being reborn, now that it is possible to practice them freely. However, the strength of military traditions in the Soviet Union is likely to ensure that the army will still attract more of the ablest young men than in most Western countries.

The military instructors who work in every school in the Soviet Union (see Chapter 4) are supposed to keep an eye open for pupils who might make good officers, to encourage them and to prepare them for the entrance examinations to military colleges. The voenkomats (military commissariats) that see every teenage boy in connection with national service also have instructions to look out for likely candidates. Although the military instructors are pretty ineffective, the voenkomats often give sensible and useful advice that enables boys who might not otherwise have done so to meet the colleges' entrance requirements. Most would-be officers seem to have been attracted by a general impression of military life based mainly on myth, folk history, newspapers, novels, and films. However, a significant number of applicants to military colleges are the sons of army officers. This tendency is officially encouraged, since it is thought that those who have grown up in military families know what they are doing when they join the army. They are familiar with the difficulties of army life, and are already steeped in army culture by the time they arrive at military college. Therefore, not only are they themselves likely to stay the course, since they have realistic expectations, but they are supposed to have a stabilizing influence on their peers.

It is also noticeable that a great many boys who grew up in children's homes end up in the army. This trend was strengthened during the war by the extension of the special Suvorov and Nakhimov military boarding schools to cope with some of the children who had lost their parents. In any group of a dozen full colonels or generals it is common to find at least one who grew up in an orphanage. In such a group of senior officers the long-term orphan is often the man who seems most attached to the army, frequently a popular extrovert. So in the past the system of encouraging orphans to enlist has been beneficial both to the army and to the men concerned. It is not clear whether or not this tradition is continuing. Since the war, the number of orphans has declined, and it is more common to find children who have one or more parent, but whose parents have proved unsatisfactory. It is worth pointing out that the Soviet officer corps is overwhelmingly male. There are no women in combat positions, and the few women who do join up usually work as doctors, nurses, clerks, or in communications. This is how the army wants it – everybody I spoke to considered that women should be kept away from the front line, unless, as during World War II, they were needed because of a shortage of men.

The Suvorov and Nakhimov schools

It is still generally accepted that the best way for an officer to start his career is to attend one of the very smart Suvorov or Nakhimov schools, the military boarding schools. Several of the original schools have closed, leaving eight Suvorov schools (which prepare boys for any of the armed forces) and one Nakhimov school (which prepares boys specifically for the navy). These schools no longer cater only for orphans, although the official admission regulations still state that priority should be given to orphans, or to children with one parent. This preference can, in certain circumstances, be extended to other boys who have suffered hardship. For example, after the Armenian earthquake in December 1988, the schools were encouraged to take any boys from the region who passed the medical examination and wished to apply for admission. However, the majority of 'Suvorovtsy,' the boys in the Suvorov schools, now come from normal families and a significant number are the sons of officers. At the Leningrad Nakhimov School, for example, 30 per cent of the Nakhimovtsy are from military families. Of the others, 32 per cent are the sons of workers or peasants and 40 per cent are children of professionals. Nearly a third have only one parent or are orphans. There are no school fees, but parents supply their sons with pocket money (recommended maximum of five rubles a month).

Any boy who would like to attend a Suvorov or Nakhimov school may apply through his local voenkomat. The first difficulty is to persuade the voenkomat that he is healthy and intelligent enough to deserve a place. The next hurdles are the oral and written examinations at the school. There is a great deal of competition for places, but the schools seem to be more interested in the boys' motivation than in academic or athletic brilliance. The first-year pupils at the Leningrad Nakhimov School, who met all the other applicants during their selection procedure, say that it was the boys who most wanted to get into the school who succeeded. Since 1969 the schools have taken pupils for two years from the age of fifteen. Earlier, the courses lasted for six years and pupils could be admitted at the age of ten or eleven.

In those days, pupils studied a much wider range of subjects, including fencing, riding, and dancing. The standard of foreign-language teaching in the schools was especially high and the graduates were considered to be qualified interpreters. The schools' curriculum, based on the nineteenth-century idea of a gentleman's education, aimed to produce polished officer cadets, and it certainly succeeded. The old-style Suvorovtsy really know their stuff, and a lot of the most brilliant men now serving in the army were molded by the old six-year Suvorov school courses. In the two years now allotted to the course, it is simply not possible for the schools to exert such a profound influence, nor to offer the same standard of education. However, the standard of education is still generally considered to be much higher than in normal secondary schools.

The purpose of the Suvorov schools is to prepare their pupils for admission to military colleges: in general, a Suvorovets will be able to get into whichever college he chooses. The Suvorovtsy certainly give the impression that they are an élite within the army. An extraordinary number of the most promising young officers still come from these schools, despite the changes. There are many stories of much-decorated heroes

OVERLEAF: Suvorov school pupils during the November parade. At the general rehearsal, the Minister of Defense advised them to be less tense in their marching. The airborne troops, he said, were the smartest (followed by the border guards). 'Although I dearly love the Navy,' he added, 'I felt that they had the most work to put in.'

A naval lieutenant during maneuvers in Vladivostock.

At the Nakhimov School for Naval Cadets in Leningrad, boys study ordinary academic subjects as well as specifically naval ones. The 730 boys are divided into six companies, each of which is divided into four platoons (in effect, classes). Between the first year of study and the second the boys spend 15 days training on a ship at sea.

Great emphasis is placed on physical training at every level in the army, from the military boarding schools upward, and success in sport will improve an officer's chances of promotion. Many of the country's most successful sportsmen on the international scene are serving officers or *praporshchiks* (warrant officers).

who say that the medal they value most is the old school badge. A Suvorovets is never unworldly, and so he knows that a young officer wearing that badge is likely to be taken more seriously than the rest by his superiors.

The contrast between the Nakhimov School in Leningrad and the Suvorov School in Moscow is striking. The Nakhimov School, housed in a lovely eighteenth-century palace on the Neva River, is clearly very successful, by any standards. The atmosphere in the school was serious and disciplined, the boys seemed bright, confident, and excited by the prospect of the naval careers that lay ahead of them. Most of the boys I spoke to at the Moscow Suvorov School, on the other hand, seemed keen to avoid a mainstream military career. They wanted to be military journalists or military lawyers, anything except soldiers, it appeared. One or two had ambitions to fly, but none of those I met had any intention of commanding a unit. Of course, the comparison between the two schools is unfair, because at that time the whole world was discussing the cuts that were to be implemented in the Soviet Army, but there was no talk of reducing the navy. So perhaps it was understandable that the Suvorov boys should be considering careers that could be followed just as easily outside the army. Nevertheless, the morale among the boys at the Moscow school did not appear to be very high. There are, however, eight of these schools, and some of the others, such as those in Minsk, Kiev, and Khabarovsk, seem to have a better reputation.

Military colleges and academies

Most future officers enter higher military colleges having completed the ten years of secondary-school education. Soldiers who decide, in the course of their national service, that they would like to enlist as officers are warmly welcomed if they have adequate academic qualifications. With them, the army at least knows what it is getting. The courses at the higher military colleges usually last for four years. Anyone who wishes to attend a military college has to apply through the local voenkomat, in the same way as boys hoping to go to Suvorov schools. The level of competition for places at military colleges varies a great deal. The most prestigious are described as 'command colleges,' and the authorities at these establishments can demand higher levels of physical and intellectual achievement from their potential officer cadets. Certain colleges are described as 'all arms,' which means that they prepare officers for all infantry jobs; others specialize in training gunners, airborne officers, pilots, naval officers, and so on.

According to some influential figures in the army, the officer selection procedures at the voenkomats and military colleges are seriously inadequate. It is said that the colleges make no attempt to identify the applicants' leadership potential, and that this should become their first priority. Nor, apparently, do they pay enough attention to selecting young men with the specific abilities necessary for the different branches of service. At the moment far too many of the colleges are just looking for good all-rounders, who, they assume, can turn their hands to anything.

In general, military colleges devote about 60 per cent of the timetable to relevant military subjects, such as tactics and weapons, about 30 per cent to various academic subjects, such as mathematics, physics, and a foreign language, and 10 per cent to

The commander of the independent airborne regiment in Fergana, Hero of the Soviet Union Colonel Aleksandr Solyuyanov. Like many of the country's most distinguished soldiers, he is a Suvorov school graduate.

political training. The *kursants* (officer cadets) also spend an average of six weeks before their final year working as platoon leaders in military units, to gain practical experience.

All graduates of military college leave with a civilian diploma (usually in some sort of engineering) as well as an army qualification, so that they should be able to find jobs if for some reason they have to leave the army. However, the standards of the military colleges (and, therefore, the marketability of their diplomas) vary considerably. The Leningrad Military Topographical College is said to be as good as any in the world in its field, and the Ulyanovsk Higher Military Engineering Tank College is said to have exceptionally high academic standards. The College for Underwater Training Named After Lenin's Komsomol and the Higher Naval Command College Named After M. V. Frunze, both in Leningrad, also have very good reputations. The Ordzhonikidze Higher Combined Arms College and the Kiev Higher Tank Engineering College are both considered to be excellent officer-training establishments. The Airborne Officers College at Ryazan seems to be by far the best-known military college in the Soviet Union, and is thought to offer fine professional training.

A *kursant* at a military college earns about 20 rubles a month if his marks are satisfactory, 25 rubles if they are good, and 30 rubles if they are very good. Many colleges also have five or six special bursaries (usually named after Lenin, Frunze, and so on) worth about 75 rubles a month, which replaces the standard payment. A student who gets married while he is at college (and over a third of them do) will get a further grant of about 40 rubles a month. However, he stands virtually no chance of being given a separate apartment, either by the local authorities or by the college. Most *kursants* marry girls who live in the towns where they are studying, whose families manage to accommodate them somehow. However, a married *kursant* will still usually be required to spend several nights a week in the students' barracks. Most of those who marry do so in their final years, perhaps because they do not want to be split up from their girlfriends when they are posted to their units.

If an officer is to advance to a staff or command position he will have to attend one of the sixteen military academies, which prepare the ablest in each generation for posts up to the level of divisional command. Most people spend two or three years at an academy, but officers who have not been admitted as full-time students can sometimes take correspondence courses, which may take an extra year. In this case they usually attend short residential courses each year at the academy itself. They end up with the same paper qualification as full-time students, but they miss out on the intellectual stimulation of academy life. Most of the students at these academies have the rank of captain or major, or perhaps lieutenant colonel at the more important Frunze Academy. In a class of its own is the Voroshilov Academy of the General Staff, where most of the students are colonels who have already graduated, a few years earlier, from the Frunze Academy. Attending the Academy of the General Staff is the definition of a real high flyer in the Soviet Armed Forces. Here they groom the men who will occupy the highest positions in the army, and equip them to take command of formations in any service — and even of a service itself — in which they may have no direct experience. The academy is not only an educational establishment — it is also the most important center of military research in the country.

A student (with the rank of captain) at the Yuri Gagarin Military Air Force Academy for pilots, in the cockpit of an aircraft simulator.

The first posting

In many colleges the students with the highest marks are allowed to decide, out of the available postings, where they would like to serve. These high flyers often make a point of asking to be sent to far-flung outposts, where life is generally supposed to be most difficult. This is a smart career move for several reasons. It demonstrates the young man's seriousness and devotion to duty. It will ensure that he is well-received in the unit to which he is sent, in the difficult conditions of the far north, the east, or the south. A further consideration for some may be that if an officer serves in an unpopular area during his first few years in the army, he can expect an easier posting afterward.

A young officer's first job after he leaves military college is almost always as a platoon leader. This will teach him everything that the college failed to mention about army life. It is not easy to control conscripts, especially those who are the same age or even older, physically stronger, and see newly fledged officers as fair game. But the platoon leader has to accept responsibility for their personal welfare and their training. At the same time he will have to attend political lectures and spend time on the continuous in-service training known as 'commander's preparation.' This is an aspect of life that generally makes officers groan, since it is often just a less inspiring version of the sort of education they received at military college. Few officers seem to consider that it stretches their ability or improves their skills in any way at all. The time that an officer spends on this depends on the strength of the unit. If the regiment is at very reduced strength it may occupy a day or so every week, but if the unit is more than half-strength no one is likely to spend more than a couple of hours a week, on average, on 'commander's preparation.' In addition, officers, like soldiers, have to take their turn going on guard duty in the regiment for twenty-four hours at a stretch, and this is universally considered to be another of life's undesirable features.

Life is tough for young lieutenants. Apart from the difficulties of the job, many of them are not provided with proper accommodations, and end up living in rooms without proper cooking facilities in 'hotels' in their regiments. But others are even worse off, and have to sleep in the barracks with the soldiers, although as a mark of their rank they are sometimes given two mattresses. Then it takes some time to get used to garrison life, especially for those who are city-bred. For the wives too, the first year or two may be difficult. But, of course, a great deal depends on the relationship between the young officer and his superiors. A favorite army joke describes the arrival of three young lieutenants at a regiment.

Early in the morning the first of them arrives and knocks on the colonel's door:

'Comrade Colonel, Lieutenant Ivanov has arrived to continue his service in your unit.'

'Did you have all excellent marks at military college?'

'Yes, Comrade Colonel.'

'Good. Then you will be a platoon leader.'

After lunch the second lieutenant arrives.

'Comrade Colonel, Lieutenant Petrov has arrived to continue his service in your unit.'

'Did you have all excellent marks at military college?'

48 Life in the military academies

Attendance at a military academy is an essential part of a high-flying officer's career, as can be seen from the biographies in the Selected Who's Who in the Soviet Armed Forces (page 224). Study at these academies includes strategy, operational art, and discussion of tactics and weapons technology. At the Gagarin Academy for Pilots, computers are used to test the speed of the students' reactions to unexpected developments during flight (right). The radars and other electronic equipment of the command and control simulators (far right) are much like the real thing in an aviation unit. Students at aviation academies generally have no opportunity to fly, so flight simulators are particularly important to them (far right, below). In the center right picture, students at the Frunze Academy discuss tactical questions and, below, the Mi-24 attack helicopter is being studied at the Zhukovsky Academy. Many of the military academies are important not only as educational establishments, but also as centers of research.

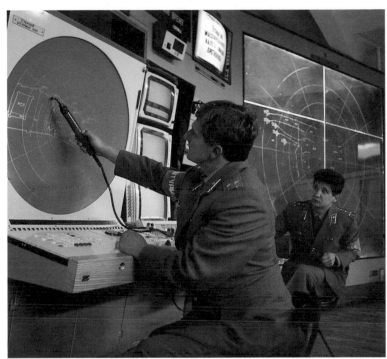

'Not all of them, Comrade Colonel.'

'Don't worry, Comrade Petrov. You'll be a platoon leader here and you will improve.'

Time passes, and the sun sets and the commander gives up waiting for the third lieutenant. In the middle of the night he is awakened by a knock at the door. He gropes his way to the door, in the dark. He sees a young lieutenant, leaning against the door post, hands in his pockets, too drunk to stand up, who asks:

'Are you the commander of the regiment?'

'Yes, I am.'

'Well, well, and I'm Lieutenant Sidorov.'

'So what, Sidorov?'

'What? The car is waiting downstairs, full of women and vodka.'

And the colonel shouts to his wife,

'Hey, fetch me my uniform. We've got a new chief of staff.'

Commanding a battalion seems to be the job that most people, looking back over their careers, say they enjoyed the most. Despite the responsibility of the job, they still have close contact with the men, and there is no doubt that the commanders are soldiers, rather than administrators, as they may feel that they have become later on. There is a significant leap in responsibility between company and battalion level. It is at this level that officers, especially combined arms officers, begin to assume responsibility for welding the different battlefield assets into an effective team. The battalion commander may have to direct the activities of artillery, scouts, and helicopters, as well as his own battalion – all this with a staff that usually consists of only four officers. The workload is heavy, but there is generally something invigorating about the bustle of a battalion staff.

At battalion level, some 'commander's preparation' is organized by the division. This usually entails about a week's intensive training at least twice a year for all the battalion commanders. These sessions are generally considered to be far more useful than those organized at regimental level (a couple of days a month), because they are much more directly concerned with the specific job that the men are doing. Commander's preparation usually includes tactics (70 per cent of it in the field, ideally), military teaching methods, psychology, engineering, reconnaisance, radio-electronic combat, and preparation for mobilization. On top of all this, there may be some political training. Some officers say that they have to attend about twenty lectures a year and that they have to do about three hours homework, either before or after each lecture. Others say that they no longer receive any political education. Nowadays, as such extraordinary developments are taking place in the Soviet Union, many of them say that they are finding their political lectures and seminars useful, although they used to consider them a complete waste of time.

All officers have to juggle various demands on their time and energy. First of all, they have to control and train the men under their command. Then they have to satisfy their own superiors that they are carrying out their own preparation satisfactorily. But at the same time every officer with any ambition has to begin to lay plans for getting himself into an academy. Although young officers work very long hours – twelve hours

Captain Labutkin, then company commander in Petropavlovsk-Kamchatka. His soldiers say that he is unbelievably cunning and constantly outwits them. For example, they often set up booby traps so that anyone approaching the barracks at night makes a lot of noise, giving the soldiers time to remove the evidence of whatever it is that they shouldn't be doing. 'But our Commander just steps over the traps,' they say.

a day is perfectly normal, fourteen or fifteen not unusual – they need to demonstrate their enthusiasm by taking on extra responsibilities. These might include short correspondence courses in some aspect of service, displaying initiative in organizing training or social activities for the soldiers, and taking part in serious sport. Sport is important in the army, and sports qualifications always improve the official assessment of an officer's performance.

Career structure

Young officers can expect to be moved from one unit to another, on average, about every four years. But this varies from one individual to another and between the different services. Combined arms officers seem to be moved not only from one unit to another, but thousands of miles across the country, from one military district to another. On the other hand, many of the naval officers I spoke to had spent their entire service lives in the same fleet. According to army regulations, there are statutory periods that an officer should serve between each promotion. So, for example, a lieutenant will have to wait two years before becoming a senior lieutenant, a captain three years before he can hope to become a major, and so on (see Appendix I). Only in exceptional circumstances may a man be promoted ahead of time. The further an officer progresses up the army's career ladder, the less likely he is to be promoted after the minimum time. At each stage he can only be given the next rank if he holds an appropriate job. So, for example, there are some very grand lieutenant colonels serving in army reconnaissance, who are unlikely to be promoted further because there are very few colonel's and general's jobs available in their line of work. On the other hand, there are some not very bright full colonels in the less prestigious fields. But everybody is aware of these apparent anomalies. Postings and promotions above the rank of major are dealt with by GUK (the Main Directorate for Cadres). Below this they are handled by the relevant armed service and the units themselves. Files are held on every senior officer on Soviet ES-10 and ES-35 computers. Policy matters concerning, for example, the length of postings to difficult locations are decided by the armed services, but then it is up to GUK to keep an eye on the rotation of officers, to ensure that the policy is implemented.

In the Soviet Armed Forces, an officer's status is determined by the position he holds, not by his rank. An officer will often hold lower rank than the official rank for the job he holds. In the British army, in such a case, the officer would normally be given the acting rank appropriate to the position. In the Soviet army this is considered unnecessary, on the basis that holding a job will, in itself, invest the incumbent with the authority that he needs. The possibility of further promotion is held to be an important incentive for able officers who have been given important posts. Every officer's salary is made up of three separate components. First, there is the payment for his rank, then there is the payment for the post he occupies, and a supplement for the length of time that he has served. There is also extra pay for those who serve in the most difficult locations. Of these components the most important (and the one which can vary most) is the payment for the post. It is worth pointing out that very high rank is not necessarily an unmixed blessing. A General Staff officer told me in confidence

The commander of the motorized rifle regiment in Kamchatka, Colonel Voznuk, congratulates a company zampolit on his promotion, handing him the epaulettes of a senior lieutenant. The promotion was expected, but it is nevertheless an occasion to celebrate. If the zampolit and his friends are like most officers, however, the real celebration will come later on, when the new star will be put into a glass of vodka. The promoted officer must drain the glass in one gulp and catch the star in his teeth as he does so. This is an old army tradition, still loyally observed.

that 'colonels have the most fun.' Majors do not have enough power, it seems, but generals are so hemmed in by convention and regulations that their lives, too, are very restricted.

The officer's career is punctuated by the regular 'officer's check,' whereby his performance is assessed. This can be purely routine or it can be very unpleasant if he is thought to have stepped out of line in some way. The results of each training exercise in the unit are recorded and are considered to reflect the abilities of the officer concerned. In addition, confidential reports are prepared on each officer every year. An officer whose superiors feel that it is necessary to exert more than usual control over him may well find his life dominated by these checks. Some people appear to suffer from these checks constantly.

Basically, officers alternate between command and staff positions during their careers, but there are, of course, exceptions. The Selected Who's Who section provides summaries of the careers of a number of officers. Unless he is hampered by ill health or by enforced early retirement, an officer will for the rest of his working life be part of the vast Soviet military machine. How this career works out depends on the man himself, on the vagaries of international politics (influencing the size and character of the armed forces), and on simple luck.

Life in the garrison

Although an officer might be called upon to serve in any part of the Soviet Union under almost any conditions, each unit to which he goes will feel like home. Everything will be immediately familiar to an officer or an experienced wife the minute they arrive. Army garrisons produce recognizable character types. There is the talkative zampolit, and the jolly deputy for rear services (*zampotyl*), always universally popular because he controls the supplies. Then there is the tough spinster schoolmistress, fearless in arguing with the commander of the regiment and his deputies on behalf of the wives and children. She is often the only person who can do this, since the wives are either afraid to damage their husbands' prospects or else they are themselves married to the commander or his deputy. The chief of staff is inevitably harried, since he is responsible for the smooth running of the unit.

There is a very strong sense of community within the army. Wherever you go you find that people know each other. The deputy commander of this regiment was at military college with the commander of that one, the chief of staff here met the acting commander there on vacation at a 'rest-house' a few years ago. The big military families and the Suvorovtsy play an important part in forging the connections that make the army world seem so cozy. There is also undoubtedly something very reassuring in the constancy of the military system.

When an officer is given a new posting, the unit that he is leaving pays for the relocation of his family and will transport household equipment and possessions free of charge: if he has one child the allowance is three tons, with two children the allowance is five tons, and so on. Upon arrival at his new regiment he will be given an allowance of one month's salary to cover the costs of setting up his new apartment. (Often, a family leaving an apartment will sell some of their furniture, or fittings, such as shelves

Inside an officer's apartment in Kazandzhik. This woman is lucky – she has an apartment and her child has a place in the local kindergarten. Even so, there is not much to do in a place like this. But the women's lives are generally not as gloomy as they might seem. They have a world of their own, often based on the local officers' club. There is usually a cafe where the wives meet and plot improvements and amusements. They organize their lives efficiently to share chores like shopping and child-minding, and to pool their resources when necessary. But if you marry an officer you have to be able to get along with everybody. Quarreling wives can wreak havoc in a small garrison.

and curtains, to the new arrivals.) KECh, the service responsible for housing, either carries out any necessary repairs to the officers' apartments, or it gives them the cost of the repair work, so that the officer can either find somebody to do it for him or carry out the repair himself. But this is assuming, of course, that there is an apartment available for the officer. For thousands and thousands of them there is, quite simply, no proper housing. They end up sharing apartments or renting rooms, often at inflated rents in substandard buildings. The community will generally go to some trouble to make the newcomers to the regiment welcome, even though the facilities provided for them may be grossly inadequate. I visited units where, despite all the hardships, the friendships among the officers and some of their families had created remarkably happy communities where life was clearly fun.

Despite public resentment of the privileges that they are supposed to enjoy, from the officers' own point of view life is anything but easy. Many of them have to live for years on end in some of the most inhospitable territory on earth. Others are moved around so often that neither they nor their families ever have the chance to establish themselves or put down roots of any sort. It is not uncommon for people to spend their whole working lives on one housing waiting list after another. Each time, before they reach the top of the list and can be given an apartment, they are posted elsewhere, to the bottom of yet another list. The shortage of housing creates a widespread sense of insecurity. Even if a family has a decent apartment now, they never know what their next posting will be. Admittedly, in the past officers could sometimes earn more money than their civilian peers, but this is no longer so. In any case, most Soviet families operate financially on the assumption that the wife will work full-time. For many officers' wives this is impossible. In many places where they are sent to live, there are no opportunities for them to find the sort of job for which they are qualified (nor indeed any other). If they don't work, they will lose their pension rights and therefore the family will have to save for the future. So although the officer himself might have a good salary, the household often has less to live on than comparable civilian families.

This gives rise to another of the difficulties with which many officers have to contend: living with a wife who is bored out of her mind, thousands of miles from her family and friends, and unable to afford to visit them very often. Many civilians believe that the military benefits from its own exclusive shops, in which there is a dazzling array of goodies, totally unavailable to ordinary people. We visited shops in some garrisons that did appear to be better supplied than ordinary Soviet shops, but not, it seemed to me, dramatically so. These tended to be in regions such as the Ukraine where the living is, in any case, relatively easy. In fact, it is not unusual in the Soviet Union for factories or other large employers to provide better-than-average shops for their staff. In other places, such as the deserts of Turkmenistan, where no sane European would choose to live, the military shops were poorly stocked even by Soviet standards. Now that rationing is widespread throughout the Soviet Union, military families are, in any case, often not given coupons to buy food in civilian shops, so officers' wives may be unable to buy even those goods that are available to everyone else.

Another problem arising from military life is that of the education and welfare of children. Not only are army children forced to change schools whenever their father

Captain Second Rank Ostrovsky (foreground) playing in the snow with his daughter and another officer. There are Ministry of Defense 'rest houses' all over the Soviet Union, comfortable hotels with good sports and recreation facilities for officers and their families. In order to spend his vacation at one of these, an officer has to get a voucher, and even this is not always easy.

A typical scene on the drill square, in front of the barracks, in the 304th Red Banner Motorized Rifle Regiment based in Petropavlovsk-Kamchatka. Those who are about to go on guard duty line up for their instructions.

A marine with his wife and child during a sports competition outside Vladivostok.

changes his job (so it is not unusual to find children who have been to four or five schools in ten years), but in many remote garrisons the schools are staffed almost entirely by officers' wives who have no training at all as teachers. Another source of worry to the officer is health care for his family. Although every military base provides medical treatment of a sort, there are not usually the resources to provide specialized care for the women and children. I met a senior lieutenant who had been on the point of leaving the air force because his severely handicapped child desperately needed treatment that was not being made available to her in the area where he served. In this case the political workers in the regiment managed to surmount colossal bureaucratic difficulties to ensure that she was seen by the best specialists in the field. So this young officer will stay in the armed forces. But others are leaving, for similar reasons.

The officer corps has always taken these conditions for granted. Officers used to grumble among themselves and complain through the proper channels. Even before the current openness in the press, there was discussion in the military newspapers of the difficulties under which the army served. However, the overriding assumption of the officer corps was that, although their lives were difficult, they were proud to be soldiers and, together with their wives and families, proud of their tradition of coping, no matter how hard the circumstances. There always was, and from my observation there remains, a very strong moral code among the officer corps which dictated that they would get on with the job, whatever the cost, and not whine in public.

The Russian cult of service

The characteristics of the officer corps are undoubtedly part of a common European military culture, but it seems to me that the concept of service has deeper roots and more complicated ramifications in the Soviet Union than elsewhere. In the Russian army, and indeed in the Soviet, endurance has often been seen as a major military virtue, in the popular imagination if not in theory. This emphasis on heroic endurance has had a great influence on the country, for good and for ill. Russia — both Christian and Socialist — has always tended to make a cult of self-sacrifice. The first Russian martyrs, Boris and Gleb, remain in some way the quintessential Russian saints, remembered and loved by the Orthodox Church because of their willing self-abasement. When Orthodox theologians consider the character of Christ they tend to dwell on the idea of *kenosis*, on the 'emptying out' of power and glory that was necessary if God were to become man. To Russian Christians the idea of God humbled and sharing in our humanity is almost unbearably moving. In Orthodoxy, humbleness is prized above cold righteousness, compassion above the legalistic observation of the law. Cleanliness is certainly not next to godliness.

The notion of the elect has no meaning for the Russian Church: there the prince and the prostitute, the boyar and the beggar were always felt to be bound together in one community where redemption lay in the acknowledgment and forgiveness of other people's frailty. If early Protestants thought that they would get to heaven by being better than the common herd, Russian Christians know that they will get there by sharing fully in the humanity of that herd. In the same way, the commanders who have been most loved by the army have been those who seemed to partake of the hardships of the troops. Suvorov (d. 1798), the greatest Russian military hero of them all, canonized in the popular memory, is always described as having shared his porridge with his men. He is loved still, mostly because of the love that he is supposed to have felt for the men. It was not that he treated his men better than his contemporaries: General Potemkin, the commander of the Semenovsky Regiment, was by all accounts kinder to the soldiers and more careful of their lives. But the men believed that Suvorov understood what they were going through. He was a ruthless disciplinarian and a fierce upholder of the distinctions between the ranks. But his cultivated eccentricities and his ability to address the peasant soldiers in a language they understood made him the enduring Russian symbol of the good commander. The representative of authority, of the power that ruled the land, he nevertheless knew what it was to be a common soldier.

In the Soviet period, World War II produced a healthy crop of good military leaders. Historians are fascinated by the intellectual and sophisticated Marshal Konstantin Rokossovsky, who served throughout the war under a sentence of death passed on him in 1938, but the common soldier, on the other hand, preferred a man such as Marshal Georgi Zhukov, who, like Suvorov, had risen to eminence from the ranks. Again, what the soldiers wanted was not soft discipline or liberal principles. They could forgive what might, with hindsight, seem like cruelty; they could admire ruthlessness. Like Suvorov, Zhukov was sometimes wasteful of the lives of his troops. But, again like Suvorov, he was felt to empathize with their hardship. That, in the end, was what counted with the men.

Western observers have been alarmed by the evidence they have picked up of the Soviet officer corps' growing spirit of Russian nationalism. But the longing to rediscover their lost past is an understandable reaction of any people trying to recover from seventy years of enforced amnesia. Much of the Soviet period, and many of its supposed achievements, are now seen by many Russians to have been fraudulent. The state into which all the officers now serving were born is considered to have become morally bankrupt. So it is hardly surprising or reprehensible that at a time of political upheaval and moral bewilderment people, including soldiers, should look to this national past for some understanding of who they are, and for some guidance as to how they should behave in the future.

Realistically, the dark side of nationalism is xenophobia. The strongest racial hatred in the Soviet Union is reserved for the Jews, and anti-Semitism is endemic in the army. It ranges, in my experience, from collusion in inoffensive jokes to rabid fervor. The oddest aspect, to a Westerner, is that many Russians have evidently never encountered the notion that overt anti-Semitism is socially unacceptable. On more than one occasion I have witnessed the topic of the Jews being introduced into a conversation intentionally, on the basis that this is an entirely uncontroversial subject, about which everyone will agree. I need hardly say that anti-Semitism in the Soviet Union is not restricted to the army. In their own defense, the officer corps would say that although they admit that they do not like the Jews, if there were ever to be widespread pogroms it would be they, the army, who would go in to save the Jews. This is undoubtedly true.

The experience of World War II has unquestionably contributed to a certain sentimentality about Mother Russia among army officers. They understand that the war

Reservists writing operational
messages during maneuvers.

was won, in the end, by Russian peasants fighting on Russian soil. After the Revolution the country went through paroxysms of fantasy about the future. Machinery, tractors, and aviation, these were the things that would liberate a benighted people from dark superstition and oppression. It was a crazed millennial dream that had to be forced on those too slothful to grasp its possibilities for themselves. The earth, the mud, and the dust of Russia were despised and forgotten in the heady days of building socialism. But then came the German invasion – and the army had to cope with hard reality. There is a war song remembered by almost all Russians of a certain age that recalls the violent reawakening of an understanding of the land:

Do you remember, Alyosha, the roads round Smolensk,
How the foul rains fell without cease . . .
I think you know that after all the motherland
Isn't the city where I merrily lived.
It's these villages where our grandfathers passed before us
With the simple crosses over their Russian graves.

After the war, the Future was never the same again. The worst abuses of the land were still to come and probably the greatest triumphs of the Soviet system, in the breathtaking, pioneering days of the space race. But the blithe optimism of the early days of socialism could never be recaptured. And, from the military point of view, the importance of the countryside and its people would never again be overlooked. But the army's interest in the land is not only professional. The ablest officers now talk endlessly about the environment, and about the series of man-made catastrophes that, they fear, Russia now faces. It seems to me that the military give higher priority to the ecological crisis, compared with the country's many other problems, than most civilians. Again and again, I was told of initiatives on the part of commanders to preserve the countryside and minimize the risk of pollution of the air, rivers, and lakes, by any activities of their units.

Sentimentality about old Russia is not the only basis of the officers' culture. They are also influenced by classical ideals of masculine excellence. I have noticed an almost Roman idea of manly virtue among some officers, a virtue that involves intellectual fastidiousness, atheistic courage, and ruthless criticism of self and others. A man who is noble should aim to perfect himself in his lifetime. For some officers this means that the cultivation of physical fitness seems to acquire moral overtones. Equally, brilliant commanders will talk quite simply about the importance of men being handsome. Physical bravery is, of course, prized in the Soviet Army as much as in any other.

The Heroes of Afghanistan

Perhaps the most interesting and significant group of officers currently in the Soviet Armed Forces are those who fought with distinction in the better units in Afghanistan. The ten-year campaign in Afghanistan was the first real action that the army had seen since 1945, so the able veterans of this now have experience that, otherwise, only the old men in the armed forces possessed. Most of the relevant young officers now hold ranks between lieutenant colonel and major general. Those of higher rank had already

OPPOSITE: Troops of a motorized rifle battalion and their BMP-2s gathered at an assembly point near Termez in Uzbekistan after they had been withdrawn from Afghanistan in February 1989.

Inside the museum of the Zhukovsky Military Air Force Engineering Academy, whose graduates include the first cosmonaut, Yuri Gagarin, and important former Soviet military leaders, such as Marshal of Aviation Vershinin.

60 FACING PAGE: Major Valentin Ivanov, commander of an air assault battalion, communicating during maneuvers.

Colonel Ruslan Aushev (he has been promoted since this photograph was taken), seen here with the troops of his regiment in Ussirisk, is one of the best-known of the Heroes of the Soviet Union from Afghanistan. Like many other officers he has to reconcile the demands of army life with those of his position as a member of the Congress of Peoples' Deputies. Some deputies now admit that they had not realized how much time the Congress would take up. So it is possible that fewer officers will stand for election in future.

passed their formative years in the army before they were sent to Afghanistan. Those of lower rank are still very young, insufficiently confident for it to be clear where they stand on the vital issues. What is clear, however, is that the experience of Afghanistan was deeply traumatic for them, because they were simply unprepared for the responsibility they faced, and for the reality of war.

The group of Afghan veterans, the young colonels and generals, includes a significant number who have been decorated as Heroes of the Soviet Union. Some of them, young men aged between thirty-five and forty-five, have become household names, and have had Komsomol groups, schools, and streets named after them throughout the country. Others have received much less attention, although the importance of the Hero of the Soviet Union award is such that no one who has received it will ever again be entirely out of the public eye. It is not really clear why some recipients of the award have become so much more famous than others. One of the best known of the Afghan heroes is (now Colonel) Ruslan Sultanovich Aushev, who has had just about everything that can possibly be given a name called after him, and is an active member of the Congress of the People's Deputies. This entails going to Moscow whenever the Congress is in session and taking an interest in the welfare of his constituents back home. Authoritative and self-possessed, he is everybody's idea of an army officer. He is not a man who airs any doubts that he may feel, and his style of command, in Afghanistan and back home in the Soviet Union, has been characterized by an ability to identify problems and to devise practical and often innovative solutions. This is clearly valuable, not only to the army but also in his work as a member of the Congress. The fighter pilot Aleksandr Rutskoi (also now colonel) is another wellknown figure. He was hit four times during his 428 combat flights in Afghanistan. Twice he managed to land safely, and the third time he had to eject after being hit by a Stinger missile. On the fourth occasion, a Pakistani F-16 equipped with Sparrow missiles brought him down in Pakistan. He was on the run for five days, without food or water and losing blood. Finally, he passed out and was captured by an Afghan group. He was not gently treated. For twenty-four hours he hung in the air, slung onto a pole with his hands and feet tied. He was later handed over to the Pakistanis, and subsequently to the Soviet authorities. At the time of this incident he was waiting to be presented with the Hero of the Soviet Union award for bravery that he had shown earlier. But he assumed that the award would now be canceled, in keeping with the traditionally unforgiving Soviet attitude toward any of their own people who were taken prisoner. But the times were changing, and Rutskoi was presented with the Hero of the Soviet Union award on 8 December 1988.

Aushev and Rutskoi seem to be more famous among civilians than most of the other Heroes, but seen from inside the army, they are only two among many. A great many of the recipients of the award are airborne officers. Afghanistan was not a mechanized war, so it was the paratroopers, airborne infantrymen in fact, who carried out the most difficult missions. Among these, the immensely likable Valery Vostrotin and Sergei Kozlov (described by Ruslan Aushev as one of the best officers in the army) are influential. So too is the Hero of the Soviet Union Aleksandr Petrovich Solyuyanov, who was the commander of the independent airborne regiment at Fergana in Uzbekistan when I first met him. As commander of the airborne regiment he was also

Aleksandr Ivanovich Lebyed (now Major General) at Ryazan. 'My job,' he says,' is to make one fist out of the regiments in my division.'

the chief of the Fergana garrison, and, therefore, in a sense, the descendant of the old Russian military governors of the area. He was very aware of this tradition and referred more than once, quite knowledgeably, to his predecessors and the contributions they had made to the development of the area, planting orchards as well as introducing the more intangible fruits of civilization. A perk of the Fergana job is the lovely old governor's house, with its vine-covered arbor and pretty garden. But despite this background of colonial elegance, Aleksandr Petrovich gives the impression that he is constantly alert to what might be happening behind his back as well as in front of him. He is evidently highly scrupulous in his stewardship of the army's resources (human and material) and in the execution of any decision that he has reached.

One of the most formidable of these Afghan veterans is Major General Aleksandr Ivanovich Lebyed, now the commander of the 106th Guards Airborne Division, based in Tula. He worked as a platoon and company commander at the Airborne College in Ryazan for a couple of years, and is therefore very well known to paratroop officers of his own age and slightly younger. Afterward he led a battalion in Afghanistan with distinction. Few people in the armed forces command as much affection. He strides around his territory in riding boots and breeches, usually with a cigarette in his mouth. He is an imposing figure by any standards. Self-mocking, he says that his deep bass voice is his principal asset as a commander. It is certainly arresting when you first hear it. When I first encountered Lebyed, by chance, at his regiment in Ryazan, he wanted to know what the hell we were doing in one of his regiments and he saw no reason for delicacy in asking us. Later he was to be kind and hospitable far above and beyond the call of duty. But never did he allow himself to be sucked into the mire of bourgeois niceties. At his regiment in Tula we were shown how vehicles are prepared for air-dropping. Just afterward we ran into Aleksandr Ivanovich who asked us, gruffly, how we were doing. I told him what an interesting time we were having. He lifted his upper lip at one side, screwed up his nose, and growled in disgust at this unmanly reply. But Lebyed's rudeness is deployed with undeniable aplomb. He is notorious in the mess for his kind heart, and among the paratroop conscripts, who often make cults of their commanders, he is probably the single most respected figure in the airborne forces. Everybody I know who has met him believes that they have a special understanding with Lebyed, and everybody, conscript or world-weary intellectual, values the relationship.

These Afghan veterans are all impressive individuals and evidently good officers, but their real significance is as a group. Taken together, they are very much more than the sum of the individuals concerned. Their affection for one another is evident. They relax in each other's company. They clearly share strong opinions about a wide range of matters. They keep in touch with each other, and they put themselves out to arrange meetings. Whatever happened in Afghanistan bound them together more strongly than any of the normal bonds that exist among soldiers who have studied or served together. They seem to identify with each other's successes and failures. They give the impression that they are very much older than their actual age, and that they have far more experience of the world than can possibly be the case. They have a confidence, authority, and gravitas often not to be found in much more senior army officers. They are impatient with the noise and nonsense of cities and staffs, after the certainties of the battlefield. Having confronted physical danger and the horrors of war, they are certainly not now intimidated by any of the perils that sometimes dog the imaginations of other officers — the displeasure of superiors, the loss of promotion, or the wrath of the security forces.

In the past, the Soviet socialist system did not foster the development of enterprise or resourcefulness. The Soviet Army, by Western standards, has traditionally placed less reliance on individual initiative and more on well-rehearsed drills. But in the conditions that prevailed in Afghanistan the lessons that had been taught in the military colleges back home were quickly found to be useless. The officers had to think for themselves, and they had to act fast. They had to be concerned with reality, not ideology or making the correct reports. Almost everybody in the Soviet Union now claims to be impatient with bureaucracy. Unlike most people in the country, however, the officers from Afghanistan are used to taking radical action to overcome bureaucratic (and other) difficulties, and at the same time accepting responsibility for the results of these actions. Their prestige and fearlessness make this group of great importance in the army now, and in the future they are likely to have even greater influence.

It is often said that the military is the most conservative element in Soviet society. To some extent this is undoubtedly true — professional soldiers in most Western countries also tend to be more conservative than other sections of the community. The officer corps is very worried about the breakdown of law and order in parts of the Soviet Union, and keen that the country's political leaders should avert such disorders. But I think that the army is unfairly accused of being a relic of the bad old days. Everybody I spoke to in the armed forces, from the very top down, is aware of the errors, the mismanagement, and the tragedies of the past. However, the most intelligent people in the army, in the General Staff as well as in the units, manifest a self-awareness that is often absent elsewhere in Soviet society. They remember that, whatever the ills of the past, the army was one of the pillars of the state and therefore in part responsible for what happened. From my experience, they are aware of the implications of the recent revelations, alert to the charges of collusion that must now confront every adult who was not openly dissident. As we have already seen, an influential section of the Soviet media is happy to lay the blame for almost everything that has happened (for ill) during the Soviet period at the door of the armed forces. They expend some energy and much newsprint on promulgating their view that the army has been the root of all evil. But were not all Party members, all journalists, all those employed by the ministries, all those who cooperated in what are now known to be falsehoods and repressions equally culpable? If the state was rotten, the responsibility lies with everyone who functioned within it, especially those who now say that they always hated the system. Those who use the army as a scapegoat for all the horrors of the past perpetuate the real evil of the system, which was that it encouraged people to abnegate moral responsibility. In Moscow one is likely to be deafened by the flapping of turning coats. The army's caution should in many cases be read, in my opinion, more as a dignified awareness of the painful ironies of the present situation than as ingrained resistance to change.

4 CONSCRIPTION

Between January and March of each year, every young male Soviet citizen who has reached his seventeenth birthday must report to his local voenkomat (military commissariat). There he will be assessed for military service, for which he will be eligible as soon as he is eighteen. The spring visit to the voenkomat is not, however, the first contact that the young man will have had with the military. Not only are the armed forces far more visible in the Soviet Union than in any Western country, but from childhood all Soviet citizens have been made aware of the importance of defending the motherland. Even the prizes given for the school physical training tests are called Ready for Labor and Defense awards. Many children's books, even those aimed at seven- or eight-year-olds, describe the exploits of military heroes (real and fictional) and extol the virtues of bravery and resistance to the tortures and wiles of the enemy. The heroes of these stories are often children themselves, reminding the reader that defense is the responsibility of every Soviet citizen, however young. Of course, the Civil War and World War II provide a rich source of material for adventure stories, and in occupied Soviet territory there were well-documented cases of heroism among Soviet children and teenagers (although it is a pity that the official treatment of their lives so often tended to turn them into unbearably sickly martyrs).

In the past, the country's youth organizations laid the foundations for the military and patriotic education with outings to war memorials, and so on, for children from the age of seven onward. The Young Pioneers (the Party organization for children between nine and fourteen) developed these activities and also ran annual summer camps that included a game called *zarnitsa* (summer lightning) — a mixture of hide-and-seek and a scaled-down military exercise. The Komsomol (Young Communist) movement, which children can join at fourteen or over, also organized camps, where a more sophisticated quasi-military game, *orlyonok* (little eagle), was played. Most children still attend Young Pioneer camps, and they seem to enjoy them (and, according to their mothers, they return home with greatly improved manners). But by the time they are teenagers they lead more independent lives and so far more of them opt out of the organized fun of the summer camps.

In some areas *zarnitsa* and *orlyonok* are still organized, and well supported. But elsewhere, especially in the cities, schoolchildren have only vaguely heard of them and have certainly never been invited to take part in them. Even where these games are still

Conscripts at the recruiting point in Kiev. The slogan on the mural tells them that 'Defending the socialist fatherland is the sacred duty of each citizen of the USSR.'

played the military element is not labored much these days, and it would be a mistake to attach too much significance to them. After all, when the games are well run, they are fun.

Throughout the educational system (schools as well as political organizations) considerably less stress is placed on military matters than in the early 1980s, and military and patriotic education often seems to be concentrating more on civil defense and on Soviet peace initiatives than on preparation for defense. Nowadays, a bright thirteen-year-old Moscow schoolboy may not be able to tell the difference between the uniform of a captain and that of a colonel, a failure that would have been unimaginable a few years ago. Even in the mid-1980s a boy would have known the main Soviet Army insignia by the time he was about ten, and he probably would have been able to identify the principal small arms, tanks, and planes used by the Soviet Union and by Germany during World War II. Nevertheless, a teenager, especially in Russia or the Ukraine, is still likely to have been exposed to more information concerning the military than his Western counterpart.

Preliminary military training

During his fifteenth year every schoolboy has an army medical examination at a local clinic, with further check-ups and treatment if anything is found to be wrong with him. An unofficial estimate at a Ukrainian voenkomat suggested that 20 per cent of the boys needed further attention after their initial examination, a figure that would presumably vary considerably from one region to another, according to the health of the local population and the thoroughness of the doctor conducting the examination. In the tenth grade at school (when they will be fifteen or sixteen), boys begin their specific preliminary military training. During the next two school years, 140 hours will be allocated to this military training, in the course of which the instructors will endeavor to instill in the boys some idea of basic drill, the handling of firearms, and so on. This is a compulsory part of the school curriculum, taught by military specialists under the control of the local voenkomat. The marks awarded for this military training are included in the student's graduation certificate. The military instructors should, ideally, be retired officers, but they are often former *praporshchiks* (warrant officers), and I have been told of cases where former sergeants (in other words, conscripted soldiers) have been employed in this capacity. Similar premilitary training is provided in factories and on farms, in technical schools (*tekhnikums*) and special professional and technical schools (SPTUs). In many schools it is made clear that the educational staff as a whole, including the head, have little respect for the military instructor. If there is a need to interrupt some part of the school routine, it will inevitably be his lessons that will suffer. Some schoolboys say that skipping military preparation is quite safe, and not considered to be an offense comparable to missing math or science lessons, for example. There are even stories of schools allocating the last period in the day to military preparation, so that for part of the year these lessons will have to take place in the dark. Many accounts suggest that military training in technical schools and work places is taken even less seriously there than in schools. Although every educational establishment or enterprise employing young people is legally bound to

Saying good-bye at the recruiting point.

ensure that its pupils or young workers receive premilitary preparation, some soldiers, especially those from the Asiatic republics, seem to be uncertain about whether or not they, personally, were given any such training.

In addition to the weekly military lessons, there are summer camps, described, somewhat alarmingly, as 'military sports and sanitary camps,' which boys used to attend for a fortnight when they were sixteen or so, and for five days the next year. Russian youth often still attend such camps, but in large parts of the country they have virtually died out now. Here, orienteering and hand-grenade throwing are added to drill and small-arms training, along with basic camping and survival skills, such as lighting fires. Teenagers (girls as well as boys) are also encouraged to enroll in DOSAAF (the Voluntary Society for Collaboration with the Army, Air Force, and Navy), a vast organization that provides facilities for all sports in any way relevant to the military. DOSAAF has recently been renamed the 'Union of Societies and Organizations Assisting National Defense,' but it is still always referred to by its former acronym. Flying, shooting, parachuting, driving, sailing, and diving are among DOSAAF's more obvious activities, but others include model-aircraft making, go-carting, radio-operating, and model-ship making.

Conscripts usually travel to their units by train.

The annual DOSAAF subscription is thirty kopeks, and anyone over the age of fourteen may join — there is no upper age limit. Some older people, especially war veterans, pay the subscription as a way of making a donation to the organization. Others, according to a DOSAAF spokesman, are less altruistically motivated, and simply pay the thirty kopeks in order to be allowed to buy tickets for the very popular DOSAAF lotteries. There may be as many as 100 million nominal members, but the authorities are currently trying to reduce this and ensure that in the future only active members are allowed to remain on the rolls. Apparently it is easy to spot the organizations that are not serious — they are the ones with lots of members but no cars, aircraft, or sports equipment. All sports training is free for members, and the DOSAAF facilities are usually far better than any others available to teenagers. It is thought that about three and a half million people regularly take part in shooting (the most popular sport) with DOSAAF. But it is difficult to give accurate figures for the number of participants in the different sporting activities because of the huge number of nonactive members, and because many active members take part in more than one activity.

It is not clear how successful all these activities are in preparing young men for military service. Although some newly recruited soldiers appear to be well informed about the facts and requirements of military life, others seem to be so unprepared that it is difficult to believe that so much time and effort has gone into their pre-military training. Army General Lizichev said, in 1989, when head of the Main Political Directorate, that many young men arrived in the army straight from school, 'insufficiently trained physically, not adequately trained to take independent decisions, and still less able to bear the stresses and privations of military service. Many have parents who, because they themselves went through difficult times, think that their sons shouldn't suffer. And as a result, they bring up a little flower of the field that is afraid of the wind and only used to consuming, not to doing or producing anything. I cannot be satisfied with this.' Various practical measures have been taken to improve the standard of premilitary training. For example, a campaign was organized in the late

1980s to provide at least one firing range or shooting complex for every two Moscow schools. But in many schools the problem seems to lie more with the quality of the instructors than in the equipment. In big cities military instructors often appear, to the boys, to be less sophisticated and less aware of the developments in contemporary society than their other teachers. In the countryside it is often even more difficult to recruit instructors of the necessary caliber. The boys' reaction to the military lessons, and to the instructors, is obviously strongly influenced by the antimilitary attitudes current in society. With an influential section of public opinion so hostile to the military, and to military values, it becomes virtually impossible for any teacher to arouse much enthusiasm for premilitary training. An interesting development of the last few years has been the formation of independent military-patriotic clubs, usually under the leadership of Afghanistan veterans. These clubs are meant to supplement the deficiencies of the official program of military preparation. They offer activities such as rifle and pistol shooting, unarmed combat, and drill, but, unlike the military lessons in schools, these clubs are very popular, especially, from my observation, with working-class urban boys.

Assessing the conscript

Each year the Second Department of every voenkomat (the department responsible for conscription) compiles a list of all the young men who should be summoned the following spring. These lists are drawn up on the basis of information supplied by every educational establishment and every employer in the area, and by the housing authorities, who have a record of all the inhabitants of each residence. (Each voenkomat serves an area with a population of up to half a million people.) During the spring visit to the voenkomat each young man is interviewed by a selection commission, consisting of the senior doctor in charge of the medical examinations, and representatives of the district executive committee, the local Party and Komsomol organizations, and the chief deputy of the Ministry of Internal Affairs in the area. The chairman of the commission is always the head of the voenkomat, a post usually occupied by a retired colonel. A representative of the local *militsia* (police) also works with the commission in the cases of boys who have been in trouble with the law (25 per cent in 1989, according to Army General Lizichev).

By the time of the interview the commission will have received the school, Komsomol, and DOSAAF references and medical records for each conscript. The 'Character Reference of Conscript' (see Appendix IV) indicates the sort of information that should be included in these references. Section Four, headed 'individual psychological qualities,' is a revealing illustration of the meaning usually attached to the word 'psychology' by Soviet officialdom. The subheadings make it clear that what the military authorities are interested in are those mental and physical qualities that may affect the youth's ability to perform certain tasks – there is no desire here to delve into the dark recesses of his mind. The army is simply interested in finding out what the soldier can do. The 'Conscript's Family Details' (see Appendix V) gives an idea of the sort of information that is collected by the commission. This chart will be sent with the conscript to his unit. The call-up takes place twice a year in May–June and November–

Army medical inspections pick up many complaints that have been overlooked by the boys' civilian doctors.

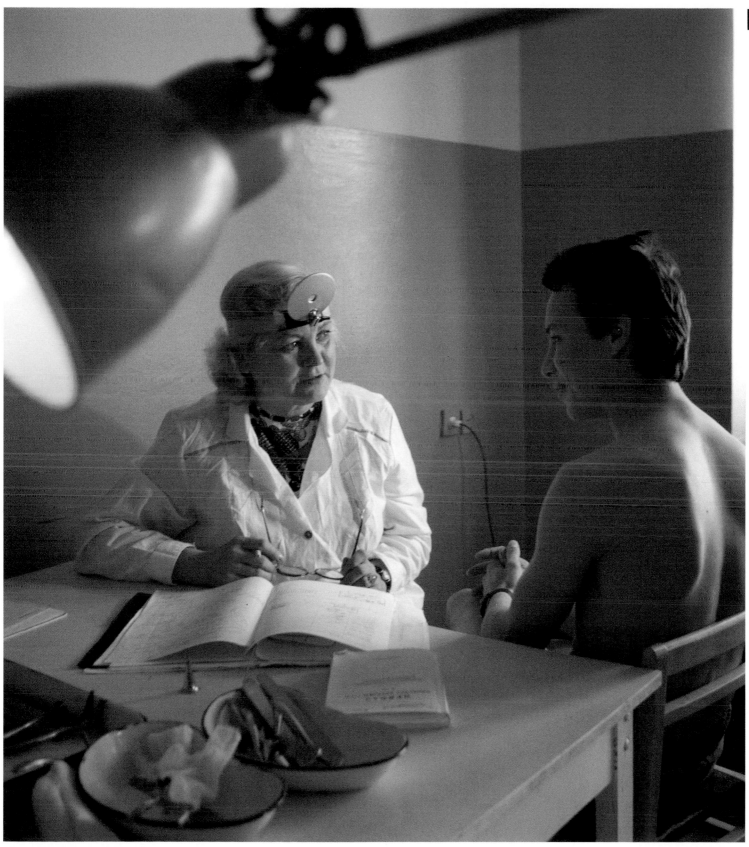

No Russian mother would send her boy off to join the army without something to keep body and soul together on the journey.

December. The task of the voenkomat is not to find the perfect niche for each young man but to fill the quotas sent by the Main Directorate for Organization and Mobilization (a department of the General Staff) two or three months before each call-up. These give the numbers of conscripts that they will be expected to supply for the various services in the different military districts and fleets. Voenkomats often have difficulty meeting the quotas for particular services, but they also sometimes have more well-qualified young men than they have been asked to provide, so they often form a pool of conscripts from the area – any shortfall in one district can then be supplied from the excess in another. Conscripts are not only needed for the Ministry of Defense. The border guards and the Kremlin Guard (both are part of the KGB), the Ministry of the Interior forces and the *militsia* also want them (the latter only a small number). The Kremlin Guard, the border guards, and the strategic rocket forces are said to be given the best all-rounders, and the airborne forces the outstandingly fit. The naval infantry gets good conscripts, and so does the navy, but the air force has lower priority since its conscripts are only involved in maintaining the aircraft and performing routine duties. The Ministry of the Interior forces traditionally need soldiers who are politically reliable and psychologically stable, since these forces are the first to be called in to deal with any civil unrest in the country. But it has been reported that the Ministry of the Interior forces are to stop conscripting young men and become entirely volunteer. Obviously the different services have specific physical requirements, as well as the more general qualities that they demand. The physical regulations include the rules that a tank man should not be more than 5 feet 8 inches tall, and a paratrooper should not weigh more than 198 pounds. These guidelines are officially acknowledged, but there are many widely held theories about the selection of conscripts that are clearly inaccurate. For example, it is often said that only the most reliable would be sent to serve in Eastern Europe – in other words, no one with Jewish blood or any religious beliefs. In fact, not only are there Jews and believers serving there, but I met the son of an Orthodox priest who served in East Germany in 1982, long before *perestroika* could have affected the policies of the voenkomats. The less able conscripts are usually sent to the rear forces or the engineering troops and the least reliable, politically and psychologically, tend to end up in a Stroybat (*Stroitelnyi Batalon*), a construction battalion.

At about the same time as the spring visit to the voenkomat, the young man has a second, more thorough medical examination, including an assessment of intelligence and manual dexterity, which will influence the commission's decision as to where to send the conscript. This medical offers the likeliest opportunity for escaping national service, for those who want to use the law to do so. Such evasion is becoming more and more difficult, for several reasons. First, the army's medical standards have been lowered in the last few years, partly due to the need for as many conscripts as possible during the Afghanistan war, partly because the low birthrate among Slavs has reduced the pool of young men available for conscription. Therefore a complaint such as 'flat feet,' which would once have been sufficient to secure exemption, now merely means that the conscript will probably have to serve in a construction battalion, where drill and an ability to march well are not high priorities. Second, inflation has affected the cost of bribing a doctor to produce a document describing a serious medical condition from which you have not suffered. The price of the ultimate deterrent to call-up, the totally unnecessary operation whereby a doctor simply administers an anesthetic, makes a dramatic incision, and then sews it up so that it scars nicely, would now be prohibitive for all but the very richest parents. (Rumors of the price vary from 10,000 to 50,000 rubles, or even more.)

The most serious difficulty facing a young man trying to escape military service nowadays is likely to be the increased alertness of the army's doctors. In the past, complicated techniques involving fasting, drinking a great deal of black coffee, or bruising oneself to show that one had fallen over in an epileptic fit (and other routines to feign serious illness) were often successful. But they had side effects, such as the necessity of undergoing nasty medical treatment and repeating the procedure whenever the voenkomat might decide to summon one again. And the army doctors are known to be very sharp. A famous scene in *Command 33*, a film of army life, is not unrealistic according to some unhappy soldiers. In the film a youth attempts to avoid conscription by pretending to have an appalling stutter. He tells the doctor, through his almost incomprehensible stammer, that he would very much like to serve in the army. The doctor discusses the peculiarities of stuttering in general and says how strange it is that all genuine stutterers can pronounce a certain polysyllabic word without difficulty. He asks the boy whether he can manage this word. Without any hesitation the boy pronounces the word perfectly. 'Gotcha!' (or Russian words to that effect) says the triumphant doctor.

Not only do the doctors know all the tricks, but they know exactly the types who are likely to try to get out of army service; apparently the ailments of the children of liberal intellectuals and wealthy profiteers deserve special attention. Young men without rich parents often organize their own exemption. The favorite method of doing this is not without risk. It entails cutting one's wrists wide open, making a lot of mess with the blood, then holding one's hand firmly against one's shoulder and calling the emergency services. It is advisable to have a friend standing by to do this for one, if it should be necessary. An attempted suicide will undoubtedly gain the status, envied in certain circles – '7b': State of Insanity – which ensures permanent exemption from military service. The Moscow and Leningrad police, who try to stamp out the activities of the *fartsovshchiks* (the young men who hang around foreigners trying to exchange money illegally or buy Western clothes), never bother to ask them why they are not in the army. The evidence of their insanity is there for all to see. During the mid-1980s the number of people attempting to feign illness to avoid military service increased dramatically. This was partly because of the Afghanistan war and partly because *dedovshchina*, the institutionalized bullying that plagues the army, was then at its worst. Now, however, some young men say that they are more resigned to performing military service than they would have been at that time.

Deferment and exemption

For many young men, the question of evading army service has now become irrelevant. Since August 1989 students who have been given places at universities and institutes have an automatic deferment. For many this means, in practice, that they

72 The Call-up

We followed the progress of these boys for eighteen months, from the day they joined up, through their time at a sergeants' training center, to their posting to a tank unit near Minsk. They were all drafted in spring 1989, just after the withdrawal from Afghanistan. For the first time in ten years young men joining the army knew they would not be sent to war. However, within twelve months most of this group were to find themselves peacekeeping in the Caucasus.

Upon arrival at a training center in Borisov, near Minsk, Yuri Badeshko is given a proper military haircut.

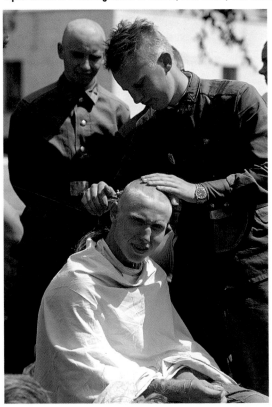

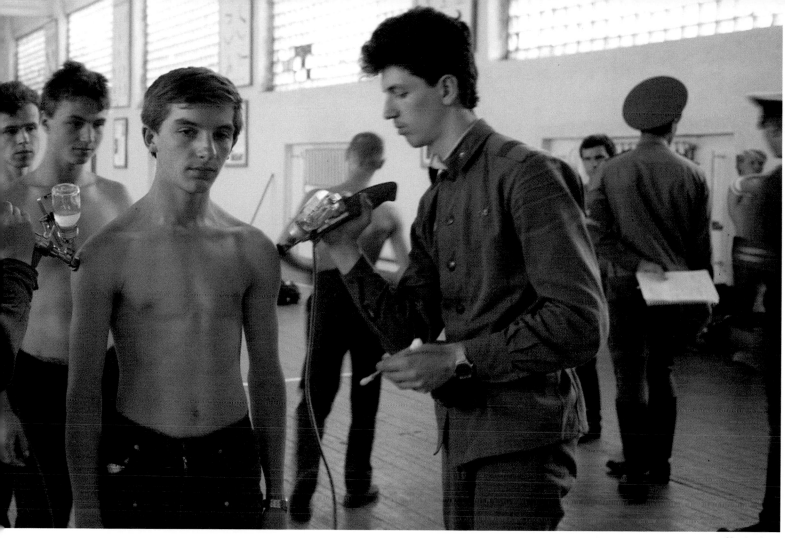

Vaccinations.

The first army meal.

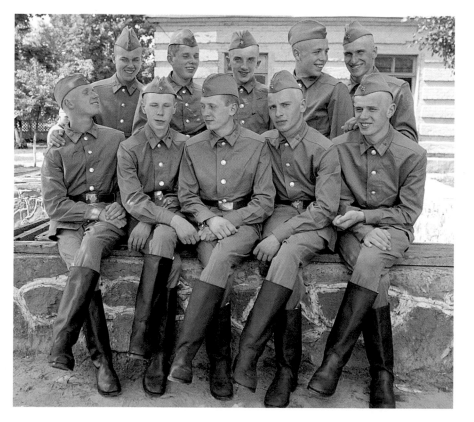

The new recruits are provided with uniforms — army kit can feel very strange at first.

Autumn 1989: Although they did know it when they joined up, three of the group were to enjoy army life so much that they later applied to the Kiev Higher Tank Engineering College.

are exempt. The rule is that if the university or institute has a military department, then students will be considered to be officers of the reserve on graduation, even though the military training undertaken by the students rarely consists of more than a few weeks of listless attendance at military camp. In theory, such a graduate could be conscripted (as an officer) if he had particular skills that the army needed, such as a grasp of an unusual modern language, or special scientific knowledge. In practice, this is very unlikely to happen in peacetime, according to the students themselves. However, in the past it was not uncommon for such graduates to be called up. Graduates of universities or institutes without a military department are now liable to be called up for one year's service, during which they will probably serve as sergeants.

Attendance at a university or institute is, of course, only one of the grounds for a deferment of national service. There are two reasons for which a young man may be given permanent exemption from military service. One is serious medical problems and the other is a record of more than two years in prison, or two shorter prison terms. In order to be given an immediate permanent exemption on medical grounds, a young man has to have a serious disorder, rendering him permanently unfit for army service. (In fact, nowadays such exemption is unlikely to be given except to those who are officially recognized as 'Category 1 disabled.') The minimum standard of eyesight for conscripts has also been lowered in the last few years. It is now, according to the Soviet system, 0.05 in one eye, and at least 0.5 in the other, with the young man wearing his glasses or contact lenses. The minimum height for a conscript is 4 feet 8 inches, and the minimum weight 105 pounds. If a youth is too small to be sent to serve, the medical experts attempt to devise physical training and feeding-up programs before abandoning hope and granting him permanent exemption. If a young man has been ill for between one month and one year he may be given a deferment of six months or a year. If he has been granted repeated exemptions for three years he may be granted permanent exemption. Young men who have been sentenced to youth prison, or who have been in trouble with the *militsia*, but have only been reprimanded or fined, will have to serve in the army. According to my Soviet underworld informants, young men who have not done their national service have a particularly unpleasant time in adult prisons. The older villains apparently consider that a boy should fulfil his patriotic duty before embarking on his chosen career, and that anyone who has not done so is some kind of shirker.

It is also possible to be granted a deferment of service for family reasons. A young man might be granted such a deferment if he has:

- two children;
- a wife who is officially an invalid of the first or second class;
- parents who are unable to work and who are financially dependent on him;
- no father, a mother who works, and brothers and sisters under the age of eight;
- no father, a mother who works, and two or more brothers or sisters who are over sixteen and are invalids of the first or second class — and so on.

The first two of these misfortunes would undoubtedly earn a young man an automatic deferment, but in other cases the result would evidently depend to some extent on the judgment of the commission examining the case. Every voenkomat has its difficult

Troshchinsky (center) was certainly not one of nature's soldiers. During the first few months he was constantly in trouble for talking too much, or for forgetting things. At other times he would be carrying so many clanking objects that 'you could hear him a mile away.' But his irrepressible optimism seemed to save him. Because he was always cheerful he was popular, and so the others used to help him out of his difficulties.

cases, which often remain under review for years, as the family circumstances shift and deteriorate. Deferments are also granted in order to enable young men to finish their education. For example, although most teenagers leave school by the time they are seventeen or eighteen, some do not complete the course until they are nineteen (at twenty they have to leave school in any case). So the voenkomat will allow a deferment until a young man has passed his graduation exams. They also grant reasonable deferments for young men who are trying to enter universities, institutes, or military colleges, if necessary allowing them to take the entrance examinations again.

Attitudes to conscription

As might be expected, attitudes to conscription vary considerably in the Soviet Union. By the time he is demobilized, a conscript may feel differently, but before joining the army his attitude to conscription is predominantly influenced by the opinion of his family, qualified to some extent by the opinions of his peers and of the media. The reaction of the family usually runs along fairly predictable lines, in keeping with its racial and social origins and general set of attitudes. Those who are most wholeheartedly against the conscription of their sons are the Baltic nationalities. After them come the Jews, Western-oriented liberals, and some (but by no means all) of the Caucasians and Central Asians. There is also resistance to conscription among Western Ukrainians. Those least hostile to conscription seem to be Russian, Byelorussian, and Ukrainian country people and those with family military traditions. These traditions are not confined to officers — many conscripts whose grandfathers or other relations fought with distinction as ordinary soldiers or sailors in the Great Patriotic War seem to have been encouraged by their parents to take pride in joining the army.

Young men who resent conscription tend to try to ignore the whole process, until they are actually marched off from the recruiting point to join their unit. Most of them do not really try to avoid military service, although those who have been saved from it by the new regulations concerning the enlistment of students do not conceal their glee. The attitude of this group is best summed up by the popular Russian expression, 'Life is a book and the army is two pages torn out of it.' They view national service simply as a waste of two years of life, although it is something to which they are quite resigned. In some circles anyone who has managed to get out of military service is seen as a hero, but it seems to be more usual, even among young men who are opposed to the idea of conscription, to feel contempt for those who slide out of doing their duty.

There are still many young people who are quite happy to serve in the army and who view it as a rite of passage. For some, the possibility of learning to drive makes army life worthwhile, since this increases the job opportunities available to them later. A small but significant number of soldiers volunteer the information that they made a serious effort, for a year or so before conscription, to prepare themselves for army service. Most of those who decided to do this give the impression that they considered their official military preparation entirely irrelevant. They usually say that they have tried to become as physically fit as possible by working out at a gymnasium and taking part in different sports. Many enrolled for DOSAAF training, especially in shooting, and others joined military-patriotic clubs or self-defense classes. Until a few years ago

A conscript shaving by his tank, hours after leaving Afghanistan.

the teaching of karate to civilians was prohibited, but lessons can now be given openly and are very popular. The advantages of learning to defend oneself before joining the army are obviously twofold. First, it makes one a better soldier. Second, it reduces one's susceptibility to *dedovshchina* if one ends up in a unit where there is violence among the conscripts.

In the last few years army authorities have had to contend with a new difficulty: large numbers of young men flatly refusing to obey the draft. This is quite different from the attempts to hoodwink army doctors. Youths who try to avoid national service for medical or personal reasons are operating within the law – they are simply trying to bend the regulations to suit themselves. But there are now areas where the conscription process has virtually broken down. A significant percentage of boys are simply ignoring any communication from the voenkomats. When, very occasionally, this happened in the past, the local *militsia* simply rounded up the offenders. But when enough young men do the same thing at the same time the police become unable to cope. In the spring of 1990, 26 per cent fewer conscripts answered the draft than in the spring of 1989. According to the army newspaper *Red Star* (12 July 1990), the spring of 1989 call-up in the Republic of Georgia fulfilled 94 per cent of its target, whereas exactly a year later the figure had fallen to 27.5 per cent. For Armenia the call-up rates were 100 per cent and 9.5 per cent respectively. Voenkomats are said to have been surrounded by demonstrators, and there are stories of attempts to prevent groups of conscripts from being taken off to their units. There is no reason to disbelieve any of these reports, in view of the widespread civil disorder in the Soviet Union. At the time of writing, however, most ordinary Slavic Soviet citizens still seem to be, at the very least, resigned to national service. But in such a volatile situation, where the media have such strong influence and where random events can so quickly alter public opinion, it is difficult to say with any confidence what will happen in the future.

⑤ THE SOLDIER'S LIFE

For the first few weeks in the army a young soldier will be in a state of shock. No matter how well he has tried to prepare himself for military service, he will find life very hard at first. From the moment he reports to the recruiting post, probably somewhat the worse for wear after all the farewells to schoolfriends and family, he will be under military discipline. Suddenly he will understand that this is the reality for which all the military instructors at school, the summer camps, and the visits to the voenkomat were preparing him. He may have to spend one night at the recruiting post, but not more. Unless something goes wrong, he and the rest of the group will be on their way to their unit within twenty-four hours, accompanied by an officer, probably a senior lieutenant, and a couple of sergeants from that unit.

Even if the boy is proud to be performing his patriotic duty, he will by now be apprehensive about what he is going to find. He will undoubtedly have heard horror stories about the army and just at this moment they will be uppermost in his mind. The most wretched people I saw in the army were a group of cowed conscripts at a recruiting post in Kiev, dressed almost, but not quite, in rags and shuffling along like prisoners of war in old newsreels. They were clearly not happy. Judging from their appearance they had received the commonly given advice to wear their oldest clothes because anything they took with them to their units would be stolen (advice that is now so generally heeded that it is impossible to ascertain whether or not it is necessary).

The interviews and medicals at the voenkomat are an official procedure. The future conscripts are often addressed in a curt, military fashion, but not usually with discourtesy. But their first few hours in the army provide a rude awakening. Many army jokes hinge on the fact that the language of command is a special Russian dialect, a blend of a little staggering rudeness and a lot of unpublishable obscenity. And the young officer who has to return to the unit with the correct number of conscripts is unlikely to treat them with kid gloves. It is an awesome task for any lieutenant to have to transport twenty or thirty resentful, undisciplined young men, many of them the worse for drink, hundreds or thousands of miles across the country, usually by train.

Quite a few of each batch of conscripts will have been selected in advance for training as sergeants (in the Soviet army almost all the sergeants are conscripts), and these are sent, not to their units, but to special training units, where they will spend

Paratroopers involved in peacekeeping in the Caucasus work on a new song. Soldiers put a great deal of energy into preparing for concerts and shows, usually described as 'people's theater.' This is officially encouraged, since such activities are thought to relieve the monotony of army life and improve the troops' morale. So soldiers who sing or play instruments well are welcome additions to any unit.

A conscript monitors and times the performance of a tank exercise at a training center outside Ashkhabad. Most of the soldiers' training is basic and repetitive, concentrating on teaching them to perform simple tasks confidently.

A soldier on duty inside the barracks of the First Company of the First Battalion of the Motorized Rifle Regiment based in Petropavlovsk-Kamchatka. This is one of two companies in the Soviet Army of which Lenin is considered to be an honorary member. According to the manual, the company orderly's post should be equipped with: 'a pedestal (wooden), telephone, the manuals of the Armed Forces of the USSR, and fire-fighting equipment.'

about six months. Conscripts who have been chosen for various specializations, such as driving, may also be sent for intensive training. In principle, of course, it is the ablest and most reliable conscripts who are picked out as potential sergeants. In practice, many officers are dissatisfied with the sergeants who are sent to them from these units. They criticize both the original selection and the training these boys have been given. The process of selecting boys to be sergeants appears to be haphazard, to say the least. Guidelines for this selection process undoubtedly exist, but no one I spoke to, either in the voenkomat, or in the units, seemed to know what they were.

Certain regiments choose their own sergeants from each intake of conscripts and train them in the unit. Although this process creates more work for the officers, there seems to be general agreement that it produces more satisfactory sergeants. Just as military colleges do not, on the whole, attempt to assess the applicants' leadership potential when they are selecting future officers, neither, apparently, do the voenkomats when selecting sergeants during the conscription process. But it is obviously a crucial asset for a conscript sergeant, who will have to take charge of other soldiers, with none of the advantages that prolonged training or proper status would have given him.

Soldiers say that the training units are much more unpleasant than normal units. The officers do not have time to get to know the conscripts, so it is impossible for them to control many of the problems that arise. There is often considerable violence in the barracks among soldiers of different nationalities and there are reports of widespread theft. However well-meaning the officers may be, working in such a unit is evidently a thankless task: as soon as the boys are beginning to be of any use as soldiers they are moved on.

Arrival and initiation

The majority of conscripts are sent straight to their regiments. Upon arrival they will have a further medical examination and they will be issued their uniforms. Apart from a few dramatic cases in which boys have been given boots they could hardly walk in, most conscripts seem to be kitted out with uniforms that fit at least tolerably well. Appendix VII lists the items of uniform issued to conscripts and the length of time for which they have to last.

Every conscript, regardless of where he has been sent, will live in basically identical barracks. The arrangement of the rooms may vary, but the plan of each barracks is broadly similar all over the Soviet Union. Each floor is designed, usually, to accommodate a company, in other words up to 100 soldiers. On each floor of every barracks there is an armory, often to the left of the entrance, protected by iron bars. A small amount of ammunition is kept here. Straight ahead of the entrance is the guard post where the soldier on duty stands. From the guard post there must be an unimpeded view of the armory. There is also a storeroom for uniforms and bed linen (the *kaptiurka*), a room where soldiers may cut each other's hair, clean their boots, iron their clothes, and so on, and usually a warm room (the *sushilka*), where wet clothes may be dried. Then there will be the company commander's office and a room where young officers may work or interview soldiers. Every barracks has a 'Lenin Room', with a small library containing a few political and historical books and some newspapers and magazines of a serious and supposedly uplifting nature. This room is used for political lessons and for private reading or studying.

At the far end, running the width of the barracks, is the dormitory, with plain iron bedsteads arranged in pairs and beside each bed a plain wooden locker. Even the size of bed is standard (26 x 76 inches) and the army manual states that for each conscript there should be twenty-seven square feet of space. There is a television in the dormitory and often an aquarium — the presence of the fish is thought to have a calming effect and to reduce the stress and the homesickness suffered by soldiers. Next to the entrance are usually the washrooms, with lavatories and washbasins.

Every soldier in the Soviet Army begins his army service in a special company with the other new recruits for the Course of the Young Soldier. This usually lasts three or four weeks and is a basic introduction to military life, covering drill, physical exercises, small arms and simple shooting exercises, and a study of the field manual. This period, often referred to as a 'quarantine,' allows the unit to study the raw human material that has arrived from the voenkomats. By the end of it, the recruit is meant to be familiar with army discipline and routine, and ready to begin serious military training.

The first landmark in the conscript's stint in the army comes at the end of the Course of the Young Soldier, when he takes the oath of loyalty. Only after he has taken this oath is a young man legally considered to be a soldier. The oath-taking ceremony is organized at regimental level and each new soldier, in turn, will repeat the familiar words:

> I, a citizen of the Union of Soviet Socialist Republics, on entering the ranks of the Armed Forces of the USSR take the oath and solemnly promise to be an honorable, brave, disciplined, and vigilant soldier, to guard strictly our military and state secrets, and to obey without question the military manuals and the orders of my commanders and superiors.
>
> I swear to study military science conscientiously, to protect military and national property, and to serve our people, our Soviet homeland, and the Soviet government until my last breath.
>
> I shall always be prepared at the order of the Soviet government to defend my homeland — the USSR — and as a soldier of her armed forces to defend her skillfully and courageously, with dignity and pride, sparing neither my blood nor my very life if necessary for the achievement of full victory over our enemies.
>
> And if I should break this solemn oath, then let me suffer the severe penalties of Soviet law and the universal hatred and contempt of the Soviet people.

It is a text with which the conscripts should be familiar, since it is printed at the beginning of the military preparation textbook used in every school, but remarkably few of them learn it by heart. Most will read from a card that is held before them. This oath-taking was traditionally an important rite of passage for Soviet men and it is still generally taken seriously. Even boys who were unwilling to join the army say that when they took the oath they did so with sincerity. Parents and friends are always invited to the ceremony and, if the journey is feasible, conscripts' families usually turn up for it.

As well as the formal ceremony, the conscript is initiated into the world of the soldier with all its rituals and slang. A conscript who has just joined the army is referred to as a *dukh* (spirit). After he has completed the Course of the Young Soldier and taken the military oath, he becomes a *molodoi* (youth), or, in some regiments, a *slon* (elephant). *Slon* is said to be an acronym, standing for 'the soldier loves great difficulties.' After six months he becomes a *bik* (bull), a *shchegol* (goldfinch), or a *cherpak* (server of food). A man who has served for a year is described as a *fayzan* (pheasant or, in units where the term was not used earlier, a *cherpak*). After a year and a half he finally becomes a privileged *ded* (from the Russian word for grandfather), able to push everyone else around. This happy state lasts until the six-monthly minister's decree authorizing the demobilization of the most senior servicemen is issued, usually on the 25, 26, or 27 March and again on the 25, 26, or 27 September, although they may be a day or two late. With the publication of the decree the status of every soldier in the army alters. *Molodoi* becomes *shchegol* and so on, up to the *ded* who finally acquires *dembel* (one who is demobilized) status. The decree is issued about three months before most of the *dembels* are allowed to go home, and from this moment on they no longer really consider themselves to be soldiers. The terms '*ded*' and '*dembel*' seem to be universally used, although the others vary. Strangely, there is no slang term to describe a man who has actually been demobilized — the word that is used by the soldiers is the ordinary *grazhdanin* — a citizen.

Dedovshchina

In recent years there has been a public outcry over the reports of institutionalized bullying of new conscripts — *dedovshchina* — by the longer-serving soldiers (*deds*). In the army, as in any closed male institution, a great deal of the culture is based on the distinctions associated with length of service. Army life has to be tough and disciplined and the sooner the conscripts learn that, the better soldiers they will make. It became clear during the 1980s, however, that *dedovshchina*, far from contributing to the command and control system of the army, was undermining it. The bullying was so widespread and so violent, that it had, in many cases, replaced all other discipline. Experience in Afghanistan forced the army to address the problem when it became clear that, especially in some motorized rifle regiments, *dedovshchina* was destroying the vital small-unit cohesion. Relationships within *otdeleniyes* (sections) were often so bad that the soldiers hated one another more than they could be made to hate the enemy.

The full extent of the problem in those days may never be known, but there is no question that it provoked boys to commit murder and suicide. It took the army some time to admit to the scale and intensity of the bullying, partly because its own monitoring and reporting system had broken down, and no one at the top knew what was going on in the barracks. The junior officers' workloads were so intensive that they did not have the time to supervise their soldiers properly. But it should be emphasized that once the facts had come to light, it was the army itself that first publicized them. In the last few years strenuous efforts have been made to eliminate the violence, and these have had considerable success.

OVERLEAF: Repairing a tracked
vehicle under camouflage in field
conditions.

Soldiers washing in the 'tent-
town' where they live during
exercises.

Most of the cases of *dedovshchina* that we heard about involved *dukhs* being forced to carry out routine chores to increase the comfort of the longer-serving men. These might include cleaning their weapons, maintaining their uniforms, and so on. As a result the *dukhs*, who in any case find army life difficult because it is unfamiliar to them, often have very little sleep and no free time. In general, the pattern is that one generation will force another to work for its comfort. Older soldiers do not usually have a particular soldier to slave for them. This is the oppression of one group by another, rather than the exploitation by one individual of another. There are stories of horrible punishments inflicted on the *dukhs* — being forced to clean the latrines with their toothbrushes or with razor blades is an old favorite. But such cases have been unusual in the last couple of years and I did not meet anyone who was prepared to say that he had personally been forced to do anything of this kind. The accounts I heard always involved the 'friend of a friend.' The level of brutality now seems to vary a great deal from one unit to another. Violence is obviously implicit in the system, but in many places a new soldier who does what he is told by the older men will not encounter it overtly. The most unpleasant practices connected with *dedovshchina* usually only flourish these days among the least prestigious troops, especially in separate construction, supply, or engineering units. There is often a conspiracy of silence surrounding the issue in those units where it is most serious. The young soldiers quickly learn that it is better to put up with things, however awful they may be, and bide their time until they can make somebody else's life miserable, than to report the matter.

Every soldier is now made aware that violence toward a younger soldier may lead to a spell in a disciplinary battalion. A conscript who is suspected of such behavior will be given official warnings by the district military attorney twice. The third time he will be sent to a disciplinary battalion. To reinforce this message most enlisted men are now given an official document that they must sign, indicating that they are aware of the statutory penalties for various offenses, including those associated with *dedovshchina*. A board on the wall of the barracks often provides further reminders of the punishments that await convicted bullies, with the names and fates of soldiers written large: 'Private Ivanov, sentenced to three years in a disciplinary battalion for nonregulation relations.' ('Nonregulation relations,' that is, relationships not provided for by the army manual, means, of course, *dedovshchina*.) The list will sometimes be illustrated with photographs of the miscreants, usually with an arresting heading, such as 'Soldier! Stop and think!'

It is worth pointing out in this connection that some of the soldiers will have left home before joining the army. These are the boys who have attended technical schools or SPTUs some distance from their homes and have had to live in the school dormitories. No one who has stayed in one of these dormitories is likely to complain about the bullying in the army: beside the violence in these institutions, the horrors of *dedovshchina* pale. It is also the case that the army *dedovshchina* echoes the system that operates in a significant number of Soviet factories, whereby the youngest or most recently recruited workers have to do a disproportionate amount of work, so that the old hands can take things easy. As the army authorities frequently point out, the problems that exist within the army are a result of the conflicts and stresses that afflict Soviet society as a whole. They do not entirely originate within the army.

Coping with army life

A Soviet conscript will probably find himself plunged into a barracks with representatives of many different nationalities. For a conscript from one of the Caucasian or Central Asian republics, this may be the first real contact that he has had with other Soviet nationalities (although he will probably have met Russians before, unless he really comes from the backwoods). For a Slav, it can be daunting to find himself, suddenly, in a minority. According to the Russian soldiers, the worst fate that can befall them is to be put into a unit where there are a lot of Azerbaijanis, who apparently gang up and terrorize everyone else. The Uzbeks are not considered to be as bad, but they also cause trouble. They stick together and do not want to have much contact with anyone else, and if one of them makes an enemy or gets into a fight, the whole lot of them will come in on his side. It is not clear why the Slav conscripts do not band together to defend themselves; they simply say that they do not have such a strong racial identity and are not so willing to get involved in other people's battles. This tribal violence is now the most serious problem facing the soldiers. It is frequently much more acute than *dedovshchina*. It may break out between soldiers of any nationality but it usually involves Caucasians or Central Asians. Trouble often empts, initially, because one group believes that another is not doing its share of the work. The Slavs do not, on the whole, initiate such violence. They may bring with them assumptions of their racial superiority, but they are not interested in asserting this by force. The Balts are also unlikely to start trouble. From their point of view, ascendancy over the other races in a Soviet army barracks is not something that is worth fighting for, as most of them have no interest in being there at all, on any terms.

The new soldier is just as likely to be suffering from homesickness as from bullying. Most soldiers leave home for the first time when they join the army – unless you count the coziness of the Young Pioneer camps. Most of the Slavs come from small families with only one or two children. Many of them have grown up with doting grandmothers in residence or living nearby and have been taught almost entirely by women – there are very few men teachers in Soviet schools. Since Russian women are, by any standards, unusually kind and excessively protective, teenage boys tend to have been mollycoddled. So it is especially hard for many of them to leave the comfy world of mothers and grandmothers for the masculine ardors of the army. The Central Asian conscripts often come from very large families, among whom it is not uncommon to have eight or ten children. But although the pattern of family life is very different, here too there is a tradition of showering indulgence upon sons.

Especially during these difficult first few weeks, the greatest asset a soldier can have is a circle of family or friends who will write to him. Some conscripts are able to give their families their army address before they leave home, so they may receive letters almost as soon as they arrive. Others, who have to find time to write to their parents before they can hope to hear from them, may not get a letter for some weeks. A soldier who knows that his family is proud of him and hoping that he will do well in the army, is far more likely to cope with the hardships than one who is feeling lonely and abandoned. Central Asian conscripts who come from backgrounds where there is no tradition of letter writing and whose parents may well be illiterate, often suffer from

A soldier in the hatch at the rear of an artillery tractor. While he is in the army every aspect of this young man's life will be governed by the army manual. He should not say 'yes' to a superior, he should say 'exactly so' (*tak tochno*), and never 'No,' but rather 'absolutely not' (*nikak nyet*). Even when speaking to other conscripts, he should use the polite form of address, '*vi*,' when a service matter is being discussed, though this regulation is certainly not scrupulously adhered to.

homesickness and from a feeling of isolation from family and friends. This is even worse if other soldiers are receiving letters and parcels from home.

Conscripts are always sent to units with a group recruited from the same voenkomat. A soldier's life will obviously be easier if he ends up in the same unit as some of his friends from home. Resourceful boys sometimes go to considerable lengths to ensure that they are sent to serve together. I met a group of conscripts who had been at the same school all their lives and who did not want to be separated in the army. They turned up at the recruiting point on the appointed day and waited, along with everybody else, to be shunted off to their units. They knew that they were meant to be split up and sent to different parts of the country. But during the course of the day they managed to get hold of the young woman who was in charge of their documents and persuaded her to put all their papers into the same pile, with the result that they were all sent to the same regiment. Once there, it was a small matter to stick together so tightly that they ended up in the same company.

Training and duties

The army year is divided into two 'training periods,' terms in effect, from 1 January to the end of May, and from July to November. This basic rhythm of military life is governed by the biannual rotation of conscripts. Every six months a quarter of the soldiers leave the army and are replaced by new arrivals. So the army is perpetually in the process of absorbing recruits, who will themselves, within a matter of months, be helping to induct the next lot. Each spring and autumn, the conscripts who have been sent to training centers arrive at their units as sergeants or specialists, just before the next batch of conscripts, called up six months later. Every September young lieutenants arrive in the units from the military colleges. They are put in charge of platoons at the start of the important winter training period. Throughout the armed forces the conscripts' training is simple and repetitive, based on straightforward battle drills.

Between the training periods the soldiers carry out routine maintenance work in the units, but they have no lessons, apart from current affairs and political education. Repairs to the barracks and the training equipment can be hard work, but soldiers nevertheless generally prefer these periods — at least they interrupt the otherwise endless training. Soldiers often find themselves helping out on local farms especially during the summers. Although junior officers find it very annoying that the routine of the army should be interrupted in this way, the commanders find it difficult to resist the requests of the state and collective farms for assistance with the harvest. Soldiers may also be loaned to factories and other enterprises. In such cases, the unit will be paid for their labor, and this money will be spent on improving the conscripts' food and accommodations. By law, only 5 per cent of it may be used for the benefit of the officers and *praporshchiks*, even if they are homeless.

Every soldier spends his time in the same way: drill, PT, military and political lessons, and a little recreation. The daily routine is more or less the same for all conscripts, with a slight variation between the forces. Appendix VI gives the timetable for a typical motorized rifle regiment. The mornings are the worst part of the day for

Letters from home are the conscripts' lifeline. Soldiers do not have to put stamps on letters that are sent from the unit — the postal system carries their mail without charge.

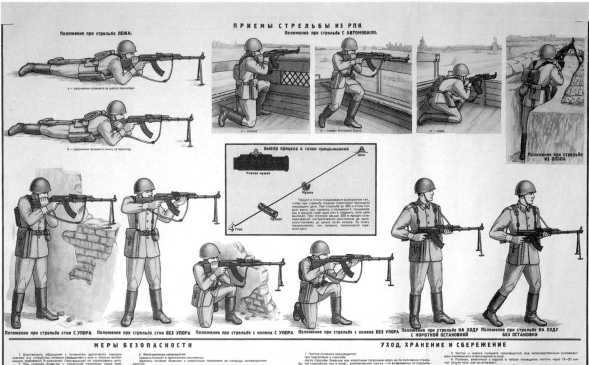

The army has a poster for almost everything – in the picture above, the soldier is standing beneath the boot-mending poster, while the example below explains firing positions and, in the center, how to take aim using the sight.

90

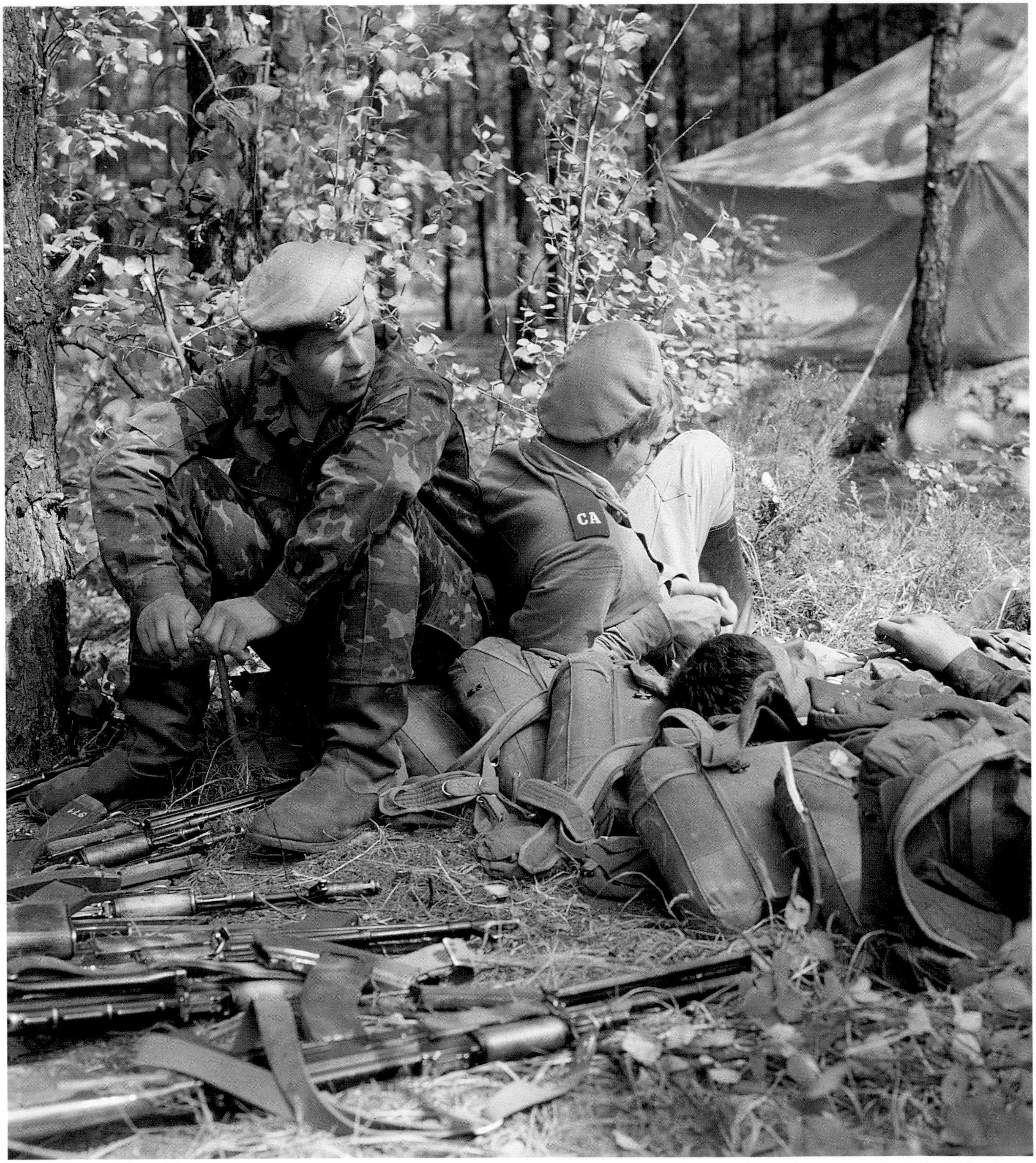

most soldiers. First there is the shock of reveille, at 06:00, when the soldiers have 45 seconds to get out of bed. They immediately pull on their long woollen underwear (in winter) or boxer shorts and vest (in summer) in which they sleep, then their trousers and boots, ready for 50 minutes of physical exercises, often including a cross-country run. In some parts of the country, soldiers regularly have to dig themselves out of the barracks in the morning, because so much snow has fallen overnight.

After the barracks have been cleaned and tidied and the soldiers have washed and shaved (often in cold water), there is the morning check. This is usually conducted by a sergeant, with the platoon formed up in two lines. In some units the entire uniform is checked every day, in others the procedure is more cursory. Collar liners are always checked, however. Usually, all the soldiers will be asked to undo their top button, so that the inside of the collars can be seen at a glance. They may be asked to remove their belts, so that the sergeant can make sure that the buckles are clean and that the belt has the soldier's number on it. Hats may be inspected to ensure that each soldier has the statutory two needles, with black and green thread, tucked into the lining. The sergeant will usually walk around the soldiers to check the back view. He will consider the neatness of their hair. He may (although not many actually do this) ask the soldiers to empty their pockets. Pockets should contain the conscript's military documents and Komsomol card, a handkerchief, a comb, a pen, a notebook (without any loose bits of paper in it), and nothing else. If any aspect of his uniform is unsatisfactory, a conscript will probably miss breakfast. At least once a week the company commander will arrive to observe the process but, in general, reveille, PT, and the morning check are the responsibility of sergeants.

During the morning check the sergeant will ask whether anyone is unwell. If any soldier says that he is ill he is taken to the medical department, where the doctor may either send him back with a flea in his ear or recommend that he should be taken off work for up to three days. The doctor gives advice; it is only the commander (of the platoon, usually) who can issue the order that the boy is to be relieved of his work. The reason for this procedure is that, during combat, any decision concerning the fitness of a soldier to fight would be taken by the officers. Any conscript who is seriously ill is to be taken straight to the medical department, without having to turn up on parade.

After breakfast the soldiers often have to listen to the morning news broadcast, and this is usually followed by fifty minutes of political information. Nowadays this may take the form of a vigorous discussion of the latest news, but there are still units where old-fashioned propaganda is dished out. Before lunch, the main meal of the day at 15:00, the soldiers have six hours of work, or training, according to the schedule. After the meal the conscripts have thirty minutes free time, during which they may buy sweets or buns in the tearoom (usually next to the canteen), have a quiet smoke, or visit the voentorg (the military shop) if they need razor blades, toothpaste, or anything for their uniform. Cleaning and maintaining weapons and machinery usually take up about an hour and a half during the afternoon. As in all armies, this is taken seriously, and inexperienced soldiers find it difficult to strip down and clean even an assault rifle to the sergeant's satisfaction in the time allowed.

Conscripts are likely to have time for private study during the afternoon, further political education, group sports, or physical training. At about 20:00 there is supper,

This soldier is sleeping during the day because he has been on duty all night. Conscripts usually sleep in their underwear, which is changed once a week, when they go to the *banya*. They are usually given clean sheets at the same time. Here the dormitory looks quiet and perfectly ordered. But at night, after 'lights-out,' it will come to life.

OPPOSITE: Paratroopers relax during exercises.

Breakfast in the field – porridge, bread and butter, and tea. Meals always taste better in field conditions. Soldiers usually complain about army food, and from my observation it is pretty unappetizing, but the soldiers eat it, and soldiers who are being demobilized almost always look stronger and healthier than the new conscripts.

after which most soldiers watch the main national television news program, 'Vremya' (Time). This is compulsory, but if the zampolit is in a good mood he may permit the soldiers to watch a feature film or a documentary as well. (All conscripts have to watch the Sunday-morning armed forces program, 'In the Service of the Motherland.') Later, there is a further half hour for the soldiers to prepare their uniform for the next day, and an evening walk, during which they sing in unison. In many regiments each company has its own song, usually an old favorite, handed down from one army generation to the next. The soldiers are usually meant to go to bed at 22:00 or 22:30, but, needless to say, anyone who has not finished his day's work will be unable to do so. There is usually a weekly platoon 'summing-up' session, during which the progress of each soldier is assessed. Such public discussion of people's strengths and failings is a familiar point of Soviet, and especially army, life.

The principal interruption to this routine is guard duty, either in the company or in the regiment, which every soldier must undertake in turn. The frequency with which the soldiers have to go on duty depends on the strength of unit: if it is drastically reduced the soldiers will go on duty more often. This is a serious matter. Soldiers on guard duty are issued live ammunition, and there are three situations in which a guard may open fire, without being ordered to do so. These are:

- If a guard post or a guard is attacked.
- If someone claims to be a commander but is not.
- If somebody approaching the guard post is challenged and then warned to stop but does not do so. The soldier should warn that he will open fire. If the intruder does not stop, the guard should then shoot, aiming away from him. Finally, if the intruder has still not responded satisfactorily, the soldier should shoot him.

A soldier cleans his boots before going on guard duty. A conscript is usually issued with a plastic belt, a *derevyashka* ('wooden') as the soldiers call it, because it is so hard and uncomfortable. By the time they have served for about six months most soldiers buy themselves leather belts from the unit's voentorg, the military shop.

Sunday is usually a day of rest (relatively), and the soldiers will probably be allowed to go into town, unless they have to go on duty.

The vital task for every soldier, every day, is the maintenance of his uniform. Boots must be cleaned, shirts and trousers ironed, and cotton collar liners must be sewn into working shirts. These collar liners may be bought ready-made by the extravagant (for 20 kopeks each) or cut out of a meter of cotton, which costs one ruble and will provide enough liners for a month. Each collar liner is used for two days (one day for each side), after which it can be washed and reused or thrown out. Some soldiers fold a large piece of cotton several times, so that by turning it to reveal a clean side each day a single piece of cotton can last for well over a week. In some units the soldiers are permitted to do this, in others it is strictly forbidden, except when the troops are in the field and unable to wash or iron their collar liners.

Conscripts have various methods of subtly altering their uniforms to denote their status and length of service, and this is done to a greater or lesser extent everywhere in the army. Colossal energy goes into modifying and improving the basic kit issued by the army. It is not difficult for the experienced eye to spot these alterations, though, needless to say, any alteration to the uniform is officially prohibited. However, since the uniforms often have to be taken in to fit properly, and since they have to be mended by the soldiers, it is difficult to enforce this regulation. The most widespread indication of the length of time a man has served is simply the tightness of the belt. A soldier is required to buckle his belt around the waist as tightly as is comfortable. For the first six months he will do this, but later the belt will get progressively looser. By the time he is demobilized it may well be hanging slackly around his hips. At the same time, the buckle itself is likely to develop from its original, almost flat state into a near semi-circle after two years. In some regiments the soldiers will then hammer the belt flat again once the relevant minister's decree has been issued.

Anyone may modify his uniform to improve comfort and efficiency, although a young soldier would certainly not have the time or energy to do so. Most Soviet soldiers wear plastic boots with leather soles which they call '*kirzachi*,' from the word *kirza*, for the synthetic material of which they are made. These *kirzachi* look a great deal better if, when they are new, they are filled with very tightly packed sand and left for about a week to improve their shape. Then they should be covered with shoe polish and ironed with a very hot iron, then covered with polish again and ironed once more. After being ironed three or four times and then brushed very hard, 'the boots will shine like a darkened mirror.' To complete the transformation the rather coarse contours of the sole should be carved with a very sharp knife to a more elegant shape.

Soldiers consider that the *shinel*, the heavy winter overcoat, looks better if it is brushed briskly with a wire brush, to make the wool look fluffier and therefore of better quality. The winter hat, the *ushanka*, made of 'fish fur,' is often modified by soldiers serving in temperate regions, who find the hat too warm in its original state. They open the seams and remove the lining material. Then they sew it up again, wash it, and stretch it over a pile of books or a block of wood. They leave it to dry for a day, then iron it to improve the shape. After this treatment it has a much more defined, square form. The soldiers think that it looks a great deal better.

Then there are niceties of fit. To be chic, the *pilotka* (the small side cap) and the soft field *furashka* (peaked cap) should be as small as possible. Trousers should either be very narrow or very wide, depending on local taste. Shirts should fit closely, and many soldiers become expert at tailoring them in such a way that no officer will ever notice that they have been touched. Enthusiastic bodybuilders will go to some trouble to get hold of a uniform that is too small, to create the impression that after all their work in the gym they are bulging out of their original clothing.

Officers and *praporshchiks*

If a soldier feels that he is mastering the job he has been given, if he feels that his family and friends back home are supporting him, and if he has been put into a unit where there is not too much bullying, then, if he is prepared to admit it, he may begin to rather enjoy his army service after a few months. There is, however, one factor that governs every soldier's experience of army life. That is, quite simply, the quality of the officers in his regiment. Some units are more likely than others to have first-class officers. Certain regiments are officially described as 'Guards,' an honorary title awarded to units that have distinguished themselves in combat. A posting to one of these smart regiments is likely to bring out the best in an officer. To encourage him there is the prestige of the regiment, the frequency with which it is likely to be officially

Repairing boots in the barracks of an infantry regiment in Byelorussia.

A *praporshchik* and a soldier discuss schedules at the airborne regiment in Tula. The soldier's armband indicates that he is in charge of delivering the day's mail and messages. The slogan on the building behind reads 'The honor of my regiment is my honor, the glory of my regiment is my glory.'

94 Laying a Pontoon

The pontoon is made up of hinged sections that unfold automatically when dropped into the water, and are then linked together by the pontooners. The PMP can be used either as a full pontoon bridge or as a raft. A full PMP set consists of 32 river sections, plus shore links, and is usually assembled in 50 minutes. Each of these sections is 21 feet wide and 22 feet long. The bridge/raft is assembled parallel to the shore and then swung across the river by the powerboats.

Traditionally, after laying their first pontoon, soldiers and officers are 'baptized' as pontooners by being chucked into the river.

Rear view of a paratrooper. All airborne troops are obsessed by their feet. If you want to make friends with a pilot, talk to him about flying. If you want to get along with a sailor, talk about ships and the sea. But the best conversation gambit with a paratrooper is feet, and what they suffer, and the relative merits of the different types of footwear.

visited, and the slightly higher caliber of the conscripts. But it is easy for the officers' standards to slip in the less glamorous branches of service. When the morale of the officers begins to flag, the standard of the unit as a whole very quickly deteriorates and, in this case, the soldiers invariably suffer. An important element here is the behavior of the senior commanders toward the junior officers. If the lieutenants in a regiment are treated contemptuously by the older officers, there is little hope that they will put much energy into improving the lives of the soldiers.

The officers who command the most respect are those who are seen to be hardworking. It might surprise the officer corps to know that when soldiers criticize their commanders they tend to accuse them of being lazy and sloppy. Brutal officers incur less hostility than those who neglect their duty. The soldiers' attitude toward their officers is also affected by their physical appearance. In the opinion of the soldiers, officers should always look neat and smart, both in uniform and in their own clothes. Oddly, the morale of conscripts can be raised dramatically if their officers, especially the younger ones, are seen to be well dressed in civilian clothes. If the officers look scruffy, the enlisted men are more likely to feel that military service is futile and that there is no dignity in their role as soldiers. This insight is guaranteed to induce depression, which is likely, in turn, to lead to insubordination in the ranks.

Soldiers invariably come into contact not only with officers but also with warrant officers, *praporshchiks*, and occasionally with extended servicemen. The *praporshchik* rank was introduced in 1972 in an attempt to create a proper noncommissioned officer class. The term dates from the days of the Russian Imperial Army and means 'standard-bearer.' Before 1972, 'extended servicemen' (conscripts who sign on for a short period after finishing their two-year stint) were all that stood between the soldiers and the officers. The status of *praporshchiks* is in no way comparable to that of the warrant officers or NCOs in most Western armies. They are seen much more as trusted soldiers than as the backbone of the army in the British mold. Individual *praporshchiks* play a vital part in establishing the morale and maintaining the standards of a platoon or a company, and we were told of instances where a *praporshchik* had been instrumental in overcoming deeply ingrained violent *dedovshchina* traditions. But such cases depend wholly on the strength of character of the individual. The army system does not, in principle, invest them with the status and responsibility that would automatically give them the influence of their Western counterparts. 'A chicken is not a bird and a *praporshchik* is not an officer,' the soldiers say. This is a view that seems to be shared by most officers. Officers will often blame *praporshchiks* for some of the shortcomings in their units. But it is unusual to hear them being given any credit for what's right. I have been told that in certain cases officers show more respect for the enlisted men than they do for *praporshchiks*. However, their resourcefulness is legendary. In every unit there is a wizard *praporshchik* who can keep vehicles running forever and prolong the life of electrical appliances far beyond any reasonable expectancy. And it was a *praporshchik* in Afghanistan, men say, who first thought of wringing out Aeroflot disinfectant tissues and mixing the liquid with lemonade. These men can fix or invent anything. Soldiers often call *praporshchiks* '*kusoks*,' meaning literally 'pieces,' but implying bounty – an allusion to the fact that they often work in positions that give them access to desirable goods. The idea that they steal is the basis of most *praporshchik* jokes. The best known of these concerns a present that arrives in the Kremlin addressed to Mr Gorbachev, from the President of the United States. Gorbachev unwraps the parcel and, since it is obviously something military, he sends for the Minister of Defense and asks him what it is.

'It's a neutron bomb, Comrade President.'

'What is that?'

'It's a bomb that eliminates human life but leaves property and material intact.'

'I see. But what can we send in return?'

The minister thinks for a minute.

'It's obvious,' he says, 'we will send a *praporshchik*. They eliminate property and material but leave human life intact.'

Praporshchiks often serve in their home area, and are not moved around the country. This is generally a sensible system, since it increases the stability of the units and makes a career as a *praporshchik* more attractive than it might otherwise be. But it caused difficulty during the campaign in Afghanistan, when some of them insisted on their right not to move. This did not win them many friends among the officer corps.

There are virtually no official regimental traditions in the Soviet army, and very few obvious differences between the units. The idiosyncrasies of military life depend entirely on the people inside the army. Within the confines of the strictly regulated army system, the soldiers of every unit live their own diverse lives, with their own morality, their own hierarchy, their own humor, and their own resources of equipment and imagination. In a good unit the secret life of the barracks revolves around bawdy and merciless jokes, community spirit, and a stern code of behavior. This soldier's code of honor seems to be based on the following principles:

- Never rat on your mates, no matter what they may have done. Cover up for them, if necessary. Soldiers should sort out their own affairs, without involving the officers.
- When caught, be willing to take the rap.
- Don't moan.
- Present a united front to the officers and *praporshchiks*.
- Going into town illicitly, meeting girls, bringing food and drink into the barracks, and concocting alcoholic drinks are all okay: a man has to live.
- Avoiding classroom lessons is also, on the whole, okay.
  But:
- *DON'T* shirk off military work. You are in the army and you should take pride in being a good soldier.
- Never feign illness. This is very shabby behavior indeed. You should always attempt to carry on working despite mild injury or ill health.

There is usually a strong sense of solidarity among the soldiers in a company, and to an even greater extent in a platoon. It is to everyone's advantage to help the weakest in order to improve the marks of the group as a whole. Soldiers have been known to carry an appalling athlete for part of the way on a cross-country run in order to avoid punishment for the whole platoon. In such a case, however, the soldier concerned will

A soldier enjoying a *'papirosa'* – the traditional, cheap way to smoke. These are cardboard tubes, containing about a third as much tobacco as an ordinary cigarette. Soldiers master all sorts of unusual skills in the army. Resourceful soldiers discovered long ago that a cigarette or two can be fitted inside the instrument compartment in the stock of a Kalashnikov. Some soldiers can also hide cigarettes inside a *pilotka*, the hat worn here, but this takes real artistry.

In many units there is a special seat reserved for soldiers on their birthday, where they sit in solitary splendor eating extra delicacies, such as sweets or fruit drinks.

be strongly encouraged to improve his physical condition. People who would otherwise never meet are thrown together in the army. A Russian factory worker might suddenly find himself standing for hours on end in a trench with a Dagestani herdsman, each of them struggling to learn to shoot straight. At first they will probably distrust each other, but after a while the barriers between them will break down.

As the soldiers get to know each other they develop running jokes concerning their common experiences and acquaintances. They swap stories endlessly, either parables or accounts of their own experiences, to while away the hungry hours out in the mud and the cold. Sometimes, after a meal or when they stop to smoke a cigarette, a soldier who has hitherto seemed completely inarticulate will pour his heart out to another in a sudden rush of confidence. It is through such friendships that soldiers survive. The companionship and the bond of everyday conspiracies against the common adversary help to mitigate the exhaustion, the homesickness, and the hunger. When a soldier says, 'let's have a smoke,' it often really means 'give me half your cigarette.' The soldiers' ethic of sharing demands that the other should give half his cigarette, even if he does not really know the man very well. Any food parcel from home will automatically be distributed among friends and a conscript will always lend his toothpaste or shoe polish to another, not only because he knows that some day he may need to ask the same favor. Of course, if the unit is plagued with racial violence, the relationships between the soldiers will not be ideal. Where there is an ingrained atmosphere of violence and distrust even the friendships among soldiers of the same nationality may suffer.

The lowest of the low, in any company, is the *stukach*, the stool pigeon, who reports everything that goes on in the barracks. In general, the *stukach* will carry his pernicious tales to the officers, although some are suspected of talking to the KGB. But it does not really matter to whom he is reporting; it is for his disloyalty to the group that he is held in contempt. Otherwise gentle soldiers are knowledgeable about the best methods of dealing with such people. The thing to do, apparently, is 'to make a *tyomnaya* for him' (from *tyomnaya komnata* – a darkened room). This means jumping him from behind, throwing a blanket over his head, and dragging him into a darkened room, there to beat the hell out of him. As he cannot see his assailants and the blanket will prevent too many bruises from developing, he will be unable to add this incident to the list of those he has reported. The same punishment can be meted out to anyone who repeatedly steals from his comrades, but this is more unusual.

'Off-duty' activities

Soldiers make army life more tolerable and enjoyable not only by mastering new professional challenges, but also by organizing little extra comforts to soften the rigors of the barracks. For this the soldier needs the cooperation of everyone else, since such arrangements are invariably prohibited. Good officers, naturally, know all about them and turn a blind eye most of the time, so long as the men behave with proper discretion. One of the principal requirements of the conscripts is a method of boiling water after lights out, so that the older soldiers who are not exhausted by their day's work can relax over a cup of tea. The standard method of doing this is to connect two razor blades to thin pieces of wire and stick them into an electrical socket. This will give the soldier a violent shock, short-circuit the whole barracks, or boil the water very quickly. But if the second worst happens there is usually somebody around with some sort of training as an electrician who can restore the power supply.

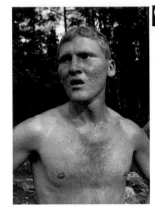

Even during maneuvers soldiers have to do their daily physical training. Here a conscript pauses for breath after a cross-country run.

In every barracks, everywhere, there is a loose floorboard in a corner or under a bed beneath which contraband can be stashed. Food, drink, and old letters and diaries (neither of which a soldier is supposed to keep) are the basic items to be found in such caches. There are even stories of sailors on board nuclear submarines storing goodies under the floor, but these, one hopes and presumes, are inaccurate. 'If he finds our hiding place our platoon commander will personally nail down the floorboard,' a soldier serving east of the Urals told me. 'And then we have to open it up all over again,' he added, resignedly. Needless to say, not everything that the soldiers want to hide is put under the floorboards. Every barracks yields several other hiding places. The storeroom invariably holds more than the officers and *praporshchiks* are meant to know about. Interesting things are often to be found among the sheets in the linen cupboard or under the parade caps, which are usually stored on a high shelf. The pockets of the parade uniforms are also useful for concealing small objects not intended for the officers' eyes.

Soldiers like to be able to watch television in the evenings, just like anyone else. In the last couple of years the coverage of current affairs on Soviet television has become very exciting. Soldiers are now keen to watch such programs as 'Vzglyad' ('Glance'), the late-night program on Fridays that deals with contemporary problems and also includes incisive interviews with public figures and recent rock videos. The soldiers also enjoy watching documentary programs, game shows, and feature films. However, it is strictly forbidden for them to watch television after lights out, so far-sighted commanders and zampolits frequently remove the television aerial cable. Therefore there is often a spare ('first-aid') cable under the floorboards.

The conscripts also like to have something to eat as they are watching television and drinking tea, but unfortunately they are not allowed to keep food in the barracks. It is easy enough for them to buy food, either from their tea room or from shops in town, but if it is to be kept in the barracks it has to be hidden. Anything brought back from town is described, in the soldiers' slang, as *samolyot* (noun or adjective), the word for an aircraft, which means, literally, 'flown off alone.' The word can be used to describe the absence without leave itself, as well as the booty gathered on such an expedition. Leaving the unit without permission (also called *samovolga*) is a serious offense, but not an uncommon one. In one well-run regiment, I was told that almost every night in every barracks at least one person spends all night out, but they usually manage to sneak back in without being found out. Indulging in these activities is not in any way incompatible with being a good soldier. Almost the opposite seems to be true. Of all the units I visited, those where the soldiers displayed the most initiative in these unofficial matters were, in general, those where they had the highest ideals and the most positive attitude toward military service. In those units where discipline and morale seemed to be lowest, the soldiers displayed a lethargy even toward the organization of fun.

If a soldier is to get on in the Soviet Army he needs to develop *soldatskaya smekalka*. This can be translated as 'soldier's tempering,' but it really means 'soldier's know-how,'

On the drill square of the regiment in Tula GAZ-66 trucks and equipment are prepared for air-dropping. In this case they are to be dropped using a multiparachute system, which costs 10,000–12,000 rubles for the set of five parachutes. The vehicles are mounted on pallets.

incorporating intuition, low cunning, and common sense as well. *Smekalka* warns the soldier when there's an officer about and lets him know when it is safe to sneak into or out of the regiment. It suggests ways of circumventing the thousand obstacles to pleasure so unkindly placed in his path, and inspires him to the prodigious feats of inventiveness that characterize the Soviet soldier. This resourcefulness is vital in the line of duty, as well as in the pursuit of pleasure. If the soldier is responsible for a weapon or a vehicle, he has to keep it in working order, come what may. He can't just whine that there seems to be something wrong with it. Making do, mending, resorting to the most unorthodox engineering and mechanical processes, it's up to him to keep the thing functioning somehow until it becomes the responsibility of some other poor bastard. As such, *soldatskaya smekalka* is an extraordinary asset to the Soviet Army and, in the necessarily less than ideal conditions of wartime combat, its importance might be vital.

A lieutenant explains a conscript's mistakes to him during company training exercises. 'If you can't do it, we'll teach you. If you don't want to, we'll force you,' as the commanders always say.

But even the best *soldatskaya smekalka* cannot always keep potential trouble away. Sooner or later every soldier will be caught in the wrong place at the wrong time. This is where the second vital soldierly skill – *otmazatsa* – comes into play. This means 'talking one's way out of it.' The basic *otmazatsa* is simple and obvious. If it is a lieutenant who finds you, then the captain has given you a special task; if it is a major, then it was the lieutenant colonel, and so on. The idea is that no officer will risk making a fool of himself by going to his superior to ask whether or not the story is true. But of course certain situations call for something more sophisticated.

Another important part of army life is the ability to *koseet* (literally, 'to cut down'), to shirk or reduce work. There are various ways of doing this. There is the tactic of making a relatively pleasant job last a long time. For example, after a barracks had been painted, a small group of soldiers was asked to scrape flecks of paint off the windows using their bayonets. This proved to be a much more time-consuming job than anyone had foreseen, perhaps because of the warm weather conditions at the time. By the same token, a physically arduous task may take longer than predicted – soldiers asked to dig a deep trench, for example, might consider it more important to conserve energy than time. Where the task concerns the maintenance of the barracks, most soldiers will consider that it is perfectly reasonable to *koseet*, but many will violently disapprove of such behavior during their military training.

Rounds of ammunition to be used during training exercises.

Soldiers are interested in drink and girls. Neither of these commodities is very easily obtainable for the average national serviceman. Conscripts are forbidden to drink anything alcoholic and it is even an offense to sell alcohol to a conscript. Of course, given time, it is always possible for the soldiers to find someone who will buy alcohol for them, or an amenable shopkeeper who will sell it to them directly. But alcohol is expensive in the Soviet Union. A bottle of cheap vodka, at ten rubles, would be more than a month's pay for a private, and drinking is an offense to which responsible officers cannot turn a blind eye. In many units, drinking, beyond the occasional beer on a free Sunday, is simply too difficult for the soldiers to arrange. Needless to say, many of them produce their own alcohol, but problems with storage limit the amount that they can make.

Drink sometimes reaches the conscripts in parcels from home. When a packet addressed to a soldier arrives at the unit, he will be summoned by the company

Food plays a large part in the mythology of every army, and all soldiers, everywhere, have some rather lurid ideas about what is actually being served up to them.

OPPOSITE: In good regiments the soldiers spend a great deal of time writing diaries and drawing cartoons of army life. These three were drawn by conscripts in Kamachatka and describe military life from their point of view.

commander (or his *zampolit*) and will be asked to open it in their presence, so that they can examine the contents. 'We trust them and check them,' as an enlightened junior officer put it. Knowing this, nobody would be stupid enough to send a bottle of alcohol to a soldier. The answer is to fill a jar with vodka and then put some apples or cherries into it, so that it looks like stewed fruit. Vigilant company commanders sniff all liquids, just to be sure. The officers know all the tricks, so there is a constant battle of ingenuity between them and the friends on the outside. Soldiers reckon that about 5 per cent of the alcohol that is mailed to the units gets past the officers, an acceptable proportion from their point of view.

Drugs, especially marijuana, are also buried in food parcels from home, often in pots of jam or in toothpaste. Since drugs can be packed inside absolutely anything, wrapped in foil, it is more difficult for the officers to detect them. In some units drug-taking is an extremely serious issue, although in others it is almost unheard of. The scale of the problem seems to be linked, in general, to the proportion of ethnic Central Asians in a unit, for the obvious reason that many of them know all about drugs before they join up. I have been told of units where the discipline had broken down entirely because of drug-taking. Soldiers were stealing anything they could lay their hands on in order to buy drugs, and when stoned they were completely uncontrollable. If the habit is sufficiently widespread it becomes almost impossible to eradicate. You can send one or two offenders to a disciplinary battalion, but you cannot do the same with an entire company. During the war in Afghanistan, soldiers certainly managed to get their hands on heroin (kindly supplied to them through the generosity of the Mujaheddin, it is said) and, partly as a result of this, there are now a great many addicts in the Soviet Union.

A good officer's *smekalka* will tell him which of the conscripts in his care is likely to be receiving presents of drugs. The officers have also become quite expert, in the past few years, at spotting the symptoms of drug abuse. Soldiers sometimes ask their friends and relations to send parcels in care of the local post office, in the hope of avoiding the officers' checks. This can be successful, but alert officers will in any case notice that the soldier has been drinking or taking drugs.

Planning the acquisition of liquor, hiding it, and reminiscing about past sprees and drinking bouts that went awry innocently absorbs a lot of the soldiers' energy. But, with certain startling exceptions, and considering their ages and sex, there is very little drinking among the soldiers. The same could be said of their quest for female company. Despite feverish interest and the effort they put into the hunt, very few of them find girlfriends in the places where they serve. From the girl's point of view, there are too many drawbacks to a soldier boyfriend. They have very little free time, very little money, and within two years they will have left the area. The girl back home is a different matter. Like all soldiers everywhere, the conscripts want to have a girlfriend to write to, even if the relationship is not, in fact, very serious. Stuck in a barracks thousands of miles away, soldiers invariably start to invest such friendships with undue significance. Others who have been going out with their girlfriends for some time join up confident in the knowledge that the girl to whom they have pledged their undying devotion will be waiting for them when they get back home.

Soldiers' maxims often complain about the inadequacy of love affairs conducted by

mail: 'Love by letter is like lunch by telephone,' for example. Nevertheless, the girl-friend's letters are a lifeline to which the soldier clings through all the hardships of army life. One thing is certain, though. Sooner or later The Letter will come, telling the soldier that she has found someone else, that she is engaged, that she is already married. 'A girl's love is like a soldier's belt, the longer you have served the looser it gets,' as they say. In any company in the army, at any time, there will be someone whose friends are trying to cover up for his bad work. He will have been plunged into a deep depression by the letter from the girl, from his friends telling him the news about her, or from his female relations who have decided that, for his own good, he ought to know what she is up to.

Teenagers often marry before the boy joins up, hoping that in doing so they will be able to meet more often. Married soldiers are given extra leave and there is now a rule that they should not be sent more than 120 miles from home. Marrying the girlfriend does not, in the experience of the Soviet soldiery, necessarily prevent the arrival of the dreaded letter from home. It just makes it much worse when it does come. The unfaithful girlfriend or wife is the classic cause of the soldier's depression. Another, less predictable source of unhappiness for conscripts is the illness or death of grand-parents. If a parent or sibling dies or is seriously ill, the soldier will automatically be given compassionate leave. However, he is unlikely to be allowed to go home if it is a grandparent who is ill, unless the grandparent is his official guardian. But many Russian children whose mothers work full-time are brought up by their grandmothers, and a considerable number of soldiers are haunted by the fear that they will never see *babushka* again and will even be unable to attend her funeral.

The high point of service, for the common soldier, is home leave. Every conscript may, in principle, be given leave to go home once, for ten days plus traveling time, during his national service. In practice, many are not sent at all, especially if they are considered to have behaved badly since being recruited. Soldiers in units that are at very reduced strength may also be unable to go home, simply because they are needed to maintain the regiment. Others may be given more than one leave, especially if they have performed well during sports or musical competitions. Conscripts who serve on submarines (especially nuclear submarines) usually have much more generous home leave. If a soldier apprehends an intruder while on guard duty, he will automatically be given ten days' home leave, whether or not he has already had the opportunity to go home.

Soldiers who live a long way from their place of service frequently gain extra time at home by flying. When traveling time is calculated, the number of days that the journey would take by train is added on to the number of days of leave granted. So, if he can raise the plane fare (usually by a donation from home), a soldier might easily be able to gain himself an extra week at home if, for example, he serves in the north of the country and lives in the south. Officers frequently use the promise of leave as an inducement to encourage soldiers to work well. This is an effective policy, unless it becomes clear to the soldiers that the date of the promised vacation keeps receding, or that the officer does not consider his undertaking to send the soldier home to be a serious commitment. From the moment that the soldier realizes that he has been duped in this way, the officer's life may become dramatically more difficult.

Discipline

According to the manual, disciplinary measures to be taken against erring conscripts begin with reproof, and build up from reprimand, strict reprimand, canceled leave, and extra duty (which must not be guard or combat duty), to imprisonment in the guardhouse for up to ten days. But some of the best disciplinarians in the army impose their own, unofficial punishments. For example, a company commander in the Far East considered shaving the soldier's heads to be an effective penalty for offenses such as going into town without permission, or being caught with food in the barracks. He points out that it is simple to administer and that it does not interfere with the routine of the units as a whole or with the individual's training. In fact, it works with his soldiers because they crave his respect, and so this public mark of his disfavor acts as a deterrent.

Inside the guardhouse in a disciplinary battalion in Minsk.

Every serviceman in the army has had leave canceled and has had to do extra duty. About a quarter seem to spend some time in the guardhouse. This is uncomfortable but tolerable. Those under arrest sleep, several to a cell, on wooden racks or folding beds without blankets. For warmth they have their *shinel* (overcoat) at night, and if the temperature in the cell falls below 18° C during the day. They are expected to do ten hours of physical labor a day, usually maintenance or construction tasks around the unit. Sergeants generally have to operate as foremen, overseeing the work. Anyone who has been put in solitary confinement for a more serious offense will not work but will be allowed out of his cell for fifty minutes of physical training. After work the soldiers have about four hours of marching exercises. The ultimate sanction, for a conscript, is to be sentenced by a military tribunal to a disciplinary battalion, or 'disbat,' as they are known.

Time spent in a disbat does not count as part of the conscript's military service. If a soldier who has served for one year commits an offense and subsequently spends two years in a disbat, he will then have to serve for one further year in order to complete his army service. No record is made on the military identity card, which adult Soviet men carry throughout their lives, of the fact that he has done time in a disbat: only the numbers of the units and the time spent there are listed. But it is difficult to think of any other reason why an ordinary soldier, not an extended serviceman or *prapor-shchik*, would have spent four or five years in the army. For a good many of the inmates the shame of being sent to a disbat is the greatest punishment. Even in circles where there is little support for the principle of conscription it is seen as a disgrace for a soldier to have been sentenced to a disbat. The feeling of shame is strongest among Slav soldiers (but by no means unique to them) and among those who served formerly in prestigious units. At a disbat I spoke to an inmate who had been a paratrooper. It seemed likely, from what I was told, that I knew the commander of his old unit. But he evidently could not bear to talk about that previous existence. He just did not want to be reminded that he had once served in the airborne troops.

Everybody in the army knows that conditions in the disbats are appalling: the inmates sleep on wooden bunks, without mattresses, three tiers high, they say. Certainly, from the outside, the battalion I visited in Minsk looked like a prison camp in an old war movie. The high walls of the battalion were topped with ugly rolls of barbed wire, and the watchtowers were clearly manned. But, bizarrely, the first dormitory I saw was the most comfortable that I had seen anywhere in the armed forces, including those in the officer training colleges. The paint was fresh and the floor recently varnished. The blankets on the standard soldiers' beds were clean and new. The whole place sparkled with an air of efficiency. There were only two clues to the nature of the establishment: Each bedside locker stood with its door open, revealing the contents neatly laid out, and the entrance to the dormitory was barred with heavy metal gates with a serious lock. At first I assumed that one dormitory had been revamped for the foreign journalist's visit, but a detailed inspection revealed that they were all more or less of the same standard.

Then I went to the canteen where I found the inmates eating better than average meals. Later, Lieutenant Colonel Bortnik, the commander of the battalion, told us why the life of the young men sent here as punishment for serious offenses is so much more comfortable than that of everybody else who lives in a barracks. These battalions are no longer described, as they were in the past, as 'punishment battalions.' They are now meant to reform the inmates with much stricter discipline than that found in the normal units. Here life really is lived by the manual. But the manual, in fact, provides for better food and better living conditions than those that exist in many units, and the disbats make a point of ensuring that the barracks are clean and the food as good as possible. The basic conditions should be conducive to decent living and the regime strict but fair. The inmates do manual labor for eight hours a day, but this includes traveling time, so in practice they usually work for about six hours a day. So, if you work hard and keep your head down, life here is not intolerable. But any infringement of the rules is dealt with severely. Anyone who tries to escape will be shot. In the past eight years four people have attempted this: two of them survived and were given extra punishment. Photographs on the bulletin board of the dead in their coffins, surrounded by their weeping families, encourage the inmates not to make a run for it. From time to time there are cases of homosexual rape inside the disbat. Two years ago two such cases came to light, and the offenders were each sentenced by a military tribunal to five years in a civilian prison. Most of the serious offenses committed within the disbat involve alcohol. All too often the ordinary workmen on the building sites give drink to the boys in order to be kind to them. Punishments within the disbat begin with reprimands. These should be taken seriously, as the next stage is 'strict arrest' in the guardhouse, a *zalyot* as the soldiers call it (literally, 'a flight into trouble'). In the guardhouse the men are kept in solitary confinement, permitted to sit down only for ten minutes in every hour. The rest of the time they must stand up, without attempting to make contact with other prisoners.

Most of the inmates have been sentenced to two or three years, the majority of them for offences in connection with *dedovshchina*. Others are sent here for theft (usually breaking into dachas and taking wine, jam, and so on), serious hooliganism, and rape. About 10 per cent of the inmates had been in trouble with the police before they were conscripted. According to Lieutenant Colonel Bortnik, most of the others should never have ended up here; he blames their fate on their first commanders. As Suvorov said, 'There is no bad soldier, there are only bad commanders.' Those who are here as a result of the violence associated with *dedovshchina* and many of the petty thieves were,

Inmates of the disbat return from work.

The security surrounding the disciplinary battalions is tight. Armed guards will shoot any inmate who tries to escape.

Many units, not only disbats, have their own farms that provide good, fresh food for the conscripts. The surplus is usually sold, and the money raised must, by law, be used to improve the soldiers' living conditions.

Parents visit their son in a disciplinary battalion. Families are invariably horrified when their children are sent to such units, but the conditions there are much better than might be expected.

in effect, corrupted by the atmosphere of the units in which they found themselves. Young men who come here because they have gone AWOL from their units are also, Lieutenant Colonel Bortnik says, victims of poor army discipline. Soldiers who desert are often married men who have just received the classic letter from home reporting on their wives' activities. But this is no excuse: the army is the army.

Eighteen to twenty per cent of the conscripts who end up in disbats do so as a result of unfortunate accidents. These might include road crashes, incidents where people have been shot by mistake, and so on. In such cases the military tribunal, when sentencing the soldier, often attributes the accident to the negligence of the officers in charge, who will then be punished accordingly. Up to 40 per cent of the inmates of the disbat in Minsk come from stroybats (the construction battalions), at least five times as many as there should be, if the percentage reflected accurately the number who serve there. This is partly because troublemakers are likely to be sent to the construction battalions, and partly because these soldiers work on large building sites where it is difficult to provide constant supervision. At the other end of the scale, soldiers who began their military service with very good references may end up in disbats after abusing positions of trust. A common example of this is the conscript who has been chosen as driver to a regimental or division commander – a plum job for a soldier and one that may entail a lot of waiting around and the opportunity to disappear for quite long periods of time. 'The busier the soldier, the less likely he is to get into trouble.' Soldiers who come here from the airborne forces usually do so because of a fight in the barracks, those from the air force for stealing alcohol or gasoline in order to sell them.

In the Soviet underworld most tattoos have a precise significance. The roaring tiger, shown here, is one of the most unpleasant. It signifies unbounded contempt for the law and for society. These disbat inmates are clearly not boys who fell into trouble accidentally. No one would dare to wear such tattoos unless, in the eyes of other villains, he had earned them. This culture prizes violence and the more ruthless its exponent, the greater the respect that he will be shown.

Soldiers who are being considered for remission must appear before a meeting of the Council of Society's Representatives, consisting of representatives of the local military and civil communities. These are, in effect, courts to decide whether or not to release the inmates after they have served one third or one half of their sentences. In each barracks the list of subjects on which the conscript may be questioned when appearing in front of the Council is displayed. It is as follows:

- The National Anthem
- The Military Oath
- The Soldier's Duties (from the manual)
- The Disciplinary Manual, Chapters 1, 2, 3
- The Manual of Internal Service, Chapters 262, 263
- The Manual of Rank and File Procedures, Chapter 25
- What is Communism?
- Perestroika in the Armed Forces of the USSR

The real trouble is that even one *zalyot* makes it much less likely that the inmate will be released ahead of time. Early release is the basic instrument of discipline. More than 90 per cent of those sent to this battalion do not serve their full sentence, although many ask to complete their military service there rather than returning to their original units. Broadly, about half of them seem to be anxious to get back to an ordinary regiment as soon as possible, to escape the stigma of the disbat. The rest prefer to stay and finish that military service as ordinary soldiers here, convinced that life in the disbat is simpler.

110 Dogs of War

At the Army Dog Training Center near Moscow, conscripts and dogs are trained for five months, and then sent to the units. Between 20 and 30 per cent of the soldiers here bring their own dogs into the army. These are boys who belong to dog-training clubs and own a suitable animal. The dog will serve with them and will go home with them when they are demobilized (unless the boy chooses for some reason to leave the dog behind). The rest of the soldiers train with dogs bred in the unit, which belong to the army and will remain in the unit when the conscript leaves. There are usually about 800 conscripts training in the unit.

Usually an army dog handler is responsible for four animals, so that when a soldier arrives at a unit he takes over responsibility for dogs whose handlers have been demobilized.

The animals are trained to guard all kinds of installations, to search for explosives, to find wounded people on a battlefield and to blow up tanks. For this they are taught to run underneath a tank with a box strapped to their backs. In times of war the box would contain explosives. They are also trained to attack when given the order.

Former paratroopers with a good record are welcomed by the *militsia*, the Ministry of Interior forces, and at most military colleges.

Demobilization

After a soldier has served for a year or so he will start to think about his demobilization. After eighteen months he will begin to make serious plans, and after the minister's decree concerning his release from the army has been issued he will worry about nothing else. He will think, talk, and dream constantly about what he will do and who he will be when he is demobilized. There will be no joys denied to him then and nothing that he will be unable to achieve in his *dembel* persona. Soldiers from the Baltic republics usually just want to get out of the army as soon as possible. They have no other interest in the matter. But for most conscripts the rituals of demobilization become vitally important. They list the days left on the back of pictures, inside textbooks, and on the furniture, and tick them off each day. Many of them compile albums of photographs, cartoons, poems, reminiscences, and proverbs of military life.

Soldiers are often prohibited from making such albums, but the more enlightened officers realize that they are, at the worst, harmless (even if they do contain irreverent cartoons of characters in the regiment) and at the best a wholesome indication of positive and even sentimental attitudes toward military service. Soldiers invest extraordinary energy in creating these albums, illuminating the lettering and drawing the cartoons a hundred times until they are satisfied with the result. One of the main difficulties they encounter is obtaining photographs. Even if the officers permit the soldiers to have cameras there may be certain restrictions, such as the ruling, which does not seem to be official, but which is enforced by some commanders, that they may not photograph army vehicles. Or that, if they do so, they must ensure that no number plates can be seen. Then there is the difficulty of finding film and photograph paper. But the soldiers usually manage to get hold of everything they want in the end.

The most important part of demobilization for many soldiers is arranging their physical appearance for their arrival home. Whatever they may have said about military service in general, it is clear that there is a great social prestige for most of them in being seen to have done well in the army. They are determined to go home looking like heroes. To this end they employ all their initiative to acquire what they consider to be the most desirable uniform possible. Many who did not bother to modify their uniform earlier will do so now, giving the hot iron treatment to boots and wire-brushing their *shinels*. Some will grab nice new items of uniform that have been issued to newly arrived *dukhs*, leaving their own worn-out clothing in exchange.

Soldiers who are demobilized in the autumn usually return home wearing a *shinel* and boots (although they may wear shoes), while those who leave in the spring go in parade uniform and shoes. Some soldiers shave their heads 100 days before the minister's decree so that the man who is demobilized will even have a new head of hair for his new life. This practice is frowned on, or banned, in most units. All soldiers are eager to acquire any medals or badges to which they may be entitled before they leave the army. Some will beg, borrow, or steal anything that can be pinned to a uniform, whether or not they have the right to wear it. And this is only the beginning. Soldiers manufacture every kind of badge and emblem that their riotous imaginations can devise and hide them in the pockets of their parade uniforms until the great day comes. Tie pins with elaborate insignia (sometimes the emblem of the Soviet Union from a two-kopek coin, soldered onto the tie pin), enormous, bejeweled medals and braided and fringed (yes, fringed) shoulder boards are all perfectly normal. The letters CA (Sovetskaya Armiya) on the shoulder boards are often replaced with copper or other gleaming metal equivalents.

In the spring and again in the autumn on trains all over the Soviet Union, there are soldiers to be seen taking off their jackets to reveal emblazoned shirts more appropriate to Ruritanian generalissimos in comic operas than to Soviet servicemen of the 1990s. There are many reports of unofficial museums of confiscated *dembel* ephemera, but these rumors are so far unsubstantiated. Although these extravagances are strictly forbidden, once the soldier has left his unit he is generally considered to be beyond the control of the military, and as long as he looks reasonably normal in his coat or jacket most officers do not inquire too closely about what the *dembel* is wearing underneath. They have enough to do worrying about the new intake of hopelessly raw recruits, and, by their own account, they consider it churlish to interfere with the departing soldier's moment of glory.

The wildest flights of *dembel* fantasy usually spring from the minds of conscripts from simple backgrounds. These are the boys from the provincial towns and the farms who were relatively happy to join the army in the first place. Soldiers from more sophisticated backgrounds do not manufacture decorations for themselves, but even they go to some trouble to ensure that they will arrive home in as smart a uniform as possible. The overwhelming majority of conscripts, as they end their period of service, express a sense of achievement. Some, who say that conscription should be ended, nevertheless concede that they, personally, have benefited from their time in the army. When asked what they have gained from their military service, soldiers usually say that it has made them physically fit, self-reliant, and adult. They often mention that army life has taught them the value of time and that in the future they will make better use of their recreation as well as of their working hours.

The soldiers' contentment, as they leave their units for the last time, can be utterly destroyed if they feel that the officers have not said good-bye to them properly. But on the whole, Soviet commanders take great pains to make demobilization dignified and to treat the men who are leaving with affection and respect. So, after two years of soldiering, the young men go back home to face the different reality of civilian life.

On a train bound northwestward in the autumn of last year a demobilized soldier was describing his feelings: 'I know that this is one of the happiest moments of my life. Once I actually get home new problems will start. But now I have finished my army service successfully. Everyone in my unit was pleased with me and my family is looking forward to welcoming me home. I want this train journey to last forever.'

6 THE GROUND FORCES

The ground forces (*Sukhoputniye Voiska*) form the largest branch of the armed forces, consisting of over 1,500,000 men in over 140 motorized rifle and tank divisions, and other units, including independent heavy artillery brigades and helicopter regiments. The ground forces have at their disposal over 50,000 main battle tanks, about 30,000 armored personnel carriers, 9,000 self-propelled artillery pieces, 4,500 helicopters, and so on. Over 70 per cent of the country's conscripts end up serving here in one capacity or another, manning and servicing this huge armory. Although the ground forces are likely to be those most affected by cuts in equipment and personnel over the next few years, they will continue to provide the basis of any significant fighting force. Even if the eventual outcome of the war were to be decided by the strategic rocket forces, the Soviet General Staff usually assumes that the ground forces would be involved in the initial stages of the conflict.

The ground forces consist of the following branches: motorized rifle troops, air defense troops, tank troops, and rocket troops and artillery. In addition, the airborne troops are administered by the ground forces, but they have their own commander and more autonomy than other branches (see Chapter 9). There is no chief of the motorized rifle troops — because this branch is the backbone of the ground forces, it comes directly under the commander-in-chief and its affairs are dealt with by the ground forces staff as a whole. Each of the other branches has its own chief and its own administration, responsible for the overall development and supply of the ground forces, in other words, for training and equipping them. Operational planning, however, is carried out by the commanders of the military districts and by the General Staff.

It is important to remember that, in Soviet military thinking, all ground forces combat is a combined arms operation. This is the basic principle of modern Soviet conventional warfare, whereby the activities of all the branches of troops and special troops are completely coordinated and integrated. So tanks operate together with motorized rifle troops, air defense, and artillery. Combined arms operations can also involve aviation and naval units. In these operations all the forces involved come under the command of a combined arms officer, who belongs to the ground forces. According to Army General Varennikov, the commander-in-chief of the ground forces, 'The

Artillery tractors belonging to the 304th Red Banner Motorized Rifle Regiment, based in Petropavlovsk-Kamchatka, driving through the fog toward the Pacific Ocean.

A great deal of work goes into planning and organizing maneuvers.

A field forge during maneuvers.

combined arms officer bears responsibility not only for his own unit, he coordinates the combat activities of units belonging to other armed services and branches. He is the main person responsible for the cooperation of different units.'

Each military district has at its disposal between two and five ground forces armies and corps. In the last couple of years some armies have been transformed into corps. Armies are described as either 'combined arms' or 'tank' armies, although both are in fact combined arms armies. The difference is that a tank army has more tank divisions. There is no fixed structure for armies, but they generally consist of two, three, or four divisions. Tank and motorized rifle divisions traditionally include a three-to-one combination of regiments: motorized rifle divisions have three motorized rifle regiments to one tank regiment, and tank divisions have three tank regiments and one motorized rifle regiment. This mix continues within the regiments – in a motorized rifle regiment there will be one tank to three motorized rifle battalions, and a tank regiment will have one motorized rifle and three tank battalions. In addition to the four motorized rifle tank regiments, each division also includes an artillery and an air-defense (surface-to-air missile) regiment. However, the ratio of motorized rifle to tank and artillery units appears to be in the process of changing, to provide a better balance of weapons within formations. Regiments, as well as divisions, are provided with combat and logistical support units (antitank, anti-aircraft, engineer, reconnaissance and signals, and motor transport, maintenance, and medical), so that they will be able to operate independently for a limited period of time. Wherever possible, soldiers who have trained as a unit will fight as a unit, from the platoon, right up to the divisional level. The most likely exception to this rule would be the tank battalion of a motorized rifle regiment, each of whose three tank companies might be attached to a motorized rifle battalion, and then split up further so that eventually each company commander would have at his disposal a combined arms force of BMPs (*Bronevaya Mashina Pekhota*, armored military vehicles) and tanks.

The motorized rifle regiment in a tank division, or the tank regiments in a motorized rifle division, might be broken down and used either as battalions (attached to regiments) or as companies (allocated to battalions), or they might be split up further still and allocated to companies. The assets of these regiments, usually in the second echelon, would thus be used to reinforce the first echelon. However, if the second echelon were to be deployed, the regiments would revert to their normal structure. Artillery units may also be formed into groups and attached wherever they seem to be needed. Again, this is likely to be done, initially, to fortify the first echelon.

In Afghanistan, regiments and divisions tended to include units and subunits that were not organic to them, depending on the specific character of the tasks. In general, however, combined arms units train in the formations in which they would be deployed during combat. Within this system, the officers and men usually wear the uniform and insignia of their profession, no matter what type of unit they serve. So a tankman in a motorized rifle division will wear the black tank tabs and cap-band, with the appropriate insignia, while a gunner in a tank division will wear artillery emblems. This is not, however, invariably the case. Some officers and even soldiers seem to get away with electing to wear the uniform that is appropriate to their regiment, or division, rather than to their own job.

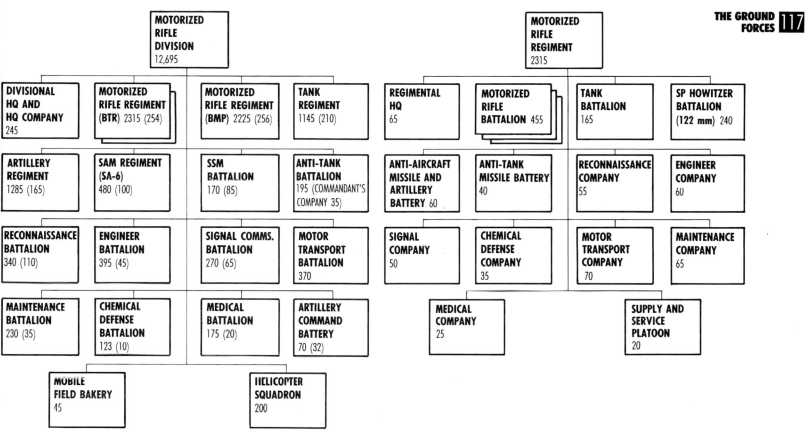

There are four recognized strengths for Soviet divisions:

- 100% full strength – *razvertivannaya*
- 70–80%   normal peacetime full strength – *polurazvertivannaya*
- 20–50%   reduced personnel – *sokrashennogo sostava*
- 5–10%   very reduced strength – *kadrovaya*

Within the Soviet Union there are virtually no divisions at full strength. These only exist during wartime or in the Group of Forces abroad. At normal peacetime strength a motorized rifle regiment consists of up to 2,500 men and a tank regiment around 1,000. But many are now at reduced strengths. The units with the least manpower are able to do little more than guard and maintain the equipment that would be used, were reservists ever to be called up to flesh them out. Many regiments are at such low strength that the soldiers are on duty every other day, with the result that they have virtually no time available for training. (For a comparison of a standard division with the actual strengths of a division in the Turkestan Military District, see above diagram.)

The motorized rifle troops are often referred to by other soldiers as the *pekhota*, literally, the 'infantry.' But, in fact, there is no real infantry in the Soviet Army: a motorized rifle squad may dismount, but it can also fire from inside its BMP. However, the importance of well-trained infantrymen was demonstrated in Afghanistan, and it seems likely that, in the future, more attention will be paid to improving the training of motorized riflemen.

LEFT: Standard Strength of a Motorized Rifle Division (actual strength, 1989, of 58th Motorized Rifle Division, Kizyl-Arvat in brackets) Information supplied by Army General Varennikov, Commander-in-chief of the Ground Forces (data from Kizyl-Arvat supplied by Acting Commander Colonel Mishin). *Note*: These strengths vary considerably.

RIGHT: Standard Strength of Motorized Rifle Regiment

This camouflage pattern, designed by computer, was first worn by the border guards, but is now also used for the uniforms of other units.

Training

Soviet military art recognizes three levels of combat activity – strategic, operational, and tactical – and deals with them separately. Strategy is the overall planning and preparation for wars that may occur, the conduct of those wars, and the general furtherance of the aims of the state in the military-political sphere. Operational art is the theory and practice of the combat activities of large formations, up to army or front level, while tactics covers every aspect of fighting a war, up to divisional level. These distinctions govern military thinking to a remarkable extent. A Soviet officer will say, 'This is a tactical weapon,' or 'This is a tactical exercise.'

Just as academic military theory grades combat activities according to their scale, so the training of the soldiers progresses from the smallest fighting unit – the individual – up to larger formations. At the beginning of every training period each *otdeleniye* (section or squad) is taught separately, with particular attention being paid to the new conscripts who have just been attached to it, after finishing their Course of the Young Soldier. Once each soldier seems to have mastered the rudiments of his job, the officers can concentrate on coordinating the activities of the unit. In the past couple of years, training exercises have been revised to reflect the fact that the army now expects future operations to be predominantly defensive. Some officers say that the training methods should be further revised. In Afghanistan, they say, soldiers who performed perfectly well on the shooting ranges were unable to cope in the unpredictable conditions they found there. After two or three months it should be possible to train an entire company to act together, and a month or so later battalion-level exercises are usually held. Regimental or divisional exercises may take place at any time, but they usually coincide with the end of the training period. Larger-scale exercises, at military-district level, occur more rarely, and the Minister of Defense, Marshal Yazov, announced in July 1990 that operational-strategic maneuvers would, in the future, be cut by a third.

Soldiers spend six hours a day training, usually from 09:00 to 15:00, with a ten-minute break every hour. As a rule, the training process begins with theoretical explanations in a classroom. Then the soldiers try out what they have been taught on simulators, and then they practice using real weapons or vehicles. But live ammunition is strictly limited. The conscripts in a T-64b tank regiment, for example, fire live rounds twice a year, during their training sessions. According to the regulations, they should fire six live rounds a year – in other words, three each time they are used. But they may have the chance to fire more live rounds during large-scale exercises. Real weapons or combat vehicles are only used, in general, at the *poligon*, the training ground, some miles away from the regimental base. The opportunities for physical discomfort – heat, cold, damp – are much greater at the *poligon*, but many soldiers, nevertheless, prefer days spent there to those when they are stuck indoors in the regiment. *Poligon* exercises are much more interesting and it is harder for the officers to keep a close watch on every soldier. At the *poligon* there may be scale models, charts and other teaching aids, and there will be a control tower for each training area. From the control tower, a basic rectangular structure with an upper floor reached by open iron steps, the soldiers' performance will be observed and automatic targets, stationary, or mobile, will be controlled. The training processes are planned to enable anyone,

Camouflaged command post during the Byelorussian Military District maneuvers.

A T-72 tank company attacks during these maneuvers. Note the mine-plough on the tank in the right foreground.

Shooting exercises in Kamchatka

The officer wearing the armband, the instructor, uses the flag to communicate with the command post, from where the automatic targets are positioned. The exercise will be repeated again and again. Eventually, most of the soldiers will get it right. As Suvorov said, 'repetition is the mother of education.' *Left* Soldiers load the magazines of their Kalashnikovs with ammunition. *Center* Standard paper targets for pistol shooting.

During a T-72 tank assault on maneuvers, a tankman carries out running repairs. This photograph calls to mind the case of a conscript in the Far East who had landed a job as a driver. Part of his job was to maintain the jeep he drove. He discovered that if he tied his wrists to the underside of the jeep he could lie underneath it, sleeping happily. To anyone passing by it would seem that he was doing something to the vehicle, and he would be left alone.

even the simplest peasant with little Russian, to learn enough to be useful in the army, so the exercises are simple and repetitive. Each activity is broken down into parts and these are rehearsed continually, so that each soldier will feel absolutely sure of his ability to carry out his own task successfully. Motorized riflemen who enjoy their work derive satisfaction from the feeling that they are proficient with small arms. So they quite enjoy the hour and a half that they have to devote to maintenance of weapons and machinery every weekday afternoon. For anyone who dislikes army life, though, it is simply tedious.

Tankmen profess affection for their tanks, and, discreetly flouting the regulations, will often keep personal photographs or a good-luck charm inside it. The commander of a T-64b tank told me that 'inside my tank I always feel high-spirited. I have great responsibility and it makes me feel very brave. I feel as though I were inside a Zhiguli [a Soviet car].' But I have never heard a motorized rifleman express affection for his BMP. These are the infantry combat vehicles in which each *otdeleniye* moves. With between seven and nine people on board, it is very cramped inside a BMP, and every time it drives over so much as a pebble, the soldiers bash their heads on the roof. It is also dark and often too hot. The commander of the BMP (and hence of the *otdeleniye* itself) is usually a sergeant, who sits next to the gunner in the turret (in older models the commander sits behind the driver). The gunner operates the automatic cannon, which fires armor-piercing rounds. The rest of the squad include a sniper, a grenadier and riflemen armed with AK-74 assault rifles.

Of the three BMPs in each platoon, one will be commanded by the platoon commander (an officer), in which case the sergeant in charge of the *otdeleniye* only takes over when the men dismount. At this stage the platoon commander concentrates on coordinating the activities of the unit as a whole. His deputy (a sergeant) will remain in the first BMP and give commands to the other two vehicles. Each machine gunner and rifleman has a small firing port, enabling him to shoot (with some discomfort) from inside the vehicle. But the noise and the fumes are almost unbearable during mounted firing. Soldiers themselves wryly point out one advantage of this — at least they would never be unwilling to leave their BMP in combat. They also know that modern antitank guided missiles would make it dangerous to stay in the BMP on the battlefield, unless the enemy was either completely disorganized or known not to possess antitank weapons. Of course, if tactical nuclear or chemical weapons had been used the soldiers would stay inside the BMP.

Not all motorized rifle regiments possess BMPs. Some are equipped with BTRs (*Brone TransporteRs*), armored personnel carriers. These vehicles are faster than the tracked BMPs and easier to maintain. But they are less well armed, with only a 14.5 mm heavy machine gun, and their armor is less effective. Although they are more maneuverable than BMPs on good roads, they cannot cope so well with mud, bogs, and snow. Traditionally, the disadvantage, from the soldiers' point of view, was the awkwardness of getting into and out of most models of these vehicles. However, soldiers find it easy to jump out of the new BTR-80s, even when they are moving. But units equipped with BTRs have less firepower than those with BMPs and are generally considered to be lower-grade. Whenever new combat support equipment becomes available it is likely to be issued first to BMP units.

A young officer wearing heavyweight winter field uniform during maneuvers.

The three-man crew of the T-64b (commander, driver-mechanic and gunner) are given the command to take up their positions. They have four minutes to load the ammunition and five minutes to warm up the tank. The tank fires three types of shell – high explosive (OF), armor-piercing fin-stabilized discarding Sabot (B) and high explosive antitank (K), weighing 26 – 50 pounds. The crew is just about to carry out tank training exercise number two – firing from a defensive position (exercise number one is firing while on the move).

Near Odessa the crew of a T-64b tank practice loading their vehicle onto the rails, which would enable it to be transported quickly by road or rail if necessary. These tanks have seven forward gears and one reverse, and the crews complain that it is difficult to change gear when the tank is moving fast (maximum speed is about 40 miles per hour). The tanks are equipped with reactive armor, but this is removed during training, to prevent damage.

Artillery has always had a high status in the Russian Army, before the Revolution as well as since. Gunners are usually considered to be more intelligent than some other officers and they have better-developed service traditions than most branches. For example, there is a ritual whereby the church bells are rung in Kolomna on the night after the *kursants* at the artillery college there finish their exams. The importance of the artillery today is governed by the fact that almost any gun of more than 150 mm caliber is nuclear-capable. But despite its power and its prestige, the god of war cannot win a battle. It could certainly determine the outcome, but, without tanks and soldiers, artillery fire decides nothing. This is why much artillery is held at a relatively high level of command, so that it can be grouped and deployed downward, when necessary.

A recently conscripted soldier at a tank unit in the Odessa Military District.

Life in the regiment

It is in the ground forces that the conscripts are most important. The soldiers and sergeants are the basis of the motorized rifle units and they man the tanks. The air force could probably manage without national servicemen, and the navy, in certain branches (such as nuclear submarines) is already planning to do so. But a massive re-thinking of the ground forces organization would be necessary to enable them to cope without the conscripts. In most Western armies, infantrymen are trained and controlled by powerful and gutsy warrant officers or NCOs. In the Soviet Army the situation is somewhat different. Sergeants are themselves usually conscripts and the *praporshchiks* (warrant officers) are not central to the system of command. They are normally involved in technical or support positions. *Praporshchiks* may be chief mechanics, they may be in charge of training equipment, or they may run depots and stores. Some platoon leaders are *praporshchiks*, but this happens more often in support units than in combat platoons. Soldiers whose platoon leader is not an officer will make a point of saying so. Sometimes they say that they get on better with their *praporshchik* than they would with an officer, because he is nearer to them in age and background. Others cite the fact that their platoon leader is only a warrant officer to explain some fault within the platoon. But in any case, the soldiers consider it to be unusual and in a way irregular, for a platoon to be commanded by a *praporshchik*. Much of the work that in a Western army would be carried out by sergeants, is carried out by junior officers in the Soviet Army. Company and platoon commanders must supervise the training of the men and generally keep an eye on what is going on in the barracks. It is a mistake for them to end up doing the work of the sergeants — a trap that some young officers fall into, determined to ensure that everything is done properly. In the end every aspect of the soldiers' lives is their responsibility. If the different nationalities in the unit are continually fighting each other, or if the *dembels* are forcing the *molodois* to carry the brunt of the work, the platoon and company commanders have to understand what is going on and take steps to deal with it.

At the same time, the officers have a lot of paperwork to cope with. There are forms to be filled out for everything; every time somebody sneezes there are reports to be made and 'norms' to be checked. These 'norms' govern every aspect of army life. They are the approved standards for physical training, for speed and accuracy in exercises,

The soldier in the foreground appears to be concentrating hard. Apart from the job satisfaction, if he works well he is likely to be given extra privileges, including home leave.

Inside an artillery tractor.

for the length of time clothing should last, and so on. Officers also have to produce detailed lesson plans of the training periods or lessons for which they are responsible. Even for something as straightforward as 'drilling on the spot and on the move without arms,' a lieutenant is expected to write a neatly presented three-page outline, listing the time, the place, the relevant literature, and a step-by-step account of the lesson.

During the last few years the ground forces have been determined to raise the standards of the worst regiments, and the army is perfectly open about the necessity for this. But salvaging a unit that has been badly run is an awesome task. Years of mismanagement will have undermined the morale and the professionalism of the officers, and the conscripts' lives are most unlikely to be following the lines laid down in the army manuals. The officers and *praporshchiks* may have been falsifying the training records to make things look better than they really are for years on end. While it will be perfectly clear that the unit (usually a regiment) is in trouble, with everybody covering up for other people and for themselves, it can be difficult to rectify the underlying defects. The Hero of the Soviet Union Ruslan Aushev had achieved spectacular success in transforming his regiment in Ussirisk, which used to be considered one of the worst in the Far East Military District. This is the 'Romanian Regiment,' so called throughout the army because some years ago it was issued uniforms that were so bleached out that the troops ended up looking like Romanian soldiers. Within a year of Aushev's arrival the regiment took first place in the military district's annual assessment. The very fact that one of the most distinguished soldiers of his generation was given command must have had a dramatic impact on the morale, but this in itself was not enough to improve its performance so dramatically.

Aushev says that he concentrated his reforms on the sergeants in the unit, giving them all sorts of advantages, with the intention of improving their status. These include privileges such as more free time and leave, more independence, and extra financial incentives. He did this because it is, in the end, only the sergeants who can really ensure higher standards of morale, discipline, and professional proficiency. He has also introduced what he calls 'trust mail,' a system whereby anyone in the regiment may write to him personally, using a special mailbox, about any aspect of the life of the unit or about their personal problems. This system is not unique to Colonel Aushev's regiment, but nor is it by any means universal. I was surprised by the easy accessibility of the commanders, usually up to the commander of the regiment for soldiers, and up to the divisional commander for all but the most junior officers. Most commanders allocate certain times each week during which they will receive any soldier or officer who wants to speak to them. A conscript who is thought to have wasted the commander's time or otherwise abused the system will of course regret it. At the motorized rifle regiment we visited in Kamchatka there is a special telephone box with a hotline to the colonel in command, installed with the same aim of giving everyone access to the commander.

Ruslan Aushev says that, in order to improve his regiment, he made a point of spending much more time working than was necessary. Where the officers are lazy and ineffective, he says, they will quite naturally lose control: 'The commander must be the leader in everything, in combat training, sports, and recreation. He must exercise authority over his subordinates. If the commander is weak, the soldiers will find their

These bridges in Kamachatka are sturdier than they look. Nevertheless, they have to be approached with caution.

own leader.' Certainly, a good commander can transmit his professional enthusiasm to the men. In good regiments the conscripts make it clear that they are proud of the weapons and equipment they have mastered. But only an officer who spends a great deal of time with the soldiers can instill in them any keenness for soldiering and respect for weaponry. At the motorized rifle regiment in Petropavlovsk-Kamchatka the soldiers dragged me outside to look at their weapons. These were standard machine and submachine guns, but it was impossible not to feel a heightened interest as a result of the conscripts' evident pride in them.

Conditions of service

A combined arms officer may be sent to serve anywhere in the country. There are ground forces units near most of the cities but many are in the middle of nowhere. There are motorized rifle troops near Murmansk, in the Far East, and in Central Asia. Combined arms officers may also, of course, be posted abroad, so long as there are any Soviet troops stationed outside the country. At a place called Kazandzhik in the Karakum desert of Turkemnistan a motorized rifle regiment and a tank regiment are stationed. In the Turkman language, we were repeatedly told, the place name means 'the boiling pot of the winds.' During the summer, temperatures of 50°C (122°F) are not unusual and they are often varied only by the violent hot winds to which the area is subject. The nearest town is Kizyl-Arvat, forty-seven miles away. A lone bus rattles along the dirt road four times a day. The bus stop is half a mile from the garrison town. In the heat it seems farther. Cars do not last long in these conditions and, in any case, most officers do not have a car of their own. The divisional commander in Kizyl-Arvat says, ruminatively, that in the old days the only task of the Russian military governor was to keep the railroad from Krasnovodsk to Tashkent open, and the place still has the feel of a desolate but brave frontier town. The water supply to the garrison frequently dries up and the electricity regularly fails. Newspapers and mail always arrive twenty-four hours later than they should.

There is very little to see in the dusty streets of Kizyl-Arvat. Occasionally a sheep or a goat meanders between the low buildings, but there are not many people around. To the families of the Kazandzhik garrison, however, this is the big city. Here they can see a film, have their clothes dry-cleaned, catch a plane to somewhere else. The living conditions in this area are notoriously difficult. If you mention Kazandzhik to any officer serving in the Turkestan Military District he will nod seriously, in comradely acknowledgment of the difficulty of working there, but there will be an element of nervousness, an awareness that there but for the grace of the Staff he too might go. One man in four serving in Kazandzhik (officers and soldiers) will contract hepatitis. 'Red eyes never turn yellow,' the local people say merrily, pouring another drink to avert the ever-present danger from their minds, if not from their livers. Bodkin's disease is endemic, as are some exotic mosquito-borne ailments. The heat is so intense during the summer that children are always taken away to rest houses and summer camps, or to stay with relations. Their mothers often go with them, but since the officers and *praporshchiks* cannot all take their leave at the same time, many families are unable to have their holiday together.

A trench artillery 'command and control' point. The commander of the artillery *division* (a major) handles the target acquisition and control from here.

The women worry about the educational standards in the Kizyl-Arvat school. Most of the teachers are the wives of officers who move on whenever their husbands are transferred to new jobs elsewhere. So the turnover of staff is high and for some subjects it is impossible to find teachers at all. Apart from those who work at the school, some of the army wives find jobs at the kindergartens and a few in the local hospitals. Some are employed by the army, either as civilians, or as soldiers or *praporshchiks* in communications or clerical work. But there are really no other opportunities for women to find jobs in the area. A major complaint of the women is the shortage of kindergarten places. Although most of the wives cannot find jobs and therefore have time to look after their children all day, the Soviet education system works on the assumption that by the time children start school at the age of six or seven, they will have already received several years preschool education. So any child who is unable to attend a kindergarten begins his education with a disadvantage. Life in these garrison towns can, in any case, be boring for children, although the officers and the women go to a great deal of trouble to organize sports activities, outings, and games for them.

The army tries to offer some compensation to those who have to serve in such conditions. Throughout the Turkestan Military District (except in the easier postings of Tashkent, Ashkhabad, Dushanbe, and Alma Ata) all officers are given forty-five instead of thirty days' holiday a year, a privilege that elsewhere is only earned after twenty-five years of service (the extra leave is also given to those serving in other places where life is hard, such as the far north). It is up to the commander to decide whether to allow an officer to split up his leave, or whether he must take it all at the same time. In any case, he will only be given one fare to any destination he chooses. But unlike most officers who are given the rail fare, those serving in the most inhospitable regions such as Kizyl-Arvat are given the money to fly to their destination. Officers serving in the most difficult regions also receive a monthly bonus of 15 per cent of their function salary, and a year's service counts as a year and a half for the pension. It is not only living conditions that are more difficult here. It is also hard to train the soldiers when they can only work until noon: 'Between 13:00 and 17:00 hours you feel as though your brains are melting,' so the soldiers have a two-hour break from 14:00 to 16:00 hours. Training in the midday sun could be fatal in these conditions. As a result, night exercises are held much more often than in other units.

Despite the legendarily difficult conditions of serving in Kazandzhik, morale there seems to be higher than in some other units. This may be because the environment is so hostile and the garrison so far from any city that officers and their families are sustained by a pioneering fortitude, knowing that survival depends on a determined act of will; they cannot afford to let their standards slip. The results are impressive. In the scrubby desert hundreds of miles from anywhere the soldiers have made a garden, expending gallons of precious water to sustain a tiny patch of thin grass and some brave shrubs. The houses are better maintained than many buildings in big cities, although every nail and every can of paint has to be brought out from Kizyl-Arvat. During our travels we saw army officers' wives clearly driven out of their minds by boredom and by the constraints of life in a provincial garrison. Although they were outspoken about the difficulties of their lives, the women of Kizyl-Arvat were noticeably saner and more cheerful than these others. Their energies and imagination

These soldiers have been sent to serve in the Central Asian desert. There used to be a saying among the officers in Turkvo (Turkestan Military District): 'They can't give you command of anything smaller than a platoon, and they can't send you further south than Termez.' (But then came the Afghanistan war.)

OVERLEAF: Soldiers' washroom at a tank regiment at Kazandzhik in the Karakum desert of Turkmenistan. High standards of hygiene are vital in conditions such as these, where many dangerous diseases are endemic.

On the road between Kazandzhik and Kizyl-Arvat in Turkmenistan an officer and soldier stop to buy melons from local women.

seemed to be devoted to doing what they could to improve things for their families and friends.

Dramatically different from Kizyl-Arvat in terms of the living conditions was the regiment I visited at Belaya Tserkov in the Ukraine. This is dream countryside, each village with a pond and pretty ducks, a nice fat cow tethered outside many of the cottages, and busy chickens flapping and pecking in the gardens and along the roadside. Whatever economic and ecological problems the area may face, outwardly it presents a calm rural confidence. But apart from the differences dictated by the climate, the army routine is exactly the same in each case. Belaya Tserkov is the home of the Krasnogradsk 72nd Motorized Rifle Division. The basic structure of this division is the standard combined arms formula – three motorized rifle regiments and one tank regiment, one artillery and one air defense regiment – precisely the same as in Kizyl-Arvat. Only the levels of manpower are different: Belaya Tserkov is at a much higher strength.

Some of the support personnel of this regiment were involved in cleaning up after the disaster at Chernobyl. On 30 April 1986, the eve of the great May Day holiday, Praporshchik Grib was at home, relaxing and preparing for the next day's celebrations, when a messenger arrived from the unit summoning him at once to his boss, the commander of the mobile bakeries. For the previous three days the whole area had been alive with rumors about the terrible nuclear accident, but no one had a clear idea about what had really happened. When Praporshchik Grib arrived at the unit he was briefed about the events of 20 April at Chernobyl and told to prepare the bakery for immediate action. Thirty minutes later six Ural vehicles towing the bakeries left the regiment and four hours afterward they arrived inside the twenty-mile zone surrounding the damaged reactor. Under the command of the special operations group that was in control of the operations, they immediately began work, making bread for the specialists working there and the units who were engaged in cleaning up after the accident.

For the next few months no conscripts were employed in the mobile bakeries, only reservists. Praporshchik Grib and his colleagues worked there, in twelve-hour shifts. They wore no special protective clothing, but the bakeries are designed to be radiation-proof and the level of radiation was measured every hour. Each of the men serving there wore a DP5A personal dosimeter, whose accuracy was regularly tested. The mobile bakeries were based at Oranny: they only had to alter their position once when a change of wind direction endangered their site.

The mobile bakery company of the division's automobile battalion can feed the entire personnel of the division if necessary – every twenty-four hours it can produce twelve tons of bread. In 1989, twenty-eight people worked in the company, but it was then under strength and there should have been a few more. These field bakeries are not normally used, but they are constantly ready to operate if necessary. Within fifty minutes of receiving the order to start work, they should be producing bread. The disaster at Chernobyl seems to have brought out in the army the traditional Russian ability to pull together in an emergency. Tremendous bravery was shown by the military personnel involved in the aftermath, many of whom worked very near the damaged reactor, fully aware of the risks involved.

Boiling water in a field kitchen. These stoves are called *burzhuka*. The field kitchen includes two large boilers for soup and porridge (one of these may be seen in the background).

Specialized and support units

As well as the normal tank or motorized rifle regiments, the ground forces include units trained for specialized work. At the town of Osh in Kirghizia, for example, there is a mountain motorized rifle brigade and a cavalry squadron. The slogans on the public billboards here give a clear idea of local priorities: 'Water is Life,' they warn baldly. Osh, with a population of 250,000, is 150 miles from the Chinese border by road and 60 miles as the crow flies. Of the four motorized rifle battalions in the brigade, two are equipped with BMPs and two, consisting of specialized mountain troops, have no combat vehicles. They are trained to operate entirely on foot, carrying all their equipment with them.

The brigade was formed in 1984, as experience in Afghanistan demonstrated the need for better-trained mountain troops. Physical endurance and technical precision are the vital qualities for these soldiers. It is much more difficult to determine range and distances when firing in the mountains and yet every round of ammunition is precious, as it has to be carried by the soldiers themselves. The troops know how difficult it is to deliver extra weapons and ammunition to them. Most of the soldiers are not expected to work at altitudes over ten thousand feet. Only those who possess the 'Master of Sport' qualification in mountain climbing, or those who are working toward it, can operate at such heights. The conscripts sent to the brigade are all supposed to be experienced climbers, but some slip through the net, either by mistake or because they volunteer to serve here. These then have to be given basic training in mountain climbing. According to the officers, it is much easier to teach a soldier to use weapons in mountainous conditions than to teach him how to climb. The men frequently have exercises during which they have to survive in the mountains for two or three days, a period that often stretches to a week if, due to bad weather conditions, the exercise cannot be completed in the time. But they say that no one would die of hunger in the mountains during the summer. There are lots of berries and herbs and, on rare occasions, soldiers have managed to kill a mountain goat. They carry primus stoves (with dry alcohol), one tent for two men, sleeping bags, and the trusty 'entrenching tool' (a type of shovel), which can be used to chop wood, cut rope, hack through bushes, or dig trenches.

The cavalry squadron in Osh is currently the only combat cavalry unit in the army. It consists of nine officers. The smallest unit of the squadron is the *zvyeno* (literally, 'link'), which consists of four horses and four men. The cavalry *otdeleniye* consists of two *zvyenos*, and a platoon is made up of twelve *otdeleniyes*. There are two platoons in the squadron, totalling about 200 men. There are 400 horses at the disposal of the squadron: the assumption is that half of them would be used as pack horses. The squadron also includes a mortar platoon, equipped with the 1937-design M30 82 mm mortar, a popular weapon because it is comfortable to use and to carry, since it is small and dismantles easily. The cavalrymen carry AK-74s and sabers — you cannot control a horse and shoot at the same time, but it only takes one hand to wield a saber. The cavalry squadron is trained to operate on difficult terrain, where their speed and mobility give them an advantage over combat vehicles. These are dragoons, trained for offensive operations, for reconnaissance, and for missions such as blocking roads to

At a cavalry squadron near Osh in Kirghizia, a horse is taught to lie down. This is not a circus trick – it is vital if the horse and rider are to conceal themselves in the mountains.

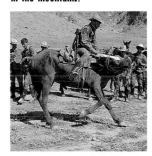

At the Kostroma Higher Military Engineering School of Chemical Defense, a relief model is used in a tactics lesson. Here they are considering how to relieve the effects of a nuclear strike and restore the troops' combat ability. Chemical defense is an unusual speciality, the officers at Kostroma say, realistically. 'There is nothing romantic about our service, but there is great intellectual interest.' Most of the officers from here were involved in cleaning up during the first few hours after the accident at Chernobyl.

prevent the passage of enemy troops. Most of the conscripts who serve in the unit have not ridden before, but those with any aptitude can be taught to do so very quickly. Most of the horses are bought locally from a handful of stud farms known to the army. There is a veterinary team attached to the squadron, consisting of two officers and two *praporshchiks*.

Other special troops provide the ground forces with combat support. These include engineering troops, signal troops, radio-technical troops, and chemical troops. Each of these branches also supports the other armed forces, however, and is administered separately. The relationship between the engineering troops and the ground forces is particularly close, since they are most likely to work with them. The morale of the engineering troops appears to be dramatically lower than that of most of the motorized rifle or tank soldiers. The men of the pontoon-building battalion and water-drilling company at Chardzhou in the Turkestan Military District prefaced several of their remarks with 'Of course our units are not prestigious . . .' They see themselves as the poor relations of the army and this colors their attitude toward military service, their officers, and life in general. In a good regiment the soldiers will always explain why their jobs are important and how the army depends on them. You might not have known that a conscript in a chemical defense unit or a rifleman in a BTR played the most vital role of all in the defense of the Soviet Union, but the soldier concerned will often explain exactly why this is the case. So it is very shocking to hear these engineering troops making it clear that they live in the knowledge of their own low status. Pushed, they admit that sappers played a vital role in World War II and would do so in any future conventional war, but this does not enhance their self-respect. It seems to be generally true that sappers do not, in the Soviet Union, enjoy the same prestige as in the British and American armies. During the war there was a famous saying: 'A sapper only makes a mistake once' (that is, when he blows himself up), which has now been revised to: 'A sapper makes two mistakes. The first is when he chooses his profession . . .' Although it is obviously a joke, it probably reflects to some extent the attitude of the officers toward their profession.

The mood of the soldiers naturally affects every aspect of their lives. Those who have served for only six months do most of the work in the barracks and the *dembels* do none, it is said. (This is the case in all the worst units.) The soldiers dream of getting out of the army – 'The day will come when the stars shining over us won't be those of the officers but those on a bottle of cognac' – but on the whole they do not go to the trouble of planning a glorious homecoming for themselves. The officers appear to be less relevant to the lives of the men than in other units. They do not spend as much time with the soldiers and they are less likely to organize recreation that will appeal to their individual tastes. The soldiers are scared of the officers; the desire to earn the respect of a particular officer that drives many conscripts is not in evidence here. But of course, given the character of the unit, the officers' task is unenviable. The soldiers have been picked for their physical strength, but in terms of intellectual ability and good character references the engineering troops have lower priority than other units. 'A drunken pontooner is harder to handle than a paratrooper,' the men say, in what may not be an idle boast. But they are surprisingly shrewd. When asked which officer of their acquaintance they respect they singled out the chief of staff of the engineering troops of the military district (Lieutenant Colonel Valery Semyonovich Timoshinov) — not, one would have thought, somebody with whom they would have had much contact. There was a theory in the ranks in the summer of 1989 that things might look up if he were to become the head of the engineering troops of the military district.

The engineering troops are not, by any means, the lowest caste in the army. That distinction undoubtedly belongs to the construction battalions — the stroybats. These come under the control of the Deputy Minister of Defense responsible for construction and billeting, and, as their name suggests, they construct things, for either the military or the civilian sector. Many of the conscripts in the stroybats have some sort of record for delinquency, not bad enough to make them ineligible for military service, but sufficiently serious to warrant exclusion from combat units. Others have failed the medical tests for ordinary army service and still others have some sort of conscientious objection to some aspect of military service. These are not usually boys who are trying to evade the army, since it is known that if you plead conscientious objection you will end up in a stroybat, and no one considers this to be an easy option. They are usually second- or third-generation Baptists or members of other Protestant sects, converted during the Brezhnev period. Many Russians see joining a Protestant group as a tragic act of double disloyalty: disloyalty to the commands of the atheistic ruling party and, paradoxically, simultaneous disloyalty to the great Orthodox Church upon which the very idea of Russia was based. Most of those who were converted were semi skilled factory workers or unsophisticated clerks. Far from having been harassed for their unorthodox beliefs, the boys I met had evidently never even begun to confront the most basic implications of their moral stand.

The conscripts in this construction battalion get up at 06:00 and begin the day with physical training, the morning check and a short period of political preparation. Their working day is usually from 09:00 until 13:00, and after lunch from 14:00 until 18:00. It is said by many responsible people in the army that *dedovshchina* is worst in these units. The boys working in the stroybat did not tell us this themselves, but then perhaps they would not. A bizarre anomaly of army life is that the conscripts working in the stroybats earn dramatically more than ordinary soldiers. Their pay depends on the work they have been engaged to do and how well they have performed, but it is rarely less than 50 rubles a month and it can be 250 rubles. The average wage seems to be 175–200 rubles. They may use the cash to buy extra working uniforms, or they may save it until they are demobilized.

The ground forces include such a wide range of units that they are, in a way, a miniature version of the armed forces as a whole, and many of the best formations, and the most impressive individuals, are to be found here. But it is also in the ground forces that many of the problems besetting the armed forces are at their most acute.

Mountain Brigade Training

One of the most important lessons of the Afghanistan war was that soldiers trained in European Russia find orientation very difficult in mountains, and were therefore unable to employ their artillery effectively. So many of the ablest people in the army now place great emphasis on the importance of mountain training. The Mountain Motorized Rifle Brigade, formed in 1984, is now the only one of its kind in the Soviet Army, although there were formerly other similar detachments. These soldiers, like many officers, have been carrying out peacekeeping functions during the past year, as trouble has broken out between Uzbeks and Kirghiz in Osh. But the soldiers and officers still have to maintain their primary professional skills. Every soldier in the brigade is taught the basic techniques of mountaineering, including the use of knots and specialized equipment. They can all climb in icy conditions and cross canyons, as here. They use flares for signaling in the mountains, especially at night or from caves.

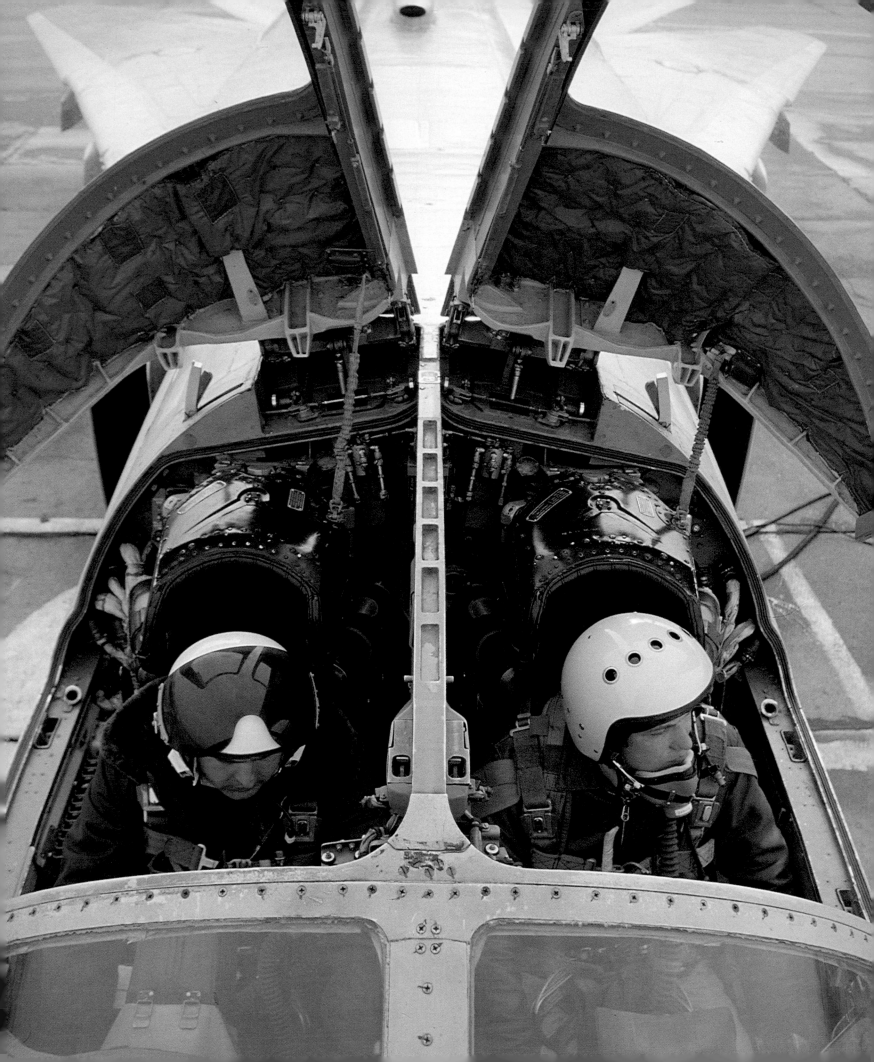

7 THE AIR

In the dark of mid-winter, in the snows of northern Russia, a Soviet major is walking along, the collar of his leather jacket pulled up, his hands thrust into his pockets. Two conscripts approach him, also in uniform, laughing and talking and looking forward to a good meal. As they pass him, the soldiers do not salute the major. He glances in their direction but pays them no attention.

This must be an air force base. You can always recognize pilots by their characteristic stance and the atmosphere of an aviation unit is considerably more relaxed than that of any other army installation: it is unusual to see soldiers salute officers if they meet in the street. Conscripts in the other services might be hungry, but it is unlikely they would be expecting anything that could realistically be called 'a good meal.' The food is much better in the air force than in the army, however, and this includes the meals that are given to the soldiers. Life in the Soviet Air Forces is rooted in a passion for aviation. The pilots and technicians alike love the aircraft. The main priority is the welfare of the airplanes. After this everything else is secondary.

The air forces (Voyenno-Vozdushniye Sily) include bombers, fighters, reconnaissance planes, fighter-bombers, attack planes, and military transport aviation. The air defense forces (Voiska Protivovozdushnoy Oboroni, known by the initials PVO), with their interceptor aviation, surface-to-air missiles, radio-technical forces (radar), and antiballistic missile defense branches have the least strong service identity of any of the armed forces. An interceptor pilot sees himself as a pilot, as part of military aviation, rather than as an air defense pilot specifically. Similarly, the missile people identify with other rocket and artillery troops. Therefore I shall consider the lives of those involved in all military aviation first and then specifically the people in air defense. It may be useful to point out here that interceptor units are not necessarily subordinate to the air defense force; in border districts they come under the frontal aviation air force.

The airmen's world

An aviation base is a completely different type of community from any other army unit. The conscripts here are not combat personnel. They work in auxiliary positions, supporting the work of the pilots and technicians. The crews of the aircraft (officers or

Pilots in the cockpit of an Su-24 wait for permission to taxi to take-off.

A technician working on a Tu-22.

During the pre-flight briefing at the Long Distance Aviation Regiment in Priliuki.

occasionally *praporshchiks*) are the 'soldiers.' But these crews are wholly dependent on their machines. If an armored personnel carrier stops working, the infantryman can hop out and keep shooting, and if his rifle jams he can fight the enemy with his bayonet, and if he loses that he can always engage in hand-to-hand combat (in a nice old-fashioned sort of battle). But if something goes badly wrong with an aircraft, the crew are finished as combatants. All they can do is hope to survive. So the engineers and technicians are vitally important. Despite the very high status of the pilots and despite the privileges they are given in terms of housing priority, pay, and so on, the aviation community seems to be less caste-ridden than the rest of the armed forces. The relationship between the technicians and pilots is close and is one of absolute interdependence. The pilots of a frontal aviation regiment at Lida in Byelorussia (near the Lithuanian border, about sixty miles from Vilnius) explained that they do not have any preference for a particular aircraft; it does not make any difference to them which of the squadron's airplanes they are asked to fly. But the pilots may prefer an aircraft that has been serviced by particular technicians. They know that the quality of the technicians affects the machine's performance. It is not just that some technicians are better than others, but that certain pilots like certain technicians' work. Similarly, pilots have been known to go to a lot of trouble to ensure that they can work with one navigator rather than another. However complex and brilliant the machinery, however much the aircraft can do by itself, the pilots know that a great deal depends on their own state of mind, and that this in turn depends on the psychological compatibility of the crew.

Conscripts in the air force have a far freer existence than in any of the other armed forces. The minutiae of military discipline are less rigorously applied to them, but their combat readiness is usually higher. They say that the officers treat them as equals and this seems to be true. Air force officers are rarely as interested in the overall education and development of their soldiers as conscientious combined arms or naval officers. The advantages of this, from the conscripts' point of view, are obvious. The soldiers are trusted to get on with their jobs and they do so with a high degree of independence.

The morale of soldiers in aviation units is sometimes undermined by the fact that they spend their time on menial tasks, rather than on military work. They complain that it is impossible for them to feel like soldiers when they are only cleaning and tidying the territory of the unit. Conscripts are usually involved in maintaining vehicles and equipment, in storing and moving fuel and other supplies, and in elementary mechanical tasks to assist the technicians. Few of them get to touch the precious aircraft. But it is churlish of the soldiers to moan about the nature of their work. On the whole they acknowledge that they have been lucky to end up doing their military service in aviation. They do not enjoy the glamour of the élite forces or the sense of achievement of those who have served in infantry regiments. But neither do the conscripts generally have to endure the excesses of *dedovshchina* or racial violence.

The most resourceful soldiers I encountered were serving at an aviation base in a remote part of the Soviet Union. Although there is a television in every barracks, the soldiers are forbidden to watch it, apart from the compulsory military and news programs and others approved by the zampolits. But soldiers often have reason to be in the barracks during the day, for example, if they are preparing to go on duty or if they have just come off duty. At such times they frequently want to watch television. So these boys have connected the main television switch to a hidden pad on the wall behind the orderly post in the barracks. Normally, the orderly leans against the wall behind him and the electricity supply to the television is switched on. But if an officer walks into the barracks he naturally leaps to attention, instantly switching off the television. The device is brilliantly conceived and ensures that the soldiers can watch their favorite programs without anxiety.

Among the conscripts there is a higher than normal proportion of Slavs, because they have to be able to read and speak Russian fluently in order to understand technical instructions. The soldiers must also be capable of carrying out elementary mechanical work, but do not have to be in peak physical condition. So although they all appear quite healthy, it is not uncommon to find boys who have some medical complaint serving in the air force.

An aircraft technician wearing protective headgear.

Pilots

Marshal of Aviation Efimov, the former commander-in-chief of the Soviet Air Force, has very definite views about the type of recruits who make the best pilots. 'The very top group, physiologically and intellectually, the people who have only had top marks throughout their whole education, are dangerous for the air force. Such men take decisions instantly, moreover a pilot ought not to rush into decisions. Somebody who succeeds very well and grasps things easily has to try less, since he has always achieved everything easily. But in life, if he comes up against difficulties he is less able to cope than a pilot who, shall we say, has a lower level of qualification. If you take the level of skill and training of pilots on a nine-point scale, with nine the highest mark, then for good pilots you need people with seven, six, or five marks. But that's just my idea.' He points out that different types of people are needed for each flying job. 'Let's take a fighter pilot. His profession forces him to be watchful, so he keeps turning his head. But if you take the pilot of a cargo airplane, he just turns slowly. His profession is like that. So when we select pilots, we have to look at the young man to decide for which type of aircraft he will be suitable. One is a born fighter pilot, another is simply a bomber pilot.'

The pilots themselves have their own ideas about the qualities they need. A fighter pilot, they say, cannot rely on anyone but himself. In action he has to assess the situation, decide what to do, and then act, all in a fraction of a second. 'Fighters can operate at very low or very high altitudes, and at great speed. But, especially at high altitudes, we cannot afford to make a single mistake – the enemy won't give us a second chance.' MiG-25 (interceptor) pilots point out that the American SR-71 flies at a height of 12 miles at a speed of 2,200 miles per hour (that is, at three times the speed of sound). 'So our aircraft have to be at least as good as that. Bomber pilots need great self-control, they should be calm, and they should be the sort of people who will not panic, even in extreme situations.' The pilots of strategic aviation need to possess all the virtues of bomber pilots, combined with extraordinary stamina (their flights may last 20 hours) and the ability to work as part of a team, since their crews consist of four people or more.

Defending Soviet Airspace

The nights are long at Kotlas in December. Here MiG-25 interceptors of the air defense forces wait as the ice is cleaned from the runway. The standard vehicle used for clearing the runway is the KPM (combined water-pouring vehicle), based on the Zil-130 truck, which has snow-plow and brush attachments. It usually works with the TGM-59 heating vehicle, which melts the ice in winter and dries the runway after it has been cooled with cold water in summer. This never-ending task is vital because when the aircraft taxi to take off they suck in a lot of air, and even the smallest pebble could damage the engine. The pilots are given their flight missions by the colonel in charge of the regiment during the early morning briefing session. An early morning reconnaisance flight will already have been performed, usually by the colonel himself, to check the weather conditions. If everything seems to be all right, the pilots fill out necessary documents and take off. *Far right* A MiG-25 starts its engines before an evening take-off. Any minute now the boosters will come on, shooting flames out of the back of the aircraft.

Flight safety receives a great deal of attention in aviation colleges and in the military press. Every *eskadrilya* engineering service includes a group, whose job it is to maintain the aircraft emergency ejection systems. Here a pilot is seen wearing a parachute harness.

In the cockpit of a MiG 25 at Kotlas.

Student pilots at military aviation colleges are taught to fly on Czech L-39 machines. When they graduate and are sent as lieutenants to operational units, they are given between fifteen days' and one month's theoretical training and then about two weeks' flight training with simulators before the commander lets them loose on the unit's combat aircraft. At this stage, although they are competent pilots they have no skill categorization. The first of these — Pilot (or Navigator), Third Class — requires 100–300 hours' flying time, but it is difficult to generalize about the length of flying time that it takes in reality. The higher categories — Second Class, First Class, Pilot/Sniper, and Honored Pilot — can be awarded after a minimum number of flying hours that varies according to the type of aircraft. In each case the pilot is assessed on his performance. An officer cannot lose a categorization, but he could fail to confirm it if he is unable to put in enough flying time. When this happens, it is necessary to repeat the entire training program for the award. Most pilots maintain their qualifications, but they frequently complain about not getting as much flying time as they would like. At the same time, each pilot must train constantly on a simulator. But there is often only one simulator for the entire regiment, so it is clear that the simulator time available to pilots is just as limited as actual flying time.

At first glance, it appears that Soviet pilots are given less annual flying time than their NATO counterparts. But in terms of the useful training time that each receives, it is not at all clear that this is the case. NATO pilots in Europe (who, in any case, say they get far fewer flying hours than they need) often have to spend a long time just cruising along to reach the area where they can practice dummy runs. Soviet aviation bases, on the other hand, are frequently located only a few minutes away from the *poligon* where pilots train. So they are able to spend far more of their flying time training in difficult maneuvers than their Western counterparts.

An aviation regiment consists of three *eskadrilyas* (squadrons), each of which is divided into *zvyenos* (flights) or, as they are called in some units, *otriads* (detachments). There are usually three or four *zvyenos* in each *eskadrilya*. The statutory rank for the commander of an *eskadrilya*, the vital combat unit in military aviation, is lieutenant colonel, but in the interceptor regiment at Kotlas in 1989 all three *eskadrilyas* were headed by majors and two out of three at Lida in 1990. The average age of the *eskadrilya* commanders was about thirty-five. At Kotlas there were three *zvyenos* in each *eskadrilya* and each *zvyeno* consisted of two pairs of aircraft (MiG-25s). There are always more pilots than there are airplanes. At Kotlas each interceptor has its 'owner' pilot, who is responsible for it, but a great many pilots do not have their own machines. Each *zvyeno* in that regiment consists of four aircraft and pilots, so each *eskadrilya* has at its disposal twelve machines. But there are usually about twenty pilots altogether in each *eskadrilya*, since the commander, three of his deputies, and others are also pilots who must complete an annual flying commitment. Each *eskadrilya* commander has four deputies — the deputy commander (who acts in his absence), the chief of staff, the political deputy, and the squadron engineer.

Usually, the commander of the regiment sets the flying schedule for the week on Monday, indicating the general principles of where the pilots should fly and the tasks they should perform. For example, when I was at Kotlas the pilots were concentrating on improving their technique in aerial target interception in cloudy conditions. The

The Tu-16 (top), an earlier
generation strategic bomber
brought into service in 1955, in
the air with the Tu-160. The
combat radius of the Tu-16
(without refueling) is 1,900
miles; that of the Tu-160, 4,500
miles.

Two Tu-22s (long distance bomber), given the command to split off. Tu-22s are to be found at five bases in the Soviet Union — Baranovichi, Gomel, Machulishe, Zhitomir, and Neshun. Several pilots, who had flown many different types of aircraft, expressed particular affection for this machine.

At the Gagarin Academy, the work of the pilot in the flight simulator is monitored on a model of the control panel of a MiG-29.

The pilots have all the glamour, but it is the mechanics, technicians, and engineers who keep the aircraft flying.

program usually includes two or three alternatives, to take account of possible weather conditions. The engineers and technicians are told what aviation equipment should be prepared. It is up to the commanders of the *eskadrilyas* to work out the details of the flights during the preliminary preparation and the *zvyeno* commanders to prepare the pilots. First they discuss how the flight should be performed and what maneuvers will be involved, where the target should be intercepted, fuel consumption, and so on. Then the pilot will practice the flight on the simulator. The commander often turns up at the preliminary preparation of one of the *eskadrilyas* to carry out his own spot check of the standard of preparation of the *eskadrilya* as a whole, or of one of its pilots. Although the flight plan is compiled in advance, the pilots and their commanders have some freedom to alter it on the day. The maximum number of flights allowed per fighter pilot per flying day is seven, but he might make only one. Each flight can last from ten minutes to an hour and a half. A normal flying day for an interceptor pilot might consist of three or four flights of about one hour each. Pilots of long-distance aviation regularly make flights lasting five hours or more.

The pilots spend flying days in the control tower, reading, watching television, or playing games. Chess is prohibited, in some aviation bases at least, because it is too stimulating. What the men need are mindless, relaxing pastimes. The young pilots in Lida have a game that certainly fulfills the first criterion, although it is played with such fervent passion that it may well raise their blood pressure. An older pilot assessed this game as taking second place, in terms of the intellectual demands on the players, after tug-of-war. *Kryutashka*, as it is called, involves rolling dice and moving checkers around the outside squares of a chessboard.

While the pilots are preparing themselves for the flying days, the technicians are working on the aircraft. Each is given a thorough check once a week by the *eskadrilya* technicians. These checks take up to eight hours. On the day of the flight the technicians arrive at the airfield about three hours before take-off to carry out the last minute preflight checks. Many engineers say that they originally wanted to be pilots, but that when, for medical or other reasons, they were turned down, they applied to military aviation engineering colleges. There is, in any case, considerable prestige attached to military aviation engineering at the highest levels. The Zhukovsky Air Force Engineering Academy in Moscow is one of the handful of top academic institutions in the country.

The *eskadrilya* engineering service is divided into groups, each with its own responsibility, such as aviation equipment, automatic flight control, radar equipment, armaments, or the engines. Each group is also responsible for keeping a certain part of the *eskadrilya*'s area clean and tidy. If the technicians discover major defects during these checks they refer them to TECh (Technical Exploitation Unit), the service responsible for serious repairs to the aircraft. Usually the relevant part will be replaced with a spare, while TECh works on repairing the original. Each section of the aircraft has its own log book, where any malfunctions that have been observed and any repairs that have been carried out are noted. The engines are periodically removed and overhauled completely, whether or not any faults have been noticed. The service life of the engines varies, but in the case of the MiG-25 it is from 300 hours for a reassembled engine to 800 for one that is factory new. TECh also carries out the annual inspection of all aircraft (Maintenance Number 1 or 'the twelve-month works'), which takes ten days, and the 14-day overhaul that takes place every two years.

From my observation, morale in military aviation is generally high because of the satisfaction that the job itself brings to pilots and technicians. However, the shortage of housing seems to be severe and I met young officers who were leaving the air force because they knew that they had no hope of being given decent housing in the foreseeable future. Flying certain aircraft, such as strategic bombers, is exhausting work, and it is important that the pilots should not be under too much stress at home. Therefore, all those who fly the Tu-160 have been given apartments. This does not include the technicians, however, many of whom share cramped flats with other families. I was surprised by how little resentment this seemed to have caused. People were angry with the system that fails to provide decent accommodations for hard-working officers, but the preferential treatment given to pilots did not seem to cause personal animosity.

Although the armed forces are being reduced and there is a need to cut some officers' jobs, the danger is that too many of the best people, confident of their ability to flourish outside the army, will be tempted to go. The personal difficulties of the officers, such as the education of their children, housing, and so on, are exacerbated by the fact that aviation, and especially air defense, bases are often located far from cities.

In connection with this it is worth pointing out that once they have been posted to bases that are several hours' drive from small towns, airmen will have very few opportunities for meeting girls. So many of them make an effort to find wives while they are at military college. Not everybody would choose to marry an airman. Any army wife is, to some extent, widowed by her husband's profession. All officers work long hours and are preoccupied by the demands of military life. But the wives of pilots have to cope not only with the ordinary stresses of military life, but also with the ever-present rival – the aircraft – whose existence they simply have to endure. Pilots and technicians are often to be found, long after working hours, pondering its intricacies, describing in the minutest detail something that happened during the last flight, or simply swapping jokes. It is evident that their working life is enjoyable. An air force officers' mess is always fun, and even the presence of a foreign visitor did not cause any awkwardness or constraint. The business of flying the aircraft and talking about them is far too important to be interrupted by any civilian. In the mess, on the airfield, or gathering in each other's apartments during the evenings, the airmen will be assiduous in their drive to ensure that no aspect of their work, or of aviation in general, has escaped their consideration.

In the armed forces the third toast always has a special significance; among the veterans of Afghanistan it is for those who did not come back and it is drunk standing up, without clinking glasses. In the air force it is *za bezopasnost* ('to safety'). That is, to safe flights and to those who have died flying (more or less the equivalent of our 'happy landings'). Whoever proposes the toast will say, 'Let's drink "za bezopasnost,"' whereupon everyone else will touch the edge of the table with the middle of their glass, saying in turn, 'Contact here.' When they have all reported contact, they move their glasses and the pilot proposing the toast will say, '*ot vinta*' (an expression dating from the days of propeller aircraft, and meaning at the same time

Colonel Valeri Seliyanov, one of the most distinguished pilots of Soviet long-distance aviation (according to Lieutenant General Pyotr Deinikin, the head of this branch of the air force) in the cockpit of the Tu-160. Colonel Seliyanov mentioned, in passing, that one in ten of those who studied at military college with him (pilots) have been killed flying, not in combat in Afghanistan or elsewhere but in the course of their work as pilots and test pilots.

The Tupolov-160, the world's largest and heaviest bomber, (weight 275 tons) carries either twelve air-launched cruise missiles or 24 short-range attack missiles. The Tu-160 is 177 feet long, with a maximum wingspan of 182 feet.

'get away,' and 'start the engine') and the others will reply, 'Yest, ot vinta' ('Roger, Wilco') and drink to the bottom, in one gulp. Most aviation rituals hinge on the idea of averting danger, not surprisingly. The word *posledniye* ('the last') is never used in Soviet military aviation circles. Instead, pilots, technicians, and even their wives and children have to use the word *krainiye* ('ultimate'). To an airman, *posledniye* brings to mind *posledniy put*, 'the last trip,' or the removal of a body from home in a coffin.

Aviation rituals are not confined to pilots. On flight days, when the aircraft has been checked by the technicians and the pilot is installed in the cockpit and about to be towed to the take-off position on the runway, one of the technicians will touch the tip of the wing, to wish the aircraft good luck and preserve it from accidents. And, so as not to tempt fate, no aircraft is ever given the number 13.

Soviet airmen have invented so much slang over the years that it is often difficult for outsiders to understand what they are talking about. Their argot is a mixture of technical language — for example fifty is always 'half hundred' to avoid confusion during radio communication — and colorful aviation metaphors. If someone leaves the table where his friends are eating and drinking, it is said to be a *shtoporno*, literally a 'spin,' as when an aircraft spins out of control and goes into a nosedive.

Air force parlance differs from that of the rest of the army in all sorts of ways. For example, a superior is normally addressed as 'Comrade Major,' or whatever. But in aviation it will always be 'Comrade Commander.' This is a perfectly accepted form of address, but pilots say that in the presence of a senior military figure, especially if he comes from another service, they might not use it. Again, the air force emblem on the officers' forage cap is usually referred to as the 'bird,' but airmen call it the 'hen.' There are also, inevitably, endless nicknames for the aircraft themselves, some official, some unofficial. Su-7 and Su-9 are known as *Truba* ('water-pipe'), Su-15 as *Golub Mira* ('dove of peace') or *Napilnik* ('instrument'). MiG-21 is *Balalaika* or *Utyug* ('a flat iron,' either because of its shape or, it has been suggested, becaues the engine has relatively little power). The MiG-23 is sometimes called *Chiborashka*, after a cartoon hero, and sometimes *Krokodil*. MiG-25 is known affectionately as *Chemodan* ('suit-case') or *Gastronom*, because of the huge amount of alcohol needed to cool some of its engine parts (it holds 160 liters of '*masandra*,' a mixture of alcohol and water, and 40 liters of pure alcohol).

The nicknames are often interchangeable — MiG-27 is also occasionally *Krokodil*, and *Chemodan* may be applied to the Su-24. Both the MiG-29 and the MiG-27 are sometimes referred to as *Lastochka* ('swallow'), but this is also a general term of affection that is used for any aircraft. Strategic bomber pilots and technicians refer to tactical aircraft such as the MiG-23 and MiG-27 as *svistks* ('whistles'), inconsequential little things, lost on the wind. These aircraft are also thought to look like penny whistles. Fighter pilots call bombers in general *utyug* ('flat iron'), implying that they are ungainly and slow. Then there are the names by which the different branches of aviation refer to each other. Pilots of cargo aviation are *messochniks* ('people carrying bags') or *odnopogoniks* ('those with only one shoulder board — because they have been carrying bags'). The men of strategic aviation, one of the most glamorous branches of the air force, are playfully described by other aviators as *ogorodniks* ('market gardeners') or mongols.

Extreme weather conditions exacerbate all the usual difficulties of aircraft maintenance.

An IL-78 refuels a Tu-95 bomber in midair.
Airmen's jokes often incorporate aviation jargon. For example, there is the story of the pilot who arrived home drunk. Unable to find his key, he rang the doorbell.
'Who's that?' his wife called out.
'8877 half hundred 9. Request permission for landing.'
'Negative. Runway too busy.'
'Roger. Making another circuit.'
A few minutes later he rang the bell once more.
'8877 half hundred 9. Request permission for landing.'
'Negative. Runway too busy,' and so on. A few minutes later the pilot again rang the doorbell and received exactly the same answer.
'Roger. In that case I'll use the alternative airfield.'

Air defense

The air defense forces include not only interceptor aircraft but also over 8,000 surface-to-air missile launchers at some 1,200 sites, a radio-technical branch, and an anti-ballistic missile branch. The surface-to-air missile forces provide anti-aircraft missile protection for fixed sites, such as airfields, and they can also offer mobile coverage. Air defense bases include outlying radio homing beacons and radar installations for air traffic control and fighter interception. These may be some distance from the unit, such as the one seven miles away from the Kotlas Air Defense Base. Three soldiers live here permanently: one, a radio mechanic, one to operate the diesel power supply, and a third man who can do both jobs. Food is delivered to the post once a month and kept in a freezer. An officer arrives during the day, but otherwise the conscripts are unsupervised. They describe the place as a 'home away from home where we have everything we need,' but admit that it can be claustrophobic: the post is isolated deep in the taiga. Another disadvantage is that the soldiers may be summoned at any time of the day or night and this is not simply a matter of telephoning for transport – it means a long walk through the snow or the rain back to base. For most conscripts, however, the relative freedom of these posts far outweighs such minor physical discomfort. There is another advantage to working in one of these radio homing posts: the conscripts have a real job to do, which is a vital part of the combat life of the unit as a whole.

Modern air defense radar, operating in the so-called Doppler mode, is tuned to a sensitivity whereby it only picks up objects moving at sixty miles or more per hour. At the same time, anything lower than 300 feet is excluded. This is a necessary limitation without which the radar operators would spend their lives monitoring the flights of ducks and geese or following ground clutter such as tractors. Even so, air defense units are successful in locating weather balloons, which apparently often conceal reconnaissance equipment. The pilots at Kotlas were very pleased to have been able to shoot down such a balloon in the autumn of 1989. It was found to hold a 'spy container,' they say, about eight feet long, six feet high, and five feet deep, equipped with cameras and devices for detecting radio frequencies. These balloons are said to offer perfect opportunities for reconnaissance – they do not need to be controlled by radio, they are cheap, they store information easily, and, in principle, they are difficult to detect because they move slowly at a low altitude. However, the balloon that was intercepted near Kotlas was spotted at a height of 300 feet. Air defense aviation and surface-to-air missile units have their own radar, but for national protective cover there are separate early-warning radar installations located mainly along the borders of the Soviet Union.

During my visit to the air defense base at Kotlas the only noticeable attempt to mislead me during the whole of my research took place. I was told that the unit was no longer on constant combat alert, as it had been in the past. But I was assured that there had been no cuts in the regiment. The changes were purely to reduce costs. I had no reason to disbelieve this, until I went into the barracks. The soldiers from the interceptor regiment said they had to wait to be demobilized until their replacements had arrived. 'You see,' they said, 'we are still needed here. There haven't been any big cuts in the aviation unit, unlike the missiles.' It transpired that, whereas there had formerly

OPPOSITE: P-12 radar (NATO designation, 'spoon-rest') at the Ruza air defense base.

A conscript makes adjustments to the chassis of an air defense missile launcher.

Ruza air defense base. Soldiers update air situation maps using information received by radar.

been 300 conscripts working for the rocket regiment, there were by then only 60. According to these soldiers and to other people at the base, half the officers had also been cut from that unit. It is completely unclear to me why it seemed necessary to maintain otherwise, especially in an air defense unit when, in general, the air force and air defense force seemed to be so open and relaxed in their dealings with us.

During the 1980s two separate incidents focused the attention of the world and of the Soviet government, military establishment, and media on the nation's air defense. These were the cases of the Korean airliner, flight KAL 007, and of the lone German teenager, Matthias Rust, who landed in Moscow in 1987 in his little Cessna 172. The reaction to these cases led the government spokesman, Gennadi Gerasimov, to complain ironically that Soviet Air Defense was criticized first for shooting down an aircraft and then for failing to do so. In fact, the air defense forces behaved quite correctly in the Rust case. The aircraft's presence was recorded more than once, but since it was clearly not military any action against it would have been unjustified. The only possible mistake was that the country's political leadership was not kept sufficiently informed. That Rust landed in Red Square and that somebody on the spot at the time had a video camera was simply bad luck for the air defense forces.

I interviewed the pilot who shot down KAL 007, Lieutenant Colonel Ossipovich, whose account of the events of 1 September 1983 is interesting not only in connection with the shooting of the aircraft but also for the light it sheds on the operating routine of interceptor pilots in the Far East in the early 1980s. Gennadi Nikolaievich Ossipovich was then regimental duty commander for flight training at one of the two air defense regiments on Sakhalin Island, off the Pacific coast of the Soviet Union. The state boundary is considered to be fifteen miles beyond the coastline of Sakhalin and beyond that a neutral zone of sixty miles extends, where Soviet aircraft can escort intruders but may not use any weapons against them. As usual there were two crews on duty on the night of 31 August/1 September, ready to take off within four to eight minutes of an alert notice.

Ossipovich was on duty with one of the unit's squadron commanders, Major Sergei Tarasov. Everything was quiet until 05:30 hours local time, when they received the order to move to alert status 'number one.' This means that the pilots are to board their aircraft and prepare for take-off. Fifteen minutes later, at 05:45 hours Lieutenant Colonel Ossipovich was scrambled and flew, as usual, towards the sea in his Su-15 Interceptor. This was all perfectly normal. The crews on duty were scrambled three or four times a day at that time, as American reconnaissance aircraft took off and flew over Sakhalin and toward Kamchatka. During this precise period, from April of that year, the Americans developed a new habit. They began to fly over neutral waters then make a 90-degree turn, as though they were heading straight for the border, then, when they were within thirty or forty miles of the border, they would swerve away again and continue to fly parallel with it. When this happened, Ossipovich says, 'We naturally turned everything on and went up, and they noted our frequencies and call signs.' These flights usually took place during the daytime.

On the night in question, Ossipovich took off and flew toward the Sea of Okhotsk. He climbed to 26,000 feet and ground control began to direct him toward the target. The intruder aircraft was coming from the direction of Kamchatka in the north. A MiG-23 from the air defense base 190 miles away in the north of Sakhalin Island had taken off some time before Ossipovich and so the actions of the two aircraft were coordinated by ground control. At 06:01 hours, sixteen minutes after he had left the ground, Ossipovich located the intruder in his radar sight. 'It was on a heading of 240 degrees directly toward our base. I was eight miles range from him and nine miles behind me was the MiG-23.' At this time the intruder was over neutral waters, so the Su-15 and the MiG-23 simply shadowed it. Major Tarasov had by now been sent up (also in a Su-15) as a backup, but he was not in the procession. The intruder was flying directly toward the border. The only information available to Lieutenant Colonel Ossipovich was its speed and the altitude at which it was flying. He assumed that it was an American RC-135 reconnaissance aircraft, as usual, and the facts available to him did not preclude this. At about 06:12 hours (according to Ossipovich's calculation) the intruder crossed the Soviet border. Lieutenant Colonel Ossipovich flashed the internationally recognized signal to an aircraft that has violated a state border. 'Do you think it's possible that he didn't see the signals?' I asked him. 'It's impossible, if they weren't asleep there. Then I fired four warning bursts from my gun. I knew that it was not one of ours because I had used the "Friend or Foe" identification interrogator. They often send up our bombers to test the air defense system and to test us.' Still the aircraft did not react. Ossipovich informed ground control of this. Like him, they had no way of making direct radio contact with the aircraft. So Ossipovich was given the order: 'Destroy the target.'

Lieutenant Colonel Ossipovich is convinced that the pilot of the airplane saw him. 'When I was flying with him we had the same speed. When I started to tell him he was violating our airspace with my onboard lights he reduced his speed so that I went on ahead of him. But we can't maintain that speed, although heavy aircraft such as the RC-135 or civilian aircraft can. They can fly at a speed which would make me stall and go into a spin, so that's why they always perform this maneuver. I often flew there. You approach to take a look at the number. He immediately reduces speed and you fly ahead and begin to come in again. They use this method almost all the time, in the hope that the pilot who intercepts them will go into a spin.' The missiles were fired from a distance of 1,600 to 2,000 feet. What can you see at that time of the morning at that height, in the skies over Sakhalin? 'Everything is sort of hazy. You understand, you could see the exhaust from the engines. You could see that, somewhere, there was an aircraft flying. As if you could see that there was someone there, but you couldn't see who. You need to be a pilot to imagine it.' The MiG-23 was still behind Ossipovich at a distance of fifteen versts (one verst = 3,500 feet), and Tarasov's aircraft and three other interceptors were by now also in the area. Ossipovich fired two missiles, both of which, from his observation, hit their target.

'Afterwards the unpleasantness began. It is easier to be up there than down on the ground. In the evening I was called by our divisional headquarters. People arrived from Far Eastern Headquarters.' At that time, air defense aviation came under the air force, not under air defense, so Marshal Kutakhov, then commander-in-chief of the air force, arrived in the Far East after the shooting. Marshal of Aviation Koldunov, the head of air defense, also visited the area as a state commission investigated the incident. In 1989 a Washington court exonerated the Soviet government and hence Lieutenant Colonel Ossipovich of any guilt in the KAL affair. Nevertheless, as a result of the case the procedure for dealing with intruders into Soviet airspace was reviewed.

8 THE NAVY

Of all the Soviet Armed Forces, only the Soviet Navy (*Voyenno-Morskoy flot*) has retained an entirely separate identity and its own traditions from Imperial Russian times. The other four services wear the same khaki-colored everyday uniform and they all have identical ranks (apart from a slight diversity of air force generals. See Appendix I). The navy, however, wear distinctive black uniforms and have their own ranks – which correspond exactly to those of the army and should never be confused with them. Woe betide any landlubber who addresses a captain of the first rank as 'Colonel.' It will be interpreted as a heinous affront to the dignity of the navy – which (if it came from a soldier) is probably how it was intended. The key word associated with the navy in military and even civilian minds is *shik* – roughly 'chic.' Sailors certainly look wonderful in their black everyday dress and in their parade whites. Even the conscripts' working clothes are redolent of the romance of seafaring in the days of steam and sail. But there is more to *shik* than this. It insinuates that only the navy knows how things should be done and how to get them done, easily and smoothly. Virtues prized by the navy include the quality of *likhost*, bold-spiritedness, that somehow suggests courage accompanied by flair and, of course, *flotskaya gordost*, naval pride.

The navy consists of four fleets and the Caspian flotilla. Each of the fleets has the suffix 'Red Banner,' including the 'Twice Red Banner Baltic Fleet,' so-called because it was the first fleet in the Russian Navy (under Peter the Great) and because its sailors fired the first shots in the 1917 Revolution. The official abbreviation for this fleet is DKBF (DK = Twice Red Banner, BF = Baltic Fleet), but it is often known as BF, which the initiated take to mean *Bivshii flot*, the 'former fleet' (in allusion to its history). The Black Sea Fleet, similarly, is KChF (Red Banner *Chernomorskiy flot*), irreverently interpreted by some as *Chi flot, Chi ni flot*, 'maybe a fleet, maybe not a fleet' (in Ukrainian). The Northern Fleet, or KSF (Red Banner *Severny flot*), is described as *Sovremnni flot*, the modern fleet, while the Pacific Fleet, KTOF (*Tikhiy Okeanskiy flot*) becomes *tozhe flot*, 'also a fleet.' As this naval joke makes clear, each fleet has its own distinct character. The Baltic Fleet is indeed highly aware of its history and, only half-jokingly, considers itself to be the first among the fleets, although it is now probably the least important. The fleet has 87,000 men and bases at Kronstadt, Liepaya, Battiysk, and Tallinn, as well as the headquarters at Kaliningrad.

A naval infantry exercise near Sevastopol. Driving off the landing ship is easy, but embarking the tanks – in reverse gear – is not. Another hazard with an exercise such as this is positioning the ship correctly, so that it is as near the shore as possible, bearing in mind the space that the landing doors need to open.

The Black Sea Fleet is inevitably influenced by its surroundings. Sevastopol, the home of the fleet, is arguably the most beautiful city in the Soviet Union. It had the good fortune to be a 'closed' city for a long time and so escaped the horrors that promiscuous tourism would have brought. There are signs now that Sevastopol is to be laid bare to the devastations of the holidaymakers, but for the time being it retains its dignity and its languid beauty. Above all, Sevastopol is a navy city, with constant reminders of the influence of the fleet in its historical buildings and monuments and in its contemporary life. The navy leads, in many ways, a charmed existence here, despite the strategic importance of the Black Sea and the strenuous schedule this imposes on the fleet. The fleet also has bases are at Balaklava, Poti, and Odessa.

The Northern Fleet, celebrated for its role in the last war, naturally benefits from most of the technical innovations of the navy because of its role in the North Atlantic and Arctic, and because of the necessity of maintaining and updating its expensive submarine fleet (consisting of over 170 submarines, 30 of them strategic). The officers and men of this fleet are proud of their ability to survive and work efficiently despite the climatic hardships of the seas they patrol. Inevitably, however, the morale of the officers and the men here was rocked by the series of submarine disasters that has cursed the fleet in the past few years. The fleet's main bases are: Severomorsk (the headquarters), the Kola Inlet, Motorskiy Gulf, Gramikha, Polyarny, and Litsa Gulf.

The Pacific Fleet is charged with the responsibility of guarding the Soviet border and representing the state's interests in the world's greatest ocean. On other shores are some of the richest and most highly industrialized states on earth – the United States, Canada, Japan, and Australia. The Cold War may be officially over, but the region remains one of vital strategic interest. This, therefore, is the biggest surface fleet, with over 300 ships and 110 submarines. The existence of Vladivostok (the fleet's head-quarters) represents a miracle of Russian perseverance. The city is reminiscent of San Francisco, with trolleybuses running up and down the hills on which it is built, and the architecture reflects the same feeling of exuberant relief at finally reaching the coast after the long trek. Vladivostok is now becoming very prosperous, its trade with the rest of the Pacific Basin flourishing and expanding. The Pacific Fleet has bases at Petropavlovsk-Kamchatka and Sovyetskaya Gavan, and abroad at Cam Ranh Bay in Vietnam and in Aden. With the Pacific Fleet one is constantly aware that its role is of great importance to the defense of the state.

In peacetime, the Soviet Navy is intended to support the state's military, political and economic interests around the world. Its missions include protecting Soviet merchant and fishing fleets and asserting Soviet rights in international waters. In the past few years it has been used to escort Soviet merchant ships in the Persian Gulf, in joint training with the Cuban and North Korean armed forces, and has made port visits to countries all over the world. In wartime the ballistic missile submarines would be vitally important, and defending them from attack by surface ships or other submarines would become one of the navy's main tasks. Another would be to eliminate enemy naval forces (surface or submarine) that might launch an attack against the Soviet Union. The navy would also be ready, where necessary, to protect and support the ground forces with gunfire and amphibious assault, and to disrupt enemy communications. Further, it could provide early warning against aircraft and cruise missiles.

Naval band playing during the Navy Day celebrations, Sevastopol.

Soviet naval ships are classified according to their function, the main distinction being between those intended for use principally against surface ships or submarines. The main task of the *Kiev* and *Tblisi* classes of heavy aircraft-carrying cruisers is anti-submarine warfare. Other antisubmarine ships are usually described as such, while the words 'rocket' and 'torpedo' are used for vessels whose primary mission is antisurface ship warfare. The navy also includes minesweepers, minelayers, landing ships, and support ships.

Running the ships

Every ship of the Soviet Navy is administratively divided into *boeviye chasti* (bay-chays), combat departments. There is a standard system of numbering these bay-chays that is exactly the same throughout the navy. Bay-chay number one is navigation, number two is missiles and artillery, number three is mines and torpedoes, number four is signal communications, number five is engineering, number six is aviation flight provision, and number seven is control (that is, radar and electronic equipment). However, each ship only has the bay-chays necessary for its own particular function. So, for example, an aircraft carrier or a large antisubmarine ship would have all seven bay-chays, but a smaller craft might have only three or four. Ships also include services and commands, according to their size and requirements. A detailed examination of the system of administration of the *Novorossisk* aircraft-carrying cruiser illustrates the general principles according to which life on all the navy's ships is organized.

Built at the Nikolaev shipyard on the Black Sea, the *Novorossisk* is the third ship of the *Kiev* class and the flagship of the Pacific Fleet. The principal modifications in the design of the *Novorossisk* are that, unlike the *Kiev* itself, it has no torpedo tubes. The other differences are mainly operational; for example, the radar equipment has been modified and there have been alterations to the propulsion and communications systems. 1,500 people live and work on board the *Novorossisk*, of whom 15 per cent are officers, 20 per cent *michmans* (the naval equivalent of *praporshchiks* or warrant officers), and 65 per cent conscript sailors. The ship can accommodate 32 aircraft, either planes or helicopters or a combination of the two, depending upon the nature of the mission in which it is engaged. It usually carries Yak-38 vertical take-off planes and Ka-27 and Ka-25 helicopters. The ship has libraries, a barbershop, a television studio that broadcasts its own programs, a ship's newspaper, *Under the Flag of the Motherland*, its own bakery, and so on. The medical facilities on board include conventional treatments by doctors, dentists, and physiotherapists, and also acupuncture. When Captain Second Rank Ostrovsky was the first deputy, he was the acupuncturist's first patient. He had injured his back and was unable to turn his head. He says that acupuncture sorted him out, although the physiotherapists had been unable to help. The acupuncturist has been successful, apparently, in helping officers to give up smoking, in alleviating asthma, and in offering mild anesthesia or supplementing anesthetic drugs.

As one of the largest ships in the navy, the *Novorossisk* has all seven bay-chays. Life on board ship is maintained by various services and commands. The main services are

A sailor during Navy Day celebrations in Sevastopol. It is believed that in future naval conscripts' uniforms will no longer identify the fleet in which they serve, but here the cap is clearly marked 'Black Sea Fleet.' On his left breast the youth wears the red pin of the Komsomol – the Young Communist League.

OVERLEAF: Navy Day is celebrated all over the Soviet Union, and nowhere with more fervor than in Sevastopol, the home of the Black Sea fleet. Here the commander-in-chief of the fleet, Admiral Khronopolou, takes the salute from a *Slava*-class guided-missile cruiser.

supply and support, chemical and medical. Then there is the financial service, the ship's orchestra, and the *botsman*'s command, which is responsible for the maintenance of the ship and its small boats and rafts. Finally, there is also the control command, which organizes the ship's library, printing shop, postal service, and club. Sailors have two jobs. One is their combat function in one or other of the bay-chays. The other is their role in the ordinary, daily routine of the ship, in one of the services or commands. So, for example, a sailor might be a typist working for the control commander, but also belong to the mine and torpedo bay-chay. The only exceptions to this are sailors working in some supply and support service jobs, which are considered to be both daily routine and combat positions.

Between 150 and 200 men work in each of bay chays one, four, and seven. The smallest combat department is bay-chay one, followed by number three. The largest bay-chay and, it is said, the most respected, is number five, engineering. Sailors working here have to be tough, since despite the cooling systems the temperature in the engine rooms regularly reaches 40°C (104°F). Each bay-chay is divided into *otdeleniyes* (sections, as in the infantry), commands, and groups. In general there are between three and five men in an *otdeleniye*, between five and ten *otdeleniyes* in a command, and four or five commands in a group. When the men line up on deck for parades and inspections they do so in *otdeleniyes*. But in the navy (unlike in the army) *otdeleniyes* are not operational units. When the alarm is given and the sailors go to their positions, they go to 'combat posts,' and at this moment each bay-chay becomes a 'control point,' subordinate to the main ship's control point. Bay-chay six, aviation, occupies a strange position in the ship's organization. On board the ship the pilots of the aircraft are subordinate to the commander of the ship. Once they are in the air, however, they are subject only to the orders of their commanders on land. The commander of bay-chay six supervises the technical maintenance of the aircraft. On long voyages an officer from the KGB will sail with the ship. This sometimes happens on shorter voyages, if it is thought advisable after consultations with the commander of the fleet.

Life on board ship is governed by bells, which must be understood instantly by everyone on board. One bell means that the officer-on-duty is calling his deputy and two rings mean that the officer-on-duty must go to the ship's entrance, because a person or persons unknown are approaching. Three rings mean that the commander of the ship has come aboard, four mean that the commander of the formation has come aboard, and five that it is the commander of the larger formation. Six rings mean that the commander of the fleet has boarded the ship (and five short plus one short ring means that he has left), and seven indicate that Admiral Chernavin (as commander-in-chief of the Soviet Navy) has come aboard. Long constant rings signify a training alarm, pairs of short rings mean 'action stations,' and constant short rings are the urgent alarm signal.

Commanding the *Novorossisk* is, in principle, the job of a captain first rank or a rear admiral, but when we visited the ship the actual rank of the commander was captain second rank. The commander has five deputies: the senior deputy, the second-in-command, who should officially be a captain first rank but was, in practice, a captain third rank, and the deputy captain, who should also be a captain first rank and was

The operating theater on board the *Novorossisk*. The entire personnel of the ship have complete medical checks twice a year, and the sailors often seem to receive better medical treatment at sea than they are used to on land.

OPPOSITE: The *Tallinn*, a large antisubmarine ship (BPK), built in 1969, which sails with a complement of 320 men (including 43 officers).

Captain Second Rank Dmitri Ostrovsky in his cabin on board the *Novorossisk* heavy aircraft carrying cruiser. Captain Ostrovsky has since left the Pacific Fleet to attend the Naval Academy in Leningrad – a sure sign that he is considered to be admiral material. When he was commanding the *Novorossisk* his function salary was 290 rubles a month – and his total, including rank payment and supplements for length of service and Far East bonuses, was between 600 and 700 rubles a month. (When at sea, 20 rubles a month are deducted from an officer's pay for his meals.)

Two conscript sailors in their cabin. The sailors are encouraged to write and perform songs and take part in concerts. Over the head of the boy on the right is his face towel. On the other end of his bunk hangs another towel, marked with the Russian letter 'N,' for legs.

OPPOSITE: Amphibious vehicles coming ashore from a *Ropucha*-class landing ship. These vessels are noted for their powerful anti-aircraft armament.

Sailor in everyday working clothes swabbing the deck. Conscripts who are sent to the navy have to get used to the traditions of life at sea as quickly as possible. For example, the starboard side of the ship is only used by officers, except during maneuvers and emergencies.

actually a captain second rank. The position of the commander's political deputy should be occupied by a captain first rank, but in fact he was also a captain second rank. The deputy for supply and support should officially be a captain third rank but was a lieutenant-captain when we met him. The aviation deputy, in reality a colonel (because he is a pilot, not a sailor, he bears army not navy rank), occupied a colonel's position. His was one of the few cases we encountered in the navy where there really were as many stars on an officer's shoulders as there should have been in theory. The disparity between the proper rank for the job and the actual rank of the incumbent seemed to be greater than in any of the other services. We did not discover why this should be so, beyond the general principle operative throughout the armed forces that the possibility of promotion offers a significant incentive to a relatively young man who has been given an important job. The command of a bay-chay is a captain second rank's position, but of the seven on the *Novorossisk* at the time of my visit, only the engineering commander actually held this rank. The other bay-chays were led by captain-lieutenants or captains third rank, apart from aviation, where the commander was a major.

The system of command on board the ship is, in practice, as follows. The deputy captain, the commander's political deputy, the deputy for supply and support, and the aviation deputy are all subordinate to the senior deputy, but of course they also report directly to the captain. The commander meets his deputies every morning and evening and the deputy captain meets the leaders of the bay-chays daily. The leaders of the bay-chays are subordinate to him, as is the chief *botsman* (a *michman*). The commander's political deputy is responsible for all the educational and welfare work on board and especially for supervising the zampolit in each bay-chay. The aviation deputy is in charge of everything concerning the aircraft on the ship and for liaison between the pilots and the naval officers. Directly subordinate to the senior deputy are the emergency commands responsible for the fabric of the ship during emergencies.

The role of the zampolits in the navy has never been exactly the same as elsewhere in the armed forces. The zampolits in a tank regiment have to be primarily tankmen and in the air force they have to be good pilots, if they are to command any respect. But the political deputies on board a large ship do not pretend to be able to perform all the sailors' and officers' jobs. 'It is possible to learn to drive a tank, but it is not usually possible for a zampolit to learn to navigate a ship,' according to Dmitri Ostrovsky, former commander of the *Novorossisk*. 'It takes years of special training to master this. You have to start out as a deck watch officer and then carry on up the ladder to become a ship's captain. We cannot demand the same level of knowledge from our zampolits. Their task is to acquire experience of life so that they know how to work with the men and help them to overcome their difficulties. Of course, a political deputy who wants to get on properly with the crew will try to understand the rudiments of their jobs. On a smaller ship the commander's zampolit may even keep watch.' When the alarm sounds and everyone takes up his combat position, the zampolit will go wherever the commander thinks he is needed to keep up the spirits of the men. It is his job to understand the strengths and weaknesses of the individual officers and steel their will when necessary. In this way the presence of the zampolits helps to prevent the crew from allowing their morale to slip during moments of crisis.

A sailor on the deck communicating with the bridge.

A *batalyorka* (store-room, equivalent of the army *kaptiurka*) at the marines base near Vladivostok.

On board smaller ships

The fast-attack craft, seen as the heirs of the brave little wooden torpedo boats of World War II, have great snob appeal. Vast ocean-going ships may be miracles of modern engineering, but in these small boats you really experience the tang of the salt air and the rolling waves. It is here, the officers say, that the old romance of naval life is still to be found. And, for all their vulnerability, the little fast-attack craft can destroy huge ships; they know that they are vital to the modern navy. The Sevastopol brigade of fast-attack craft and small missile ships consists of twenty-five ships in three groups of between six and ten. The brigade includes eight supply and support ships. The other craft are of varying sizes. The smallest have crews of eighteen, others have crews of about twenty-four or fifty. There are between three and fifteen officers on these ships. Although many of these ships provide surprisingly comfortable living accommodations, the officers and men do not normally sleep on board when the ship is in port. The sailors who serve on smaller ships live in barracks similar to those in the army.

Some of the ships in the brigade have names, often those of cities or local Komsomols. Others are known simply by numbers, such as *970*, which has forty sailors and five officers. At the time of my visit to this ship the commander was a captain third rank, the official rank for the job. The other four officers were the commanders of the bay-chays (one, two, four, and five), and the commander of bay-chay five was also the senior deputy. This is one of the few ships in the Soviet Navy without a zampolit, as there is simply no room on board the *970* for another officer. The commander of the ship is responsible for political work with the *michmans*; his senior deputy works with the leaders of the *otdeleniyes*, who are usually *starshinas* (the naval equivalent of sergeants); and one of the other officers gives political instruction to the ordinary sailors. But the crew also receives political education with others from the brigade when they are in port. A ship such as this could, in theory, spend up to thirty days at sea without needing to be resupplied, since it is able to purify sea water. But in fact it has never been to sea for more than three days at a stretch and it is unlikely to be called upon to do so, since these ships normally work in coastal waters. But *970* spends a lot of time at sea, by the standards of the Soviet Navy. According to the captain, it puts to sea three or four times a month on average, although it has been known to make six voyages within one month. It may be interesting to note that the *970* spends about half as much time at sea as do most ships of the Royal Navy.

Life here is affected by the youth of the officers. Few officers on these ships are over thirty-five, so the atmosphere on board is one of energy and raw enthusiasm. Living at such close quarters, there is scope for people to get to know each other very well and to make lasting friendships. The opportunities for dissension can also be memorable. Everyone has to muck in together on a ship this size. The 'laundry' is a single washing machine, which lives in the captain's cabin when the ship is in the harbor and is moved to the sailors' washroom when they put to sea.

In theory, all the commanders in the armed forces know their men. But it is much easier to do so if the ship's company consists of thirty or forty people rather than 1,000. The symbolic importance of the captain of the ship is strangely unaffected by the size of the vessel concerned: whether it is the *Tbilisi*, the navy's newest aircraft-carrying cruiser, or the humblest boat, the captain is the commander and is accorded a respect by visitors from other ships or from the naval staff that far exceeds the courtesy that would be paid even to a battalion commander in the infantry. The captain is always called 'Comrade Commander,' and no one else would ever be addressed thus. There is only one commander on a ship.

The antisubmarine ship *Azov* usually works as part of a formation of four or five ships in the Black Sea and occasionally in the Mediterranean or the Atlantic. Three hundred conscript sailors live on board, sleeping between ten and thirty to a compartment. There are fifty *michmans*, four or six to a cabin, and fifty officers. Young officers sometimes sleep four to a cabin, but it is more common for two to share, and of course the senior officers have cabins to themselves. When the ship was built, the main consideration was the efficiency of the machinery and weapons. The space that was left over was allocated for the quarters of the officers and men. Nevertheless, the ship has two saunas, quite apart from the ordinary showers. In accordance with the manual, the sailors here, as on every other ship, must be given a freshwater shower once a week and a saltwater wash as often as they like. They have to take a shower more often if they are working with food or if they have been involved in cleaning heavy machinery.

Naval life

The life of conscripts in the navy is no easier than in the other armed services and in many ways it is harder. For a start, if they are serving on board a ship rather than in a shore establishment, they are called up for three years, instead of the usual two. This applies to about half the sailors. Then there are the physical demands and the dangers of life at sea. But there are compensations – the navy has traditionally enjoyed a high status in Russia. It is noticeable that the navy has not been subjected to anything like as much public criticism as the other armed forces in the past few years. A distinguished Russian intellectual with somewhat hostile feelings toward the military in general nevertheless expressed great disappointment when his son was rejected by one of the Nakhimov naval schools. Strong naval traditions exist within certain families. I met a great many conscript sailors who had asked to serve in the navy because their fathers and grandfathers had done so, and several naval officers whose forefathers had been part of the Imperial Russian Navy. There is more than one senior officer wearing on his jacket burnished copper buttons salvaged from his father's uniform. Although the design is broadly similar, these are clearly different from the modern version, but no one seems to mind. Until a few years ago ordinary sailors used to do the same, but among conscripts the habit seems to have died out now.

The notion of the ship as a single community is fostered by several traditions, such as the ritual of introducing a new sailor to the rest of the personnel during morning parade. On his birthday the sailor's commander will call him out during the morning parade, congratulate him, and commend him for his service achievements. This will be greeted by 'a storm of applause' from his comrades, and then the sailor will be free for the rest of the day and allowed to go into town if the ship is in port. After the minister's decree has been published, the *dembels* on certain ships eat only with a wooden spoon, exactly like those that were in use before the Revolution. Navy Day (the last Sunday in

The maintenance and repair of ships is an endless task, but this sailor does not let it get him down.

A submariner of the Pacific Fleet. According to tradition, on his first voyage every sailor should drink a glass of water taken from deep in the ocean. This is, of course, salty, but it tastes much cleaner than shallow sea water, submariners insist.

July) and the ship's birthday are invariably the excuse for celebrations, whether at sea or not, with sports competitions and concerts, attended where possible by officers' and *michmans'* families.

Because of a lack of exercise facilities on some ships, many officers tend to get fat, and this can lead to difficulties, as they may be unable to reach vital equipment. So the medical officers are expected to check the overall fitness of the officers and men. The *Novorossisk* has a gym, sauna, and swimming pool, but on smaller ships it is very difficult to take any physical exercise, apart from the ordinary exertions of the job. Almost all routine and emergency treatment can be carried out on board ships such as the *Novorossisk*, which has its own operating room. The medical officers are also responsible for catching rats on board ship. This is a serious matter — they eat everything on a ship, even the steel cable, it is said.

The standard of accommodations for sailors and officers on board ship varies greatly, but, strangely enough, the larger ships with excellent facilities are by no means the most comfortable for the crew. For example, among the ships of the Black Sea Fleet, some of the small fast-attack craft seemed to offer greater comfort than larger ships such as the antisubmarine cruiser *Azov*.

Life in the navy has, of course, much in common with life in the other armed services. Basic principles, such as 'be as close to the kitchen and as far away as possible from the bosses,' guide sailors as much as all other conscripts. 'The shortest way is the longest route in order to avoid meeting the executive officer' is another notion that would be familiar to any conscript. But there are certain characteristic features of naval life imposed by its physical restrictions. The most obvious of these is that on board ship people salute by inclining their heads, since there is not enough space for everyone to be flinging their arms about. Sailors do not walk, they run: up and down vertical ladders and along narrow decks — an aspect of life that new conscripts find tiring and difficult. Naval slang (along with that of the air force) is one of the more impenetrable languages spoken in the Soviet Union. To a seaman, even when he is on dry land any floor is always *paluba*, a deck, and anything on which people sit (stools, chairs, benches) will be a *banochka*, in the naval term derived from the English 'bench.' Any wall is a *pereborka*, bulkhead, and, by extension, *perebor*, meaning beyond one's limits (i.e., drunk). They say that you can always tell an old sailor because for the rest of his life, wherever he may be, he will talk as if he were at sea.

Submarines

Since World War II the Soviet Union has invested colossal resources into the development of its submarine fleet. Neither the military cutbacks under Khrushchev nor those that have taken place under Gorbachev have (at the time of writing) interrupted this process. There are currently over 270 submarines in service, nearly half of them nuclear-powered. These include the *Typhoon* class (strategic ballistic missile submarines), the world's largest submarines, 550 feet in length, with a displacement of 26,500 tons (dived). Unlike surface ships, submarines do not have names. They are usually referred to by the name of the commander, although this practice is complicated by the fact that nuclear submarines tend to have two crews and commanders.

The navy is proud of the fact that its officers and sailors eat better than most soldiers. Appendix VIII gives the regulation rations for submariners, which include 250 grams of meat every day.

A senior sailor (*starshi matros*) working at the electrical control post. The figures stencilled over his breast pocket indicate, first, the combat department (bay-chay) to which he belongs, in this case number five (engineering); second, his combat post within that department, and third, the shift to which he belongs – so, this boy belongs to the first shift and his position in that shift is number one. By these numbers, therefore, every sailor on board ship is precisely identified, in terms of his combat function.

Two Victor IIIs icebound in the harbor. These fleet nuclear submarines usually operate at a depth of about 1,300 feet, with a complement of 90 men, all of them engaged in the constant battle against the sea. But submarines say that no sensation in the world can compare with that of standing in the conning tower when the boat is far out at sea. A conscript told me, 'Smoking a cigarette, breathing the cleanest air you have ever known, it is as if you are alone in the world, on a tiny island.'

But somehow everybody seems to know which boat is being discussed. I visited 'Filippov's Boat,' a three-year-old Victor III nuclear submarine belonging to the Northern Fleet and officially known as 685. Each of its crews consists of about twenty officers, thirty *michmans*, and forty men. There are five bay-chays: bay-chay one (10 men), bay-chay three (6), bay-chay four (10), bay-chay five (40), bay-chay seven (10). There is also a chemical service (8), whose job it is to check the condition of the reactor. Those who work in bay-chay five (engineering) describe those who work elsewhere as '*luxe*,' considering that theirs is elegant, white-collared work, compared to the gritty reality of the engine room.

This crew generally spends between three and six months of the year at sea, either training (usually in the Barents Sea) or on routine patrol, when it is expected to detect the location of foreign ships and submarines. The sailors say that life is much easier on patrol. During training voyages there are constant alarms, and they rarely manage to snatch more than a few hours sleep. What is more, every little mistake that they make in their work will be spotted, whereas, on combat duty, the officers may be too busy to notice. The longest voyage that this submarine has ever made was seventy days, but it could in theory spend more time at sea. Submarine voyages of three or even six months are possible, although unusual.

At sea the life of the submarine commander is dominated by communication with the authorities on shore. The commander of a diesel submarine in Vladivostock told me that his schedule for communication is fixed for the whole voyage at the outset and the frequency depends on the task of the submarine. Overall, the boat communicates with its base about once a day, but at certain times it may do so half-hourly. (If necessary, unscheduled contact can of course be made.) The day's routine is planned around the time at which the submarine is to surface and make contact. Despite the extraordinary restrictions of submarine life a normal routine has to be maintained. While they are at sea there is compulsory physical training, and political and naval education for the officers and men. But some things are impossible on boats such as these. For example, no attempt is made to wash the sailors' cotton underwear. They wear a set for one week and then it is thrown away.

The series of tragic Soviet submarine accidents in the last few years has drawn public attention to the dangers that submariners routinely face. Needless to say, this was not something of which the officers serving on board submarines needed to be reminded. The six-month preliminary training that the conscripts undergo and the daily routine on the boats both emphasize this. The training makes the realities of submarine life brutally clear to the sailors. The first man to discover a fire on board a submarine should raise the alarm, and the alert will be relayed to the central command post. From that moment the sailors are forbidden to move from one bay-chay to another. The personnel of the bay-chay concerned will fight the fire. It is up to the commander of the submarine to decide whether to send them help or to seal off the compartment so that, if the men there fail to put out the fire, there will be no risk of it spreading. The same procedure applies on surface ships (and in most other navies, too). But fire is a much greater hazard on a submarine. All the officers and men know that, in an emergency, they or their comrades may be burned to death, but that the safety of the boat will have to take priority over the lives of individuals.

This heavy diving equipment is known to the sailors as 'three bolts' for obvious reasons.

OPPOSITE: Two divers at the Sevastopol Divers' Training School. This center trains up to 500 men at a time and is the main naval diving school, although there is a separate establishment for officers in Leningrad. In general the conscripts here do not dive below 260 feet, although they may be taught to do so later, when they are sent to ships or other detachments. This diving equipment weighs 200 pounds, and enables the men to dive to a depth of 200 feet.

A sailor maneuvers the way through the busy port of Vladivostock.

A marine conscript enjoys a brief rest.

OPPOSITE: A landing operation during company exercises for marines of the Sevastopol brigade (total strength about 2,000 men). Every company practices maneuvers such as this once a month. Seven tanks were involved in this exercise, but the landing ship, the *Ilya Azarov* can carry 20 if necessary. These amphibious tanks – PT-76 – can spend up to ten hours at sea, with a maximum speed of six miles per hour in the water (28 miles on dry land).

The officers at the Vladivostok Submarine Training Center said that, although they had been watching for them, they had not noticed any symptoms of stress in their sailors since the submarine disaster, but they were aware that the boys were taking the safety precautions more seriously. Every year several conscripts arrive at the center who are unable to swim, but there has never been one who had to be rejected because he could not learn. Submariners have to be healthy, and psychologically stable. You can't have anyone who suffers from claustrophobia, or who is going to panic in an emergency, on board a submarine. Those who are color-blind or whose visual-spatial coordination is insufficient for the tasks they will have to perform are regularly sent to other units. For some of the specialized jobs the sailors need other abilities – for example, those who are to work on the sonar identification of ships and other submarines (by the sound of their engines) need an acute musical ear.

Many officers take the opportunity to study for further qualifications while they are free from the distractions of their families. The officers on board a diesel submarine expressed concern that, because they spend so much of their lives at sea, they are out of touch with the interests of each new batch of conscripts that is sent to them. 'We don't know what is going on in the real world,' they say. They consider that somehow they have to make an effort to keep up-to-date with developments in ordinary life, if they are to communicate with the sailors. But some of each group of conscripts will become fascinated by the submarine and will themselves bridge the communications gap.

The marines

The naval infantry (*Morskaya Pekhota*) or marines are part of the navy, theoretically, and yet at the same time they retain a separate identity. Conscripts have naval ranks – *Matros* and *Starshiy Matros* – but officers use army ranks. Much of their training is the same as that of the airborne forces – for example, they are all taught to parachute using the methods and equipment of the airborne forces. But, of course, marines are trained for special functions, such as spearheading amphibious assaults, conducting specialized raids, and defending the coast in critical areas. The naval infantry is not large. Its total strength is only about 17,000, divided between the four fleets. The largest detachment is based at Vladivostok, where some 7,000 marines serve.

Perhaps partly because there are so few of them, the marines do not have, in the Soviet Union, the prestige of the paratroopers. They do not have their own college: their officers are mostly volunteers selected from ordinary military colleges one year before graduation and trained specifically for the naval infantry in their final year. I was even told of sailors and officers who were rejected by the airborne troops, or forced to leave through ill health, who then served with the marines, which would never happen in Great Britain or the United States. In recent years the status of the marines may have been affected by the fact that, unlike the paratroopers, they were not involved in the campaign in Afghanistan. It is quite possible that the gap between the two supposedly élite services will close now that Soviet troops are no longer involved in the war. The marines place great trust in General Skoratov – head of the naval infantry and deputy to Admiral Chernavin. They describe him, enthusiastically, as a 'pure marine,' not a sailor in disguise.

9 THE AIRBORNE FORCES

The airborne forces, the VDV (*Vozdushno-Desantniye Voiska*), are undoubtedly the élite of the Soviet Army. Everyone in the country recognizes their blue berets, and every young man who is not entirely hostile to all things military covets them. The Soviet Union led the world in the development of airborne operations in the 1930s, and, despite a poor record in World War II, maintained this interest (whereas Western armies did not), so that in the 1950s their airborne forces grew to be the world's largest and best-equipped. This took place under the leadership of Army General Margelov, with whose death in the spring of 1990 the paratroopers lost their greatest hero. The airborne forces pride themselves on being able to do anything, and they have been used in a variety of roles over the years. But traditionally it was envisaged that they would operate in conjunction with the infantry, dropping 150–200 miles in advance of the front and holding their position for up to three days until the tanks arrived.

The Soviet Airborne Forces currently consist of six airborne divisions and four independent regiments. The divisions are: Seventh Guards, based at Kaunas; Seventy-seventh Guards, Pskov; Ninety-eighth Guards, Kishenev; 103rd Guards, Vitebsk; 104th Guards, Kirovabad; 106th Guards, Tula. These divisions are all currently at about 70 per cent strength. (Incidentally, since the disruptions on the Soviet-Iranian border, the Vitebsk Division has been operating under the control of the KGB Border Guards.)

The independent regiments include a supply and support unit in Kolomna, which provides all the airborne units with parachute platforms, multiparachute systems, and personal parachutes. The equipment is not manufactured there, but the regiment acts as a storage base and repair center. It is a full-strength regiment, but because of its particular function it has a disproportionate number of engineers and technical specialists. At Klin there is a center for the airborne forces aviation, the little AN-2 (*Anushka*) planes that can carry ten people and are used for parachute training (each division has twelve of these planes), and at Tchakalovskaya there is a signals unit.

The regiment in Fergana is the largest of these independent units and specializes in work in mountainous conditions. This regiment has had an interesting history. Fergana was formerly the home of the 105th Guards Airborne Division, which took part in the assault on Kabul in 1979 but was later disbanded. A training center, mainly for soldiers on their way to Afghanistan, was then established, but this has also been

A simulator gives the soldiers practice in dealing with their parachutes after they have landed. This requires considerable strength.

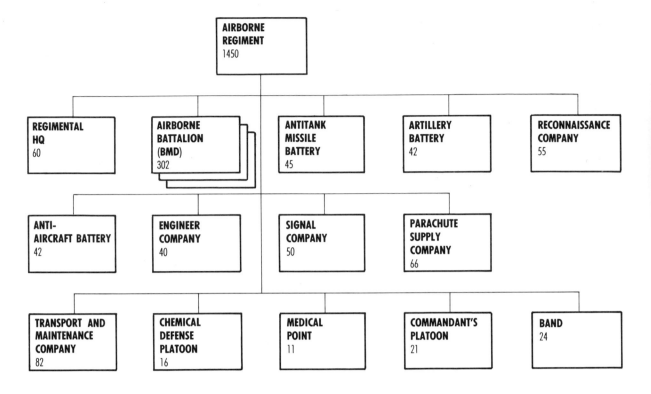

PRINCIPAL EQUIPMENT

STRELA SURFACE-TO-AIR MISSILE 36
ZU-23 23 mm ANTI-AIRCRAFT GUN 6
BRDM AT-3/5 ANTITANK GUIDED MISSILE LAUNCHER 9
RPG 7D ANTITANK GRENADE LAUNCHER 111
2S9 120 mm SELF-PROPELLED ARTILLERY SYSTEM, 'SAO NONA' 6

ARTILLERY CONTROL SHOOTING VEHICLE 'SPEKTR' 1
RPKS-74 5.45 mm LIGHT MACHINE GUN 81
BMD AIRBORNE AMPHIBIOUS INFANTRY VEHICLE 101
BTRD RECONNAISSANCE VEHICLE 44

closed. To the disgust of many of them, the airborne soldiers now based in Fergana are not entitled to wear the coveted Guards badge. Since their regiment is so closely related to the 105th Guards, this seems somewhat unfair, but the excuse is that only a unit that has distinguished itself in battle may be so designated, and that this regiment has no combat record.

There are also sixteen airborne (formerly air assault) brigades. These used to be subordinate to the commanders of the military districts, but in summer 1990 they came under the control of the commander-in-chief of the airborne forces. The number of these brigades is being reduced, as their role is less important under the new defensive doctrine. In addition, there are independent air assault battalions, but it is likely that these will be reorganized in the near future. There are two basic structures for air assault brigades. Some have about 1,800 men in three airborne battalions when at full strength. Others, when at full strength, have 2,000 or 2,600 men in two airborne battalions with BMDs (*Bronevaya Mashina Desantnaya*, airborne combat vehicle) and two light airborne battalions (or one BMD-equipped battalion and three others). The six full-strength brigades are located (at the time of writing) in the groups of forces abroad and in the Far East. Of these, five have four battalions. But all the brigades abroad are being withdrawn. The remaining air assault brigades have, in practice, about 800 men.

Paratrooper training

The paratroopers' training college, the Ryazan Higher Airborne Command School, Named After Lenin's Komsomol, is probably the most prestigious military college in the Soviet Union. Anyone wishing to enter the college should apply in the usual way, through their local voenkomat. But as with every other military college, the voenkomats are only allowed to approve a certain number of applicants. Even so, every year eighteen applicants take the entrance examinations at the college for every one of the 350–400 places available. Thousands more write directly to the college, or to the commander-in-chief of the airborne forces, begging to be considered for a place. It is well known that many unsuccessful applicants camp out in the forests near Ryazan at the start of the academic year, hoping that someone will drop out. The motivation of the would-be *kursants* (officer cadets) is straightforward. If they are to be army officers they want to be among the best, and everyone knows that in the Soviet Army the Blue Berets are the best.

The college tests applicants in mathematics, physics, history (including politics), foreign languages, and physical training. The physical training examiners are particularly interested in the candidates' running speed, endurance, and skill at bar gymnastics. One applicant was able to perform 500 revolutions of the bar and another was capable of 300 bar pull-ups. The college authorities say that they do not try to identify candidates who would be psychologically capable of performing the most demanding operations. They look for absolutely normal, stable people who can be taught to do whatever may be necessary. This is in contrast to the selection procedures of most Western élite forces, which attempt to find men who appear to be temperamentally cut out for the job.

Most of the officers in the airborne forces were trained at the Ryazan college. Only specialists in such fields as communications, artillery engineering, chemical defense and medicine are recruited from other military colleges. Most of the political workers are graduates of the Novosibirsk Higher Military Political Combined-Arms School, Named After the Sixtieth Anniversary of Great October, which has a special airborne department. Anyone joining the airborne forces from a military college other than Ryazan, or from another branch of service, will have to undergo preliminary parachute training. All the airborne officers jump and they must continue to do so if they are to remain in the service. For example, every general must jump at least twice a year, every colonel at least three times, and every lieutenant must make, at the minimum, six jumps if he is to remain qualified.

The college has eleven departments – tactics, firearms and shooting, parachute training, physical training, vehicle maintenance and driving, foreign languages, Marxism-Leninism, mathematics, physics and chemistry, material resistance (the physics of vehicle and equipment dropping), and specializations (which include topography, engineering, NBC-protection, and so on). Of these, tactics, firearms and shooting, and parachute training are considered to be the most important.

When they leave the college and are sent as lieutenants to work in the units, the graduates avoid some of the worst problems faced by other young officers. For a start, they do not have to cope with so many disgruntled, reluctant soldiers. Most of the

183

Young paratroopers fixing their parachutes. The standard D-6 parachute is used for ten years, or for 200 jumps. All Soviet paratroopers fold their own parachutes – a process that takes about one and a half hours by the time each stage has been checked.

Kursants from the Ryazan Airborne College doing their bit.

A senior airborne officer in Tula, wearing his parachute harness, waits to board a plane.

recruits are proud to find themselves in the airborne forces. Moreover, there is less violence among soldiers of different nationalities than in other units, in part because more of the soldiers are Slavs, and in part because in the past, at least, known troublemakers were less likely to be sent to the airborne forces. It is self-evident that boys who are sufficiently spirited to make good paratroopers need to be treated with a firm hand, but this is something that the lieutenants from Ryazan should be able to provide. However, there have been a few reports recently of increased disciplinary problems, as a result of soldiers with a history of drug abuse and heavy drinking being sent to the airborne forces. Nevertheless, the paratroopers' punishing training schedule tends to undermine any delinquent inclinations.

All conscripts are taught to jump in exactly the same way as officer cadets, using a variety of simulators, including the thoroughly unpleasant 300-foot-high parachute tower, which is used to prepare people for the experience of parachuting. Everyone finds leaping from the tower far more unnerving than jumping from a plane, partly because when you leave the plane you know that you are wearing the parachute, but when you jump from the tower the parachute is just lying limply nearby, inspiring no confidence at all. It is also more difficult to jump when you can see the ground so clearly. *Kursants* and conscripts are both supposed to jump at least six times a year, usually from a height of 2,600 feet; the lowest height from which most people routinely jump is 2,000 feet. Some of the instructors can parachute from 4,000 feet and there are officers who have made sports jumps from a height of 650 feet. Jumps are regularly made from 300 feet and there are reports of 250-foot and perhaps even 160-foot sports jumps (onto water). But these are the extraordinary exceptions. The airborne forces are not, in general, obsessed with leaping from absurdly high or lethally low altitudes. 'My job,' says General Lebyed of the 106th Guards Airborne Division, 'is to train my soldiers for any job that they might have to do, and to send them back to their mothers in one piece.' He is contemptuous of the tendency of some airborne officers, in the Soviet Union and abroad, to confuse military skills with those of the circus.

Normally, neither *kursants* nor soldiers jump if the wind speed is more than 20 feet per second for a daytime jump or more than 13 feet per second at night. Jumps are also usually canceled if the temperature falls below −25°C (−13°F). While he is at Ryazan an officer cadet will be expected to jump onto water, at night, and into a restricted space once a year.

Anyone who parachutes is entitled to a small payment. For the first jump the payment is three rubles. From the second to the eleventh jump the fee is two and a half rubles. From the eleventh jump onward the payment goes up to five rubles, and from the fiftieth it is seven and a half rubles. After the hundredth jump the fee is ten rubles each time. If the man parachutes carrying equipment, there is an extra payment of one and a half rubles for each jump. There seems to be a great variation in the number of jumps that are actually made. Most of the *kursants* at Ryazan parachute about six times a year, as the regulations say. We were told that conscripts at the airborne regiment in the same town jump eight or nine times a year, slightly more than the minimum. But the soldiers of the reconnaissance company in Fergana jump almost every two weeks, in other words about 20 times a year.

The worst of the simulators –
from the paratroopers' point of
view – the tower.

Parachute Training

Officer cadets (*kursants*) at the Ryazan Airborne College are trained on simulators. The first one is intended to teach them how to steer themselves in the air, by pulling the straps of the parachute. The second gives them experience of landing heavily, by jumping out of a hangar wearing a harness attached to overhead rails. Here, the training has been made more interesting by adding a smokescreen.

Below   Waiting to make the first jump from an AN-2. Anyone who hesitates will be pushed. This happens very often, it seems.

The reconnaissance company in Fergana demonstrating *rukopashni boi*, which combines elements of judo, wrestling, and jujitsu. It also involves fighting with 'cold weapons.'

OPPOSITE: In the mountains of Uzbekistan paratroopers specially trained to work in mountainous conditions practice evacuating a wounded man.

Because the Fergana regiment specializes in work in mountainous conditions, the *razvedchiks* ('scouts') are trained to a very high level. The regiment's commander, Colonel Solyuyanov, takes a close personal interest in the selection of the men for this company and in their training program. In recognition of their unusually hard schedule, the soldiers in this company do not have to do regimental duty, although they take it in turns to go on duty within the company. They are also treated in a more adult fashion than most soldiers. Unlike the thousands of conscripts all over the country who spend their time laboriously rigging up illicit systems of making tea, these soldiers have been given a kettle.

During the summer they spend six weeks living in the mountains, and they are expected as a matter of course to be able to cover ten miles a day carrying their equipment (weighing an average ninety pounds). On one occasion, the soldiers say, they covered almost forty miles across the mountains in just over eleven hours. Only two soldiers out of thirty-six were unable to complete the march and had to be revived with glucose injections.

These soldiers have an extraordinary obsession with sport and they spend as much time as they possibly can working out in the gymnasium or practicing *rukopashni boi* (a system of close-quarter combat). The men of the local MVD Spetsnaz unit were, it is said, somewhat irritated by the apparent ease with which this company beat them in a local sports competition. Bizarrely though, even these super-fit, expensively trained soldiers are used for nonmilitary jobs, working on local farms and so on. 'If I had more time with my men they would eat the Green Berets (US Special Forces) for breakfast,' one of their officers said, lamenting what he saw as the complete waste of a great deal of their precious training time, especially in the summer and the autumn.

Apart from a few little AN-2s, airborne units do not have their own aircraft. They spend a great deal of time liaising with the air force so that they will be able to have the use of the planes they need for training. Units that are located in fairly isolated parts of the country, far from most air force bases and farther from the center of interference, seem to be able to arrange what they need quite easily by speaking directly to the local air force. But others are not so lucky. Even the 106th Guards, one of the best-known divisions in the country, because it always takes part in the November parade on Red Square and because one of its regiments is based in the famous paratrooper town of Ryazan, is beset by difficulties when attempting to get the planes it needs to train its personnel.

I witnessed an extraordinary scene in Tula, the home town of the division. A big exercise had been planned, principally to give the young officers who had recently joined the division practice in air-dropping vehicles. It had been agreed with the air force that planes would be sent from Krivoi Rog, 1,800 miles away in the Ukraine. The weather forecast was fine, so the day before the exercise was to take place all the personnel went out to the division's airfield at Yefremevo and prepared the vehicles for dropping. They then settled down to what was expected to be a short night's sleep out in the open. At 2:00 A.M. the people in Krivoi Rog said that they would not be able to send the planes.

'The weather is too bad where you are,' they said.

'Rubbish,' said the staff in Tula. 'The weather is perfect where we are.'

Helicopters

During the Byelorussian Military District maneuvers, soldiers of the Thirty-eighth Guards Air Assault Brigade (now Airborne Brigade) load a vehicle onto a Mi-26 transport helicopter. These helicopters carry about 85 soldiers at a speed of around 187 miles per hour and are replacing the earlier Mi-6 model. Upon arrival, the troops will jump out of the helicopter without parachutes, from a height of about ten feet. In the early dawn, Mi-24 helicopters (on the ground) and Mi-8 helicopters (in the air) prepare to take part in maneuvers. These are to be found in all combined arms armies as troop carriers (capacity 13 men), in direct combat, support, and command roles. Designers are currently working to improve the wartime survivability of all these helicopters.

A paratrooper breaks a pile of bricks with his head. He is wearing the 'telniashka,' the blue-and-white striped T-shirt which is now an official part of the paratroopers' uniform. Originally part of the marines' uniform, it was introduced to the airborne troops by their great leader Army General Margelov, who first served with the naval infantry. In 1979 it was made a compulsory part of the uniform and since then has become, in effect, a symbol of the country's elite forces.

But still the air force insisted that weather conditions in Tula prevented them sending the planes. As a result the exercise had to be delayed, for twelve hours, to my knowledge, and possibly longer. 'Where aviation begins, order ends,' as the well-known army proverb has it. The airborne forces say that they are entirely helpless in such situations. The air force is entirely independent of them, and if there were to be any sort of flying incident after they had persuaded the air force people to send planes against their will, all the blame would attach to the paratroopers. The air force, quite naturally, tries to coordinate the requests of the airborne forces with the demands of its own training programs. This was the reason for the decision to send the planes from Krivoi Rog, rather than from one of the many nearer air bases.

The culture of the airborne forces

The world of the paratroopers is based on a pronounced cult of masculinity. Conscripts and officers talk frequently and intensely about the manly virtues that Blue Berets should cultivate. Physically they should be as strong as possible and they should constantly seek to extend their capabilities, it seems. They should conquer fear. They should be self-reliant, but always willing to assist their comrades (without being seen to do so, if possible). They should seek to educate themselves properly in many spheres, without falling into wanton and unproductive speculation. They should protect the weak. They should be self-disciplined in every aspect of their lives. All this is not just talk. The airborne forces are very different from the rest of the army. They gossip less than other soldiers and they display a stoical indifference to the vicissitudes of service and combat. Even the zampolits are strong and silent.

The type of slang used by the conscripts gives some indication of the paratroopers' view of the world. The BMD, a pretty powerful vehicle by most people's standards, becomes a *BMD-eshka*, 'a dear little BMD.' And *rukopashni boi* becomes, in another diminutive, *rukopashka*, a term that suggests a familiarity and mastery to which few soldiers would aspire. Another characteristic of the airborne forces is that their jokes are, to the outsider, staggeringly unfunny. 'A young girl asks her grandmother, "Tell me, Granny, did you have a great love in your life before you married Grandpa?" "Oh, yes." "Who was it?" "The airborne forces!"' At this, strong men collapse laughing on the floor. The problem does not appear to lie in the translation. Ordinary Russians find nothing to laugh at in the story either. The paratroopers have a catch-phrase that is, characteristically, somewhat obscure in origin. The most commonly given explanation is that an Afghan had been taken prisoner and was awaiting interrogation. To while away the time his paratrooper guards taught him an entirely meaningless Russian phrase that, to their delight, he trotted out the next day as he was being questioned as it happened, by Ruslan Aushev. The expression, 'The bamboo is blooming, long live the VDV,' is now used throughout the airborne forces as an expression of pride in the service and perhaps a celebration of paratrooper cussedness.

Officers and soldiers share a great regard for their uniform, especially the blue beret and the blue-and-white striped T-shirt (the *telnyashka*) that characterize their branch of service. 'A paratrooper can lose everything except his blue beret, his *telnyashka*, and his military identification,' as one of the soldiers' sayings goes. The soldiers, and even

A GAZ-66 truck, ready to be air-dropped, is loaded onto a transport plane. This vehicle is to be dropped using the multi-parachute system, rate of descent 16 feet per second. The airborne forces also use a reactive system, whereby a powder explosion softens the landing of the vehicle. With that system the rate of descent would be ten feet per second. It takes about 45 minutes to prepare a vehicle for dropping.

A *kursant* (officer cadet) at Ryazan showing off.

the officers, try to put on clean *telnyashkas* when they jump, and they make a point of shaving carefully. If you are to die in combat (or in practice) you should look your best. Parachuting is always taken seriously, not only because of the attendant danger but also because this is the key activity that separates the paratroopers from everyone else. The precise timing, the concentration, and the discipline that surround parachuting invest every jump with a sense of ritual. This is an activity for adults and the soldiers are well aware that not everyone is capable of making that leap into the unknown.

The paratroopers' blue berets are much sought after in civilian life, partly by young men who want to pretend that they served with the airborne forces, and partly by villains who have discovered that absolutely no one puts up any resistance if they think that their assailants might be airborne-trained. It is said that in the wrong circles people will pay up to 500 rubles for a blue beret. The price reflects the scarcity, as no self-respecting paratrooper would part with his beret, especially to the sort of people who would like to get hold of it. If a conscript loses his beret, he will be charged 10 rubles (about twice the actual cost) for its replacement. This in itself proves how carefully the soldiers look after their berets. In the airborne forces, as elsewhere in the army, soldiers and officers must pay for any piece of equipment that is lost or destroyed through his negligence. But as a deterrent they are not charged the real price, but the price multiplied by a certain factor that reflects the frequency with which the item gets lost and the nuisance of having to replace it. The knives carried by conscripts in case they have to cut their parachute ropes only cost 2.44 rubles each, but since they are much sought after as souvenirs and as useful household knives, the fine for replacement is 48 rubles. The standard D6 parachute, the real cost of which is 597 rubles, will cost anyone who loses it 2,985 rubles (five times the price). The PSN parachute, used by reconnaissance units, costs the army 858 rubles and the careless soldier 4,290 rubles. A two-man inflatable dinghy costs 167 rubles and the five-man version 546 rubles, but if they should be lost or damaged the miscreant will only be fined twice their value. This seems odd, since the dinghies would be useful in a land of wide rivers and might be expected to have a habit of getting mislaid.

Every soldier, after his maiden jump, is presented with his parachute badge in front of the whole company. There is a tradition that after his hundredth jump a paratrooper's comrades will strike him on the back with a folded parachute, and after 300 jumps he will be struck three times. Another epigram, of which the conscripts are particularly fond, tells us that 'A paratrooper's life is as beautiful as an air hostess and as short as her miniskirt.' Living beautifully and dying young are recurrent themes in VDV popular culture, but then, until the withdrawal from Afghanistan in 1989, early death in battle was not so very unlikely an end for a paratrooper. It is very important to the conscripts in the airborne forces that their officers be heroes. Tales of the heroism of the commanders are told in every barracks, and if sometimes it appears that the story is familiar, and that only the name of the hero has been changed, this does not affect the soldiers' sincerity, nor the uplifting effect of the story. Other soldiers need to be able to respect their officers and to see that they do their jobs well. But for the paratroopers it is soldierly credentials that count. To some extent this simply reflects the character of the airborne forces: the majority of their officers served in

The commander of the reconnaissance company in Fergana coordinating exercises in the mountains.

Afghanistan, most others did not.

Wherever the army has been called in to help during the recent civil disturbances in the Soviet Union, the paratroopers have been involved. Nowadays everyone is accustomed to these troubles and when there are reports of new disruptions the soldiers brace themselves to go. But two years ago the situation was very different. When the first serious trouble in Fergana broke out on Sunday 4 June, the Meskhetian Turks, who were being attacked by the local Uzbeks, instinctively sought refuge not with the *militsia* but with the airborne forces. Soldiers of the reconnaissance company were in their barracks, watching television, when suddenly an officer rushed in and yelled, 'Up! Into battle formation!' The men thought he was crazy. 'But we never have exercises on a Sunday,' they kept saying. He had to repeat the order before they realized that this was not an exercise, the emergency was real.

The story goes that, with the Turks cowering in one of his regiment's training grounds, and the Uzbeks still rampaging around the city baying for blood, Colonel Solyuyanov, the commander of the garrison, communicated the facts to Moscow and awaited orders. Hours passed and the situation was becoming more dangerous. It is presumed that the government dithered, hesitant to sanction the use of force against civilians, but uncertain of what else could be done. Solyuyanov did not vacillate. He issued live ammunition to the troops guarding the Turks and made it known that he had told them to shoot to kill if the Uzbeks mounted an attack. His resolution prevented any further violence against the Turks, who were all evacuated soon afterward. It is not clear if this story is true, but its significance is that it is believed. It exemplifies exactly those qualities that the airborne forces associate with their Afghan war veterans. That is to say, Colonel Solyuyanov was not afraid to take an action that might be criticized, nor was he prepared to kowtow to the authorities. A potential bloodbath was averted by the courage and determination of one man.

Although their values are straightforward, the airborne troops are not unsophisticated in their assessment of men's characters. Army General Margelov, their revered former leader, would have been a hard act for any commander-in-chief to follow. The gentle and soft-spoken Dmitri Semyonovich Sukhorukhov, who got the job when Margelov retired, is always described as one of the most cultured people in the army. The contrast in their styles of command was striking. Paratroopers who were used to a full-blooded bawling out when their performance was not up to scratch (which was most of the time, according to Margelov's standards) were suddenly faced with a boss who would just shake his head slowly and say, 'Comrades, I am disappointed.' But although he was so clearly not in the classic, gung-ho paratrooper mold, Sukhorukhov unquestionably commanded the love and respect of the airborne troops and they regretted his departure to the post of head of personnel. He was succeeded by Colonel-General Kalinin. The fourth commander-in-chief, Colonel-General Achalov, has to preside over perhaps the most difficult period in the VDV's history, as the paratroopers are increasingly drawn into controversial peacekeeping roles. But no one doubts his ability; as the youngest colonel-general in the army (at the time of writing) he is clearly a man to watch. During 1990, his personal prestige in the army soared, probably due to his forthright descriptions of the difficulties facing the army and his success in tackling some of them.

195

Waiting to jump during maneuvers. Paratroopers frequently jump with weapons plus full kit weighing about 90 pounds. This includes an NBC protection suit and mask, a raincoat, three days' rations, two hand grenades, an entrenching tool, a spare magazine, a mug for water or soup, a separate aluminum mug and spoon, a sewing kit, a three-color flashlight, a washbag, footcloths, matches, and a first-aid kit that includes a strong needle and syringe with which they can inject a powerful painkiller (morphine based) through their clothes if necessary. Sleeping bags are to be added to the paratroopers' equipment.

10 SPETSNAZ

Western special forces often combine antiterrorist, commando, and reconnaissance roles. In the Soviet Union the only troops who might be able to combine these functions come under the KGB, not the Ministry of Defense. (There are also highly trained special troops under the Ministry of the Interior.) Nevertheless, the Soviet Army's Special Forces are no less famous (in the West, at least) than the American Green Berets or the British SAS.

The very word 'Spetsnaz' is enough to send shivers of excitement down the spines of many Westerners and Soviet citizens alike. Since the early 1980s, when the term was first brought into wide circulation with the publication of the memoirs of the defector who calls himself 'Suvorov,' it has become a vital catalyst for all sorts of conspiracy theorists, cold-warmongers, and thriller writers. Few unexpected or inexplicable events in major Western countries have not been attributed to the stealthy hand of Spetsnaz. No miracle of logistical planning, persuasion, or coercion has been considered to be beyond their ability.

In addition to an obsession with the extraordinary power and influence that Spetsnaz wields unseen, there has been a growing tendency to spot its officers and men all over the place. It has been stated in the Western press, with absolutely no justification, that 'Spetsnaz' has been present at peaceful Moscow demonstrations, while ordinary paratroopers, especially in Afghanistan, went in constant peril of being described as Spetsnaz. There was for some time a widely held piece of folk wisdom that was responsible for some of this confusion – namely, that if ever you spotted a Soviet paratrooper who was not wearing a guards badge, you could be sure that you were looking at a Spetsnaz man. It is true that the main airborne divisions are all guards units, but neither all the airborne brigades nor the independent airborne regiments have this designation.

Part of the reason for the confusion surrounding the term 'Spetsnaz' is that it means very little – *Spetsialnoye Naznacheniye*, 'special purpose' – which could, of course, mean anything. When informed army sources speak about 'Spetsnaz' they are usually referring to the brigades that come under GRU, the Main Intelligence Directorate of the General Staff. These brigades are intended to perform reconnaissance missions deep in enemy territory generally up to a distance of 600 miles.

Spetsnaz training is much more intensive than that of other services. Here, the soldier must throw the knife into the target as he lands, then go on to throw a hand grenade, lay a mine, and shoot at various targets with different types of small arms.

Lieutenant Colonel Sergei Balyenko of the Spetsnaz staff in Moscow is an expert in the survivial skills needed by soldiers who may have to live off the land for weeks or even months.

The organization of reconnaissance

There is, at present, a Spetsnaz brigade in almost every military district, although two or three of the brigades will probably be disbanded between 1991 and 1995. The intention is not to reduce the number of Spetsnaz personnel but to create slightly larger brigades with better training facilities. At present the dislocation of the brigades appears to be as follows: at Chuchkovo, in the Moscow Military District; at Vilyandi in the Baltic Military District; at Lagodekhi (near Tbilisi) in the Transcaucasus Military District and at Perekishchkul in the same military district; at Kirovograd in the Kiev Military District; at Stariy Krim in the Odessa Military District; at Pechory (near Pskov) in the Leningrad Military District; at Kyakhta in the Transbaikal Military District (and/or Allaviyana); at Izyaslav in the Carpathian Military District; at Berdsk (near Novosibirsk) in the Siberian Military District; at Chirchik in the Turkestan Military District; at Ussurisk in the Far Eastern Military District; and at Maryinagorko in the Byelorussian Military District. There are centers for training conscripts at Pskov and Chirchik, where they specialize in intensive training for desert conditions. There are, apparently, no specialized Spetsnaz mountain troops, although some officers and men train for work in mountainous conditions in the Caucasus.

There is currently only one full-strength Spetsnaz naval brigade, at Ocharkov on the Black Sea, although during a war there could be one brigade for each fleet. There are several bases that would accommodate these brigades if necessary. These are located at Severomarsk; Primarsk at Baku; and on Russian Island near Vladivostok where there is currently a reconnaissance point. In war conditions, Naval Spetsnaz 42 Brigade would be situated there.

Spetsnaz brigades consist of between 400 and 1300 men, in two to eight detachments that are usually called *otriads*, not battalions, as they would be elsewhere. Each *otriad* usually consists of three companies and in each company there are usually three 'groups' (*gruppa*). Every group is divided into about three sections (*otdeleniyes*), generally with five men in each. But the organization of the brigades is complicated and may vary according to the mission. Each brigade includes a special signal battalion, but every battalion has its own signal company. There are also the usual supply and support services in every brigade. Most of the brigades are at reduced strength. The brigade at Chuchkovo, for example, is at about 60 per cent strength, with about 700 men. Although the reconnaissance battalions are reduced in size, the supply units are at full strength. Each brigade can call up, within a few days, 50 per cent of its current strength. Slightly more than half of these men will have served with Spetsnaz or the airborne forces. The others will be the best men available locally with experience in any of the armed forces.

In every brigade one battalion is the *upravleniye* or administration *otriad*, which would in wartime train reservists to flesh out the other battalions. Every brigade also includes one or two *otdelni otriads*, which would work in the interests of the army during wartime. These battalions would then be able to field about forty-five groups (around 200 men) capable of performing different missions. They would become, in effect, miniature brigades with their own signals companies. Information gathered by these battalions would go to the intelligence and reconnaissance chief of the army group (front). So, in a brigade that currently has eight *otriads*, in wartime five would probably work with the brigade, one would train reservists (the *upravleniye* battalion), and one or two would go to the army (*otdelnik* battalions). In peacetime the Spetsnaz brigades are subordinate to the commanders of the military districts, but in the event of war the General Staff would decide to whom each brigade should be subordinate, whether to the army or to the front.

GRU (*Glavnoye Razvedyvatelnoye Upravleniye*), the Main Reconnaissance Directorate of the General Staff, deals with army reconnaissance and military intelligence. The Fifth Directorate of GRU is responsible for the Spetsnaz brigades. The chief of this directorate, at the time of writing, was Major General Isaaev. The Fifth Directorate consists of six departments: agents in the west; agents in the south and east; Spetsnaz; army reconnaissance in the west; army reconnaissance in the south and the east; and a scientific department. Between 90 and 100 people work in the Fifth Directorate, of whom about fifteen (mostly with the rank of lieutenant colonel or colonel) work in the Third Department under the Hero of the Soviet Union Major General Vassili Vassilevich Kolesnik.

There are also two directorates that coordinate the work of the first three and the second three departments respectively. At front level the third group of the Second (intelligence) Department of the Staff controls the work of Spetsnaz. The other groups are as follows: first, army reconnaissance; second, agents; fourth, information; fifth, radio-technical reconnaissance; sixth, special signals; and seventh, ciphers. At army level the Second Department of the Staff consists of seven people (or more), one of whom, a lieutenant colonel or a colonel, will be in charge of Spetsnaz.

The backbone of Spetsnaz is the brigades, but there are also other elements in the system. Some armies currently have their own Spetsnaz companies, usually consisting of 111 men and 29 officers and *praporshchiks*, in three reconnaissance platoons and one signals platoon. Although these companies are considered to be Spetsnaz, they would only work 150 to 200 miles behind enemy lines within their own army's operational area. In wartime some armies would have separate Spetsnaz battalions, one company of which would be able to field four groups of about fourteen men and eight groups of eight men. The structure of the rest of the battalion would be more or less the same as that of a divisional reconnaissance battalion.

Every motorized rifle and tank division has its own reconnaissance battalion, although these are not Spetsnaz. These battalions usually consist of about 300 men in three reconnaissance companies and one radio communications company, although in some divisions the battalion is only half this size. The first company is trained for long-range operations (in this case 60 to 100 miles behind enemy lines within the divisional operational area) and is equipped with about twelve BTR-70 or BTR-80 armored personnel carriers. The second company usually has thirteen tanks or BTR-70s. The third, airborne, company consists of troops who have been trained in more or less the same way as real Spetsnaz soldiers, to do the same sort of jobs using the same tactics. They will be equipped with twelve vehicles, probably BRDMs (*bronevaya razvedyvatelnaya dozorna mashina*), armored reconnaissance patrol vehicles. The divisional reconnaissance chief, usually a lieutenant colonel, will control the reconnaissance battalion. Officers who have been selected for Spetsnaz and then fail to make the grade once in post are sometimes sent to work in these battalions.

A senior lieutenant, just after parachuting. One year's service in Spetsnaz will count as one-and-a-half-years' service when his pension is calculated. After this lieutenant has served for two years he will be given a bonus of 50 per cent of his monthly salary. After five years he will get a month's full salary bonus. When he has been with Spetsnaz for ten years (uninterrupted) he will receive two months' salary and after 15 years it will be three months'.

Soldiers and their training

Conscripts are picked for Spetsnaz in the usual way by the local voenkomats. There are, apparently, no special selection procedures, although some senior Spetsnaz officers would like to introduce standard tests for potential soldiers. The official minimum height for Spetsnaz soldiers is five feet seven inches, but some who are exceptionally strong are only five feet three inches or five feet four inches. The minimum weight is 130 pounds and the maximum 180 pounds, but this standard, again, is not strictly observed – some conscripts weigh 190 or 200 pounds.

Spetsnaz likes able but uncomplicated boys from the farms or small towns of Russia. In general they should have completed ten years of secondary education, but intellectuals are not welcome. Spetsnaz needs quick learners, healthy and resourceful, who will not ask too many questions or argue with any orders that might be given, no matter how odd they may seem. Virtually all the soldiers have received some sort of DOSAAF training prior to their conscription and most of them have parachuted.

When they report for national service, the soldiers are not usually told that they have been selected for Spetsnaz. The young men I spoke to said that they guessed from the airborne uniforms and the behavior of the people who came to collect them from the recruiting point that they were going to some sort of special unit, but that no one would tell them anything specific until they reached their destination. When they arrived at the brigade, the battalion zampolit addressed them and told them precisely where they were and what sort of work they would be expected to do.

Between 20 and 30 per cent of the soldiers go to one of the two Spetsnaz training centers to be trained as sergeants or in a speciality such as signal communications. The soldiers' first twenty days will be spent on the Course of the Young Soldier, the preliminary training that all conscripts follow. At the end of this period the battalion commanders can reject up to a fifth of the batch. It is vital that all the soldiers are able to make the grade, so the commanders exercise this right, but it would be unusual for them to send away the maximum possible number.

There is a general principle in the army that any soldier should be prepared to take over another's job if one of them is incapacitated, but in practice not many of them would be able to do so. In Spetsnaz, however, each group is trained to carry on operating, no matter what might happen, down to the last man. Sergeants can do the work of junior officers and any conscript can take the place of a sergeant.

The soldiers in the reconnaissance company in Fergana displayed a fascination with the idea they had picked up that in a modern war only one troop-carrying plane in six would survive. The Spetsnaz soldiers are not even interested in such notions. They know that in the event of a war or serious conflict they would probably end up dead. They believe that in such circumstances their mission would not last longer than one week, although they are trained to survive much longer. Like their officers, they do not generally tell people that they belong to Spetsnaz. They say that they are part of the airborne forces and avoid specific discussion of their service with outsiders. The fact that the soldiers are all under the official government Act of Secrecy helps to impress upon them the seriousness of their work and the need for discretion.

Like all the other conscripts in the Soviet Army, the Spetsnaz soldiers are given

Spetsnaz soldiers building a fire on the edge of the forest. They are taught how to make a fire that produces as little smoke as possible but their officers nevertheless usually forbid them this luxury.

A Spetsnaz Exercise

Two companies were involved in this exercise. Each group (about ten men) dropped separately, and then had to make contact with its company commander for further instructions. Each group was then given a route to follow (using a large-scale map and compass) to reach the objective. The groups were sent off in different directions, but they were all meant to end up at the same destination, about three miles from the zone where they landed. Having located a dummy rocket launcher and reported its map coordinates (every Spetsnaz soldier should be able to do this), they were then ordered to head for another site, about two and a half miles away and build shelters for the night. Such a shelter, called a *dnovka* in the soldiers' slang (literally, 'something for one day only') should be built out of branches, twigs, leaves, etc. Three soldiers should be awake all the time, one inside the shelter, and two watching the approach. Each *dnovka* was surrounded with wire, six inches above the ground, that would send off a signal rocket and cause a loud explosion if disturbed. The next morning each company assembled and was given new orders. From this point on, the soldiers operated in companies, rather than in the smaller groups.

Their destination was a demolition site, two to three miles away. Here, each soldier had to carry out a small explosion, and then each group had to blow up a target – either a pipe, a tractor, a radio mast, three empty barrels, or a large sheet of metal. The explosions all had to take place at precisely the same moment – one hell of a fireworks display.

These conscript soldiers parachuted into the forest. Spetsnaz soldiers are often told either to walk in each other's footsteps, so that it will be hard for the enemy to tell how many men have passed by, or to mash up the terrain by making as many footprints as possible, giving the impression that there are far more of them than there really are. One young soldier (who had been in the army for less than six months) found it extremely difficult to disentangle himself and his parachute from the tree. Eventually, after receiving advice from the company commander, the battalion commander, the commander of the brigade, and the representative of the Main Intelligence Directorate in Moscow, the conscript freed himself and managed to rejoin his group.

political lessons (four hours a week), drills, and physical training. The only difference is that in Spetsnaz the standards of physical training are higher, with the greatest emphasis on endurance, so that the soldiers regularly cover distances of twenty to twenty-five miles a day carrying full load. Their physical training includes running, assault courses, throwing axes and spades, and swimming. Between 5 and 7 per cent of conscripts are unable to swim when they reach the brigade, but they all have to learn to swim at least 160 feet carrying equipment that weighs 60 pounds. 'We aim to turn them into minitorpedoes by the end of their training,' an officer told me, with perhaps a hint of exaggeration. The soldiers also have to be able to operate on skis — anything that they can do on their feet they have to be able to do on skis in winter.

All the soldiers learn to fire pistols, machine guns, and submachine guns and to use hand grenades and grenade launchers, but soldiers belonging to reconnaissance units are given more intensive training in this than the signal and supply troops. The weapons they normally use include the standard AKS-74 (rifle); the AKSU-5.45 and PBS automatics; the RPG-7d, RPG-18d or RPG-26 antitank weapons; and the BG-15 40 mm grenade launcher (*Tishina*). One platoon in each brigade is trained to use 'Ptur' antitank guided missiles (nicknamed *fagot*, or 'bassoon'), and will be equipped with four of them.

A Spetsnaz soldier should be able to hit a stationary target at 1,600 feet with a rifle, at up to 130 feet with a submachine gun, and at 80 to 100 feet with a pistol. With a sniper rifle he should be able to pinpoint the chest of a target figure at 1,800 feet, and he should be able to hit a target figure moving at two to ten feet per second at 1,600 feet. He should be able to use an antitank grenade launcher accurately at up to 1,300 feet and an antitank guided missile at 160 to 3,300 feet. Like every other soldier he should be able to throw a hand grenade accurately from 80 to 160 feet when standing still or when running.

During small-arms training the soldiers are also taught to throw knives. Most soldiers learn to throw from a distance of 20 to 26 feet (at this range the knife should revolve 180 degrees). According to the instructors, this is one of the hardest skills to impart. You can teach anyone to shoot, it seems, but effective knife handling is a great deal more complicated. Spetsnaz men usually throw the NRS (special reconnaissance knife) 1, or the NRS 2, which can also fire a bullet and has a maximum effective range of 65 feet (20 meters). This weapon is silent and has no recoil. The most likely use of this weapon would be if the soldiers were approaching a guard who heard them. They would instantly turn the knife around and shoot him.

Everyone, except those in the supply units, is trained in basic communications. The soldiers in signal communications spend about 60 per cent of their time on this subject. The others are only given between four and eight hours' specific instruction in each six-month training period, but they also learn a great deal about communications during their instruction in tactics. Every *razvedchik* (i.e., soldier in the main reconnaissance battalions) can operate a simple radio station, and all their regular training exercises involve this skill. Each conscript usually carries an R255–PP set that picks up the signal emitted by the R354M portable radio (one per group). The signal communications battalions use larger, central apparatus, such as R360, R361, R357, R358, or R148, based on Zil-131 or Ural-375 vehicles.

Training with an antitank guided missile.

The 'path of the *razvedchik*,' a scout's assault course that involves running through smoke, fire, burning napalm, and tear gas, and jumping over obstacles and onto buildings, to the accompaniment of sound effects, gunfire, and shell explosions. But although it looks dramatic it is not as difficult as the assault course pictured on page 196.

Spetsnaz soldiers wearing chemical protection suits. It is clear from the smoke that gases have been used here for training purposes.

All the soldiers are trained in nuclear, biological, and chemical protection. They study the main chemical weapons (including phosgene, sarin, VX) and they are taught to use tear gas as a means of individual protection. *Razvedchiks* spend between six and eight hours in each half-year training period studying the organization and tactics of foreign armies and learning to identify NATO and other foreign weapons, equipment, uniforms, and emblems.

The soldiers spend a further fifty or sixty hours every six months studying foreign languages – English, French, German, Chinese, and so on. Each brigade specializes in three or four languages. There are no special language teachers; the officers instruct the soldiers. However, each brigade has one professional interpreter, a graduate who has specialized in languages, from either Ryazan, the reconnaissance faculty of the Kiev Military College, or the Military Institute of Foreign Languages in Moscow. Interpreters trained by the Institute are much sought after as they speak two languages fluently, instead of one, in the case of officers from Ryazan or Kiev. But the institute only allocates five graduates a year to Spetsnaz. The officers say that the standard of the soldiers' foreign languages is not very high, due to lack of time and because few of them have any natural aptitude for languages. But it seemed to me that the conscripts' command of English was rather good, if limited. In the class I visited the soldiers were learning some straightforward conversation gambits that might, in certain circumstances, prove extremely useful:

'What is your name, rank, and position?'

'Where is your unit located?'

'Are your missiles equipped with conventional or nuclear warheads?'

The soldiers are taught foreign languages in order to be able to interrogate prisoners and to identify personal or staff documents. I asked whether they were taught any means of encouraging foreigners to cooperate with them in this interrogation. 'They should improvise,' I was told. And are they taught to resist interrogation themselves? 'Spetsnaz men are never taken prisoner.' It seems that on occasion they have been supplied with cyanide and, in any case, 'they have bullets.' During the war in Afghanistan it was not uncommon for Spetsnaz soldiers to resort to these measures.

The soldiers in the reconnaissance units study military topography for about twenty-four hours in every training period and they learn a great deal more about the subject in their tactics lessons. This enables them to read a map, plan a route, and locate objectives using a map and compass, the stars, and local landmarks. The *razvedchiks* also study the demolition of wooden, brick, steel, and concrete construction. By the end of their military service they are given diplomas enabling them to work as demolition experts in civilian life – on the basis of this qualification several former Spetsnaz soldiers have ended up working for film studios. They are, apparently, very expert in this field. 'Our soldiers can move absolutely anything from one place to another,' the officers say.

The men are skilled in the use of trinitrotoluene and plastic explosives. The first comes in 7-ounce bars, looking like orange soap. Along with one double piece (weighing 14 ounces), 123 of these bars are packed into large boxes weighing 55 pounds in all. By detonating the 14-ounce piece, which slots into a special section of the box, the whole thing will go up, if the soldiers want to eliminate a bridge, for example, or an

Every Spetsnaz soldier (and officer) is taught a foreign language, to enable him interrogate prisoners and identify documents. He must also be able to recognize foreign weapons, equipment, and uniforms.

In the army you are always too hot, or freezing cold. You often get wet. You are driven until you think you will drop, but you also spend a lot of your time waiting around for exercises to begin, for transport to arrive, and so on. Most of all, you are always, always hungry.

armored personnel carrier. The Spetsnaz men love plastic explosive because it is so easy to direct the explosion. If you attempt to blow up a pipe with trinitrotoluene you will simply shatter it, but with plastic you can make a precise incision, with the jagged edges bent nicely inward. Plastic can even be melted down and molded into a pyramid shape, which will then adhere to a wall and, when ignited, produce a neat hole. Every soldier knows how to make live charges using detonating cord or the old-fashioned electrical fuse box – basically the World War II method, essentially foolproof and still the best for blowing up objectives some distance away.

By far the most important subject studied by the conscripts is tactics. Everything else they learn is subordinate to this and is studied in connection with it. The soldiers follow different programs according to whether they are *razvedchiks* or in signal communications or supply units. Initially they are trained individually, then in squads, then they are taught to operate as a group. Ninety to a hundred hours are allocated for this subject in each studying period. All Spetsnaz soldiers are taught basic first aid and skills for surviving in the wild under different conditions.

Parachute training is a vital part of Spetsnaz life. Every soldier is jump-trained, using the same methods and the same simulators as those employed by the airborne forces. Most conscripts parachute between eight and ten times a year, including one or two night jumps and once or twice onto water. But some 'sports parachutists' are given far greater opportunities. About a dozen conscripts in the Chuchkovo Brigade, members of the parachute team, have jumped several hundred times, and there is a famous *praporshchik*, by the name of Pokachalov, who has several thousand jumps to his credit. The officers of Spetsnaz are keen to discuss the ways in which their training could be improved. They say that they are anxious to acquire better light diving equipment and to raise the standard of their divers. They express great admiration for Italian combat divers. They also consider that they should be provided with more of the most sophisticated parachute equipment.

Perhaps the most significant difference between Spetsnaz and the rest of the army is the attitude toward conscript soldiers. Elsewhere, the national servicemen are the backbone of the army. The system revolves around the presence of conscripts; organizing their military and political training and ensuring their physical well-being absorbs an overwhelming amount of the officers' time (although this may not be apparent in the barracks). The soldiers are not the focus of attention in Spetsnaz. More attention is paid to the continuous training of officers than in other units and there is much less talk here about 'bringing up' the conscripts. The ratio of officers to soldiers is higher (about 1:12 as opposed to 1:25 in motorized rifle units) and the presumed role of the officers in combat is much greater. Many officers express the opinion that Spetsnaz soldiers should be professional, since it takes longer and costs more to train them than to prepare infantrymen and, under the present system, no sooner are they properly trained than they are demobilized. On the other hand, two-year conscripts performed well in Afghanistan by all accounts, and the officers say that in extreme circumstances they can train conscripts to a useful standard in six weeks. Despite this ambivalence about their role, the caliber of the officers, the high morale in this legendary branch of service, and the quality of their training undoubtedly mean that Spetsnaz soldiers derive more benefit from their national service than most other conscripts.

A Spetsnaz soldier with a grenade launcher and three shells.

Officer training and culture

A great many Spetsnaz officers come from the Airborne College at Ryazan or from the Higher Combined-Arms College Named After M. V. Frunze in Kiev and join one of the brigades after graduation, or after a short period in one of the airborne or air assault units. Other officers join later, usually at a natural turning point in their careers, such as upon graduation from an academy. As with the conscripts, there are no selection tests for officers and no special physical requirements, although good eyesight and a strong heart are necessary. (Spetsnaz uses, in general, the physical training standards of the airborne troops.) Many officers were successful army sportsmen before joining Spetsnaz. Some are selected for Spetsnaz, others apply. But the world of Spetsnaz is very small and almost impossible for outsiders to penetrate.

In many cases service in Spetsnaz runs in families. For example, there are the famous (in Spetsnaz circles) Kharchenko brothers, triplets currently serving in different brigades, one of whom, at the time of writing, is commander of a battalion at Chuchkovo. Only an officer with friends or contacts inside Spetsnaz would know how to apply, and to whom. The procedure (for the information of everybody else) is basically as follows. An officer who wants to join a Spetsnaz brigade should apply to be transferred by asking his current commander to include him in the next 'plan of change.' He should then apply directly to the commander of the Spetsnaz brigade. It is up to the commander to decide whether or not to accept the candidate, although every appointment must be approved by the General Staff. A significant number of officers are former pupils of Suvorov schools, but even for this privileged group, joining Spetsnaz is the pinnacle of achievement. There is an interesting hazard for those wishing to join Spetsnaz – if you are seen to be keen to enter the system, you are likely to be rejected. To maintain its standards, Spetsnaz has to be merciless. All its officers know that at any moment they may be sent back to an ordinary unit if they are not up to scratch. There is, for them, no worse fate.

Those who join the system in mid-career do not appear to be at a disadvantage when it comes to promotion. For example, at the Sixteenth Spetsnaz Brigade at Chuchkovo, the commander, Lieutenant Colonel Alexander Mikhailovich Dementiev, is a former tank man. The chief of the rear services, Lieutenant Colonel Bruknoi, used to work in chemical defense, and the commander's political deputy, Lieutenant Colonel Alexander Fyodorovich Vorontsev, began his career in an artillery unit. We were accompanied during our visit to Chuchkovo by Lieutenant Colonel Sergei Viktorovich Bolyenko, from the Spetsnaz department of the Fifth Directorate of GRU. Bolyenko, a son of a pilot, graduate of the Kiev Suvorov School (in the days when a Suvorov school education really counted for something) and of the Kiev Military College, has served with Spetsnaz all his working life. A seasoned professional, even in the company of Spetsnaz officers Lieutenant Colonel Balyenko always seems to be several steps ahead of everyone else.

Despite the extraordinary prestige of serving with Spetsnaz, its officers are not exempt from the difficulties that dog the rest of the army. Even here there is a shortage of accommodations. In the brigade at Chuchkovo there were about twenty officers and praporshchiks without apartments in the spring of 1990. Nor are Spetsnaz officers

The NRS-2 reconnaissance knife has a two-sided blade and fires a 7.62 mm bullet. The knife weighs 300 grams and can be used at a range of up to 20 metres. In the bottom picture the sheath is used to stabilize the knife when firing.

Spetsnaz soldiers at the entrance to a shelter that took 48 hours to prepare. A group could live in a shelter such as this, carefully constructed and well camouflaged for some days or even weeks.

hugely well paid. The function salary for the commander of a battalion is 200 rubles a month. He will usually be a major with a rank salary of 160 rubles, so with his length of service supplement, he will probably earn just under 400 rubles. A brigade commander will earn 230 rubles for his function and 280 rubles as a lieutenant colonel.

The Spetsnaz officers are a very different breed from other Soviet officers, even from the airborne officers, whom they so closely resemble at first glance. When talking about their work they emphasize that they have to be prepared to work alone and that they can rely on no one but themselves. They have an even more developed and even blacker sense of humor than the rest of the army. They laugh louder than other soldiers and they laugh when they feel like it. Not for them the moment of hesitation until they have ascertained that the commander, the zampolit, or the guest approves the joke.

The airborne forces are tight-lipped. The habit of discretion runs so deep in them that it can be extremely difficult to make them talk at all. The men of Spetsnaz, on the other hand, while obviously conscious of the necessity for secrecy, seem to be more extrovert. This may be because they are unused to contact with outsiders. Paratroopers enjoy fantastic prestige. They can luxuriate in the respect they are accorded by the rest of the army and by civilians. Until recently, however, the very existence of Spetsnaz was shrouded in secrecy. Their missions were carried out in stealth, known only to themselves and never to be discussed with outsiders. Even if some aspects of the bravery shown by a Spetsnaz man became public, the name of his unit and the details of his comrades would never be made known. So the closed world of the brigades developed its own myths, its own jokes, its own self-sustaining reality. Its officers reveal an almost theatrical self-awareness and an easy assumption of their superiority.

Spetsnaz men are well aware of the aura of mysterious glamour that surrounds them and they enjoy it to the full. They know about the Western myths concerning the supermen of Spetsnaz and they are realistic about suppressing the wildest of them. They are also very well aware of their own capabilities and of the mystique of the brigades. They discuss, earnestly and in detail, their own shortcomings and the improvements that they would like to see introduced in their training and equipment. But when Lieutenant Colonel Balyenko, watching soldiers train, mutters, 'Only in Spetsnaz,' smiling contentedly, you realize that despite the ruthless self-criticism, what he calls his 'Spetsnaz patriotism' is pretty unassailable.

When the Spetsnaz men have seen action (and a great many of them found their way to Afghanistan), it has been on the most dangerous missions, often involving hand-to-hand combat. The former commander of the First Battalion at Chuchkovo, Alexander Nikolayevich Slerpov, was twice wounded in Afghanistan and was awarded the Order of the Red Star for a difficult operation carried out in April 1981 in the Farakh province in a mountainous area called Anadarah. The operation involved climbing an almost sheer rock face and eliminating a Dushman (Afghan rebel) camp. But there were more Dushmans than the Spetsnaz team had realized, and one of the Soviet officers had made a crucial mistake in using a submachine gun without a silencer, so rousing the sleeping Afghans. There were very heavy casualties and it was only some time later that the bodies of the victims could be retrieved, by troops from other units. Lieutenant Colonel Balyenko describes the Afghanistan war realistically from the

Spetsnaz point of view: 'It was a perfect *poligon* (training ground), but too many wonderful people did not come back.'

Although they are capable of lying hidden in the undergrowth for hours when called upon to do so without so much as twitching a muscle, in normal conditions Spetsnaz officers roam around more than others. In some army units everyone will sit around a table for hours, happily reminiscing. Not the men of Spetsnaz. They prowl. They remember a job that needs to be done, they go outside for a cigarette, they go off to speak to the cooks or just to see what's going on. This restlessness and the fascination that they display with danger and speed may be explicable in terms of the type of mission that they have carried out. So too may the wistful tones in which some Spetsnaz officers speak, albeit not entirely seriously, of giving up soldiering. Most other officers want to remain in the army for as long as possible. Perhaps the quiet domestic life has a greater attraction for the men of Spetsnaz because they have had more than enough adventure already. But if there is for them a conflict between the alluring prospect of retiring into peace and the intoxicating fascination of service life, then it must be said that, in conversation at least, Spetsnaz wins.

The airborne forces are proud of their unfettered independence and they will behave in any situation with absolute propriety, but exactly as they want. Having understood that, you will find their behavior entirely reasonable and consistent. You know where you are with the paratroopers. You don't know where you are with Spetsnaz, though. Their charm is undeniable. So too is their panache. But what are they up to? One never knows. Take the following case. One evening as black night fell over the Russian countryside, we were all gathered together eating hare that had been trapped by the soldiers and cooked over an open fire. Lieutenant Colonel Dementiev, the commander, was there with his political deputy, his first deputy, the chief of the rear, our urbane escort from Moscow (Lieutenant Colonel Balyenko), one or two other officers, and our team (photographer, interpreter, and me).

'Did you know that our zampolit was in Angola?' asked the first deputy.

'No,' I said.

'I wasn't,' said the political deputy.

'You were,' said the first deputy.

'I said I wasn't,' said the zampolit. And so it went on. Now such a squabble, in the presence of the commander of the unit, an officer from Moscow, and outsiders, would be unthinkable in the airborne forces. Any first deputy who dared, as it seemed, not only to say something that should not be said but then to persist, obdurate in indiscretion, would simply be vaporized by the disapproval surrounding him. But this was Spetsnaz — the best, the cleverest. So what was going on? The whole episode must, one is tempted to think, have been set up in order to impress upon the mind of the foreigner, however unobservant and dim, the fact of Spetsnaz involvement in Angola. Perhaps Spetsnaz is particularly proud of its achievements there. Perhaps it was disinformation. Perhaps it was a labored kindness to give me the satisfaction of thinking that I had uncovered something about which I was not meant to know. There may be another, fiendishly complicated or utterly straightforward, explanation. But Spetsnaz is Spetsnaz and I will never know.

Postscript

At the time of going to press (January 1991), the problems confronting the Soviet Union seem to be getting worse. In many areas of the country, life is almost unimaginably bleak. Russians no longer complain about the shortages: the talk is of hunger. It is clear that Mikhail Gorbachev's government has failed in its most basic responsibility of keeping the population reasonably clothed and fed. Ever greater powers are being awarded to the president, but, since his decrees are regularly ignored, these seem to be pretty well irrelevant. Sober-minded people now speak of imminent chaos and anarchy. It is every republic and every family for itself at a time like this. In the last few months of 1990, it looked as though the government had lost all power. But this did not mean that the governments of the republics had, as a result, become stronger. In many cases, power leaked away from all the authorities and was picked up, if at all, only by independent organizations and unofficial structures, such as the organized crime network.

There is a growing feeling of despair, and, even in supposedly liberal circles, more and more talk of the need for *poryadok* (order). Many of those who, barely a year ago, seemed to attribute so many of the country's problems to the military are now saying that it must help to restore the rule of law in the most troubled regions of the country and to ensure the distribution of basic goods in the big cities. Some liberal intellectuals still believe that preserving the freedoms won during the period of *perestroika* is of paramount importance, and that this should govern all other considerations. But there are fewer and fewer such people. For most of the population it would be worth sacrificing some of these newly found liberties for the old certainty that they would be able to feed their families. This is not my speculation: it is what civilians have been saying to me during the past few weeks.

Needless to say, the difficulties facing the armed forces at present reflect those of the Soviet Union as a whole. Enforcing the draft is now a very serious problem, and the authorities in many areas are becoming ever more insistent that their young men should not serve outside their own republics. Clearly, the Soviet government is not at all keen on this plan, which would, in effect, create a series of local armies. However, armed militias have already been formed in some republics. In Armenia there is said to be a fully equipped army, some 20,000 strong. Not the least of the problems facing the General Staff at the moment is working out how to cope with these realities. The appropriate response differs in every case, since each has its own complexities.

Reports of arms thefts, including helicopters and tanks as well as small arms, continue to appear in the press all the time. With the help of this stolen equipment, a series of tribal conflicts, ancient and modern, is being pursued. Relations between the various Soviet nationalities, and between the republics seem to be deteriorating all the time. It is difficult at present to envisage any formula for the relationship between the authorities of the republics and the Union that could satisfy even a majority of the parties involved. It is the independence movement in the Ukraine that most upsets Russians. The Ukraine is not a colony: it is the ancient heartland of Russia, and if it were to secede, the loss to Russia would be truly irreparable. From the point of view of the armed forces it would complicate matters enormously, since a very large number of officers are Ukrainian. Civil unrest is most violent in the Caucasus at present, with the situation escalating fastest in Georgia. Islamic Central Asia is also increasingly giving cause for concern. The potential conflicts in that area are frightening, and the possibility that some of the neighboring countries might be drawn into these ethnic rivalries extremely alarming. So far there is not very much sign of this, but, given the volatility of that part of the world, it cannot be discounted. Civil disorder in the republics is affecting the military, of course, as it is called upon, ever more often, to restore order. In the past, officers complained vociferously that this was not their job, that if they had wanted to become policemen they would have joined the *militsia*. But the time for such self-indulgent attitudes is over. Most professional soldiers now consider that unless they and the Ministry of the Interior and KGB forces act to control the violence, they will have to cope with much more unpleasant events in future. But officers are highly aware that all such activities are fraught with danger. Either the intervention of the military might further destabilize an already precarious situation, or the army could be accused of seizing power for its own ends.

Stories of impending coups continue to surface every few months, but, although these stories invariably arouse great excitement at home and abroad, I do not believe that the army has any intention of mounting a takeover. To Russian officers the idea of government by the military sounds just as inappropriate as it does to us. From my conversations with senior and influential people in the military, it is clear that a coup is not on the cards. But as the situation in the Soviet Union deteriorates, as shortages of food and other basic commodities worsen, and as violent crime and civil disorder spreads, the imposition of martial law over much greater parts of the country is beginning to look inevitable. This will, however, be upon the order of the government. In the unlikely event of a total collapse of even the semblance of government authority, the military would only want to hold things together for the shortest period necessary for a legitimate civilian administration to be formed. Apart from anything else, nobody in the army would want to accept responsibility for sorting out the chaos in which the country now finds itself.

Civilians often suggest that they would be quite happy to lose some of the Soviet Union's republics, if stability and prosperity could be guaranteed for Russia. Army officers, in my experience, still place much greater emphasis upon the integrity of the Union. This is partly due to simple patriotism, and a feeling of sadness that a sphere of influence which Russia spent 300 years building up should be lost. But it is also due to the particular perspective on the nation's affairs that army life gives them. There are garrisons all over the country, and officers understand, perhaps better than civilians, how unpleasant the reality of the Union's break-up would be. 'The present tribal conflict in the outlying republics is as nothing to what we would see if they were to become independent. In every case there would be violent power struggles and border disputes,' as an officer from the Turkestan Military District explained it. These struggles would inevitably spread to the minorities within the Russian Republic itself. The military, knowing that it will be expected to pick up the pieces, has every reason to be concerned about the collapse of the Soviet Union. As I said before, the stereotyped view of the army as a collection of dinosaur conservatives is not accurate. The concern of the ablest officers during the last few years has been over the manner in which the reforms have been implemented, rather than with their substance. When Major General Lebyed publicly demanded of Alexander Yakovlev at the 28th Party Congress, 'Just what *do* you believe in?' he was not attacking the man's attitudes. He was confronting the humbug, opportunism and woolly thinking that, from the military's point of view, characterises too many prominent politicians and economists. The military is now perhaps becoming more opposed to further change, not because they are satisfied with the way things are, or with the way they were, but because they fear that the country is being torn apart by ill-conceived innovations.

The experience of Afghanistan is becoming ever more important. Those who were there cannot conceal their anger at the political and military mistakes that cost them so dearly. After all, they now have to face, in its most acute form, the desolation that afflicts all honest Soviet people. If they are to believe what they are now being told, then everything that they have lived for and that their friends died for was wasted. But they will not allow their experience to be neglected. These officers are making their voices heard, whatever the cost. The increasing prominence of the Afghan veterans may well lead to much more radical changes than we have seen so far. The most important of these figures was Colonel General Boris Gromov, who was the last Commander of the Soviet Forces in Afghanistan. He restored a sense of dignity and honor to the 40th Army at an impossibly difficult time and then masterminded the withdrawal so that it took place in an efficient and disciplined fashion. As a result of this, the veterans of that war have the greatest respect for him. When his appointment to the post of Deputy Minister of the Interior was announced at the end of 1990, many officers were shocked. It looked as though the military was losing one of its ablest younger men. But, after a few weeks, opinion seemed to shift and to see the move as a reassuring sign that the worth of the army was appreciated. The announcement, a few weeks later, that Colonel General Achalov, formerly the Commander-in-Chief of the Airborne Forces had been appointed Deputy Minister of Defense, pleased the paratroopers and reinforced the impression that the younger men, unafraid of radical action, were gaining greater influence. In the Soviet Armed Forces, as in all others, officers are constantly promoted, or posted to new commands. So many of the people mentioned in this book are now moving on to new positions. Major General Lebyed has been moved from the 106th Guards Airborne Division to Moscow, to be the Deputy Commander-in-Chief of the Airborne Forces, under General Grachev. Colonel Ruslan Aushev, who was a few months ago one of the rising stars of the army, has now, at his own request, moved to a less demanding job, in order to be able to devote enough time to his work as a Peoples' Deputy. And so on.

As the Gulf crisis unfolded during the last few months of 1990, there was grave concern among officers that Soviet forces would be sent to the area. Their gut reaction was clear. To a man, they were determined not to get embroiled, once again, fighting somebody else's war. I have not heard anyone in the military support Saddam's aggression. But there is a general feeling that sorting it out is not worth the life of a single Soviet soldier. There is the added complication that Central Asian youths are, it is said, hailing Saddam as a hero, and volunteering in droves to fight on the side of Iraq. So any decision to commit Soviet troops to the conflict would undoubtedly inflame further the already delicate situation in the Islamic republics.

I have not dealt, in this book, with the lives of those soldiers and officers serving in Eastern Europe. This is because I have not visited any of them, and I have been writing about people I know. But the groups of forces abroad were, in the past, a most important element in the Soviet Army. This was not only for their strategic importance during the Cold War (when, unlike almost all the units at home, they were kept at full strength), but also because of the difference that serving in them could make to an officer's life. Even before the collapse of communism, valuable consumer goods were far more easily available in Eastern Europe than in the Soviet Union, and an officer who spent his salary there wisely could make a great deal of money. But as German reunification exposed the Soviet troops to something approaching Western living standards, the advantages of serving abroad increased rapidly. By the end of 1990, *Stern* magazine calculated that a major or a lieutenant colonel serving in Germany could make as much money in six months, by buying shrewdly and re-selling the goods in the Soviet Union as in the rest of his army career put together. The 360,000 officers and men still stationed in Germany (at the time of writing) are clearly facing unprecedented temptations and stresses. These are compounded by the privations that they will face when they return home. At the moment, many of those being withdrawn end up living in tents. There is now no complacency in the armed forces about the housing shortage, or about the other difficulites in the units. The top brass is very, very aware of the hardships faced by the officers and men.

No one would deny that there is a crisis within the Soviet military. However, organizations go through crises and emerge from them stronger than they were before. With an organization as large as the Soviet Army, that had been so stable for so long, this is especially likely to be the case. There are plenty of precedents in military history of armies renewing themselves after periods of great difficulty. It is worth remembering the parlous state of the United States Army after Vietnam, when it looked as though, as the saying goes, it would be unable to fight its way out of a paper bag. But the American military has, since then, been reinvigorated and has gone from strength to strength. There is little doubt that the Soviet military can do the same, and it seems to me that there are already the first signs of a possible renaissance in the armed forces. Early in 1989, when I began work on this book, the army was still shell-shocked from Afghanistan, and it was having to cope with widespread media criticism. But the officer corps' initial horror at realizing that they are no longer to be lauded as the saviours of socialism has worn off. Press attacks are now accepted as one of the unpleasant aspects of *perestroika*. More importantly, the president is now seen to listen to the military.

Until recently, changes in the armed forces meant cuts, imposed from above and undermining the power of the military. However, by the autumn of 1990 this no longer seemed to be the case. The military was no longer simply waiting for the axe to fall. Army officers had begun to speak positively about reform and reorganization and were keen to discuss the detailed changes that had been implemented and those that they felt should be introduced. Nevertheless, problems remain, and thousands of clever officers whom the army can ill afford to lose are asking for permission to be retired early. But at the same time there is a vigorous debate, at every level, about how the armed forces should be reshaped to make them as effective as possible, taking account of the shifting international situation. The military seems to be taking control of its affairs, planning to streamline its capabilities and put its house in order.

Moscow
January 1991

218 Uniforms

Soviet officers have four main types of uniform: parade; parade-restday; everyday; field.

Officers wear parade uniform (in formation) during parades; when units or ships are presented with orders or banners; when the oath is taken; when on guard of honor, and when a unit or ship celebrates its anniversary.

Parade (out of formation) uniform is worn during parades when the officer is not marching himself or when government awards are presented. When an officer is promoted to a new rank or a new post he should report to his commanding officer wearing this uniform.

Officers' parade-restday uniform is worn on major holidays such as 7 November, 1 May, 23 February (the Day of the Soviet Armed Forces), 9 May (Victory Day), and other holidays; for important meetings, official receptions, and when placing wreaths and flowers on graves or monuments to fallen Soviet soldiers. It is permitted to wear this uniform when off duty.

Officers wear everyday uniform (in formation) during lessons and combat training, and during exercises according to the instructions issued by the commander of the unit, and when on 24-hour duty. Everyday uniform (out of formation) is worn when working in the staff, at divisional level or above, in various departments, and off duty. It is permitted to wear this uniform when working in units, if the work has no connection with formations, in indoor classrooms, laboratories, repair shops, and during service meetings.

Officers wear field uniform during exercises, maneuvers, combat duties, and during lessons and exercises in training centers.

Soviet soldiers and sergeants, officer cadets, and pupils of Suvorov Schools have five main types of uniform: parade; parade-restday; everyday; field; working.

Parade uniform is worn on the same occasions as for officers and when guarding the combat banner of the unit.

Parade-restday uniform is worn as for officers and when soldiers are given permission to leave their unit. It is worn when going on home leave and on other occasions, according to the order of the commander.

Everyday uniform is worn during all lessons and exercises; when not occupied in lessons or exercises (in the unit); on 24-hour duty, and on other occasions, to the order of the commander.

Field uniform is worn during exercises, maneuvers and combat duties, and during lessons and exercises in training centers. Working uniform is worn when working, building, or maintaining armament and equipment.

Naval uniforms are broadly similar to those of the other services.

Officers and soldiers also, of course, wear special types of clothing for different activities – for example Nuclear, Biological, Chemical (NBC) protection suits.

Parade Uniforms

Marshals and generals

1 Summer parade uniform, in formation
2 Summer parade uniform, out of formation
3 Summer parade-restday uniform
4 Winter parade-restday uniform

1   2   3   4

Officers, *praporshchiks*, extended-service men

5 Summer parade uniform, in formation
6 Summer parade uniform, out of formation
7 Winter parade uniform, in formation
8 Summer parade-restday uniform
9 Summer parade-restday uniform

    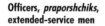

5   6   7   8   9

Sergeants, soldiers, *kursants*

10 Summer parade uniform
11 Summer parade uniform (airborne forces)
12 Winter parade uniform
13 Summer parade-restday uniform

Everyday and Field Uniforms

Marshals and generals

1 Summer everyday uniform, out of formation
2 Summer everyday uniform, in formation
3 Winter everyday uniform, out of formation
4 Winter field uniform

Officers, *praporshchiks*, extended-service men

5 Summer everyday uniform, in formation
6 Summer everyday uniform, out of formation
7 Summer field uniform
8 Winter field uniform
9 Winter field uniform (airborne forces)

Sergeants, soldiers, *kursants*

10 Summer everyday uniform, out of formation
11 Summer everyday uniform, out of formation (airborne forces)
12 Summer field uniform
13 Summer field uniform, full load (front)
14 Summer field uniform, full load (back)

10   11   12   13   14

Branch of service sleeve patches

Motorized rifle   Artillery   Armored   Air force   Airborne

Engineers   Chemical defense   Bands   Signals   Topographical

Motor transport   Railway transport   Medical   Construction   Pipeline

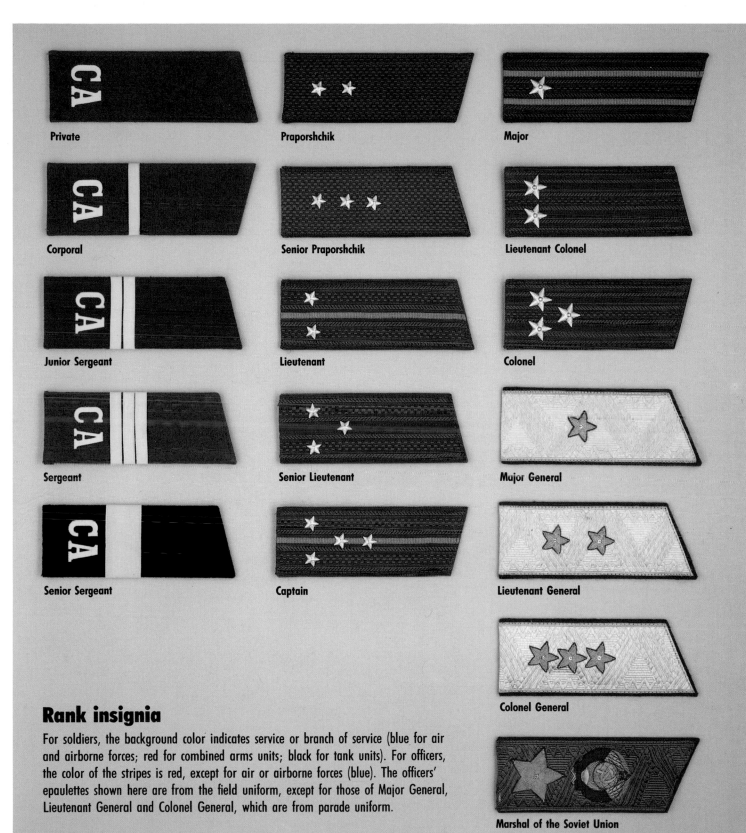

Private

Corporal

Junior Sergeant

Sergeant

Senior Sergeant

Praporshchik

Senior Praporshchik

Lieutenant

Senior Lieutenant

Captain

Major

Lieutenant Colonel

Colonel

Major General

Lieutenant General

Colonel General

Marshal of the Soviet Union

Rank insignia

For soldiers, the background color indicates service or branch of service (blue for air and airborne forces; red for combined arms units; black for tank units). For officers, the color of the stripes is red, except for air or airborne forces (blue). The officers' epaulettes shown here are from the field uniform, except for those of Major General, Lieutenant General and Colonel General, which are from parade uniform.

Badges

Some of the most commonly seen army badges.

Guards regiment

Graduation badge, Suvorov School

Graduation badge, Nakhimov School

Graduation badge, military colleges

Graduation badge, military academies

Graduation badge, General Staff Academy

First Class

Third Class

Classification for officers and *kursants*:

Second Class

Master

Military navigator, First Class

Military navigator, Second Class

Military navigator, Third Class

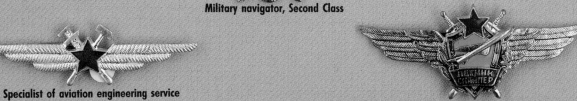

Specialist of aviation engineering service

Master pilot (pilot-sniper)

Long service, navy

Long service, air forces

Long service, ground forces

Badge of honor, air defense forces

Parachutist

Best parachutist
(10 jumps)

Parachute instructor
(over 200 jumps)

Specialist badges for soldiers and sergeants:

Specialist, First Class

Specialist, Second Class

Specialist, Third Class

Master specialist

Military sportsman, First Class

Military sportsman, Second Class

Best of unit, construction

Best of unit, navy

Best of unit, ground forces

Military sports champion

Best of unit, air forces

Selected Who's Who in the Soviet Armed Forces

This is a short and entirely subjective selection and is not intended to be a complete or authoritative guide. It provides examples of the lives and careers of prominent senior officers and of some younger men to watch. The biographies were provided by, or on behalf of, the individuals concerned.

ACHALOV, Colonel General Vladislav Alekseevich Born 13 November 1945, Atamish village, Arski District, Tatar Autonomous Soviet Socialist Republic; Russian; son of Aleksei Afanasievich, peasant collective farmer, and Evdokiya Dmitrievna, housewife. *Education*: ten years of secondary school; Kazan Red Banner Tank Military School named after the Praesidium of the Supreme Soviet of the Tatar Autonomous Soviet Socialist Republic (graduated 1966); Malinovski Armored Troops Academy (graduated 1973); Academy of the General Staff (graduated 1984). *Military career in brief*: leader of tank platoon; commander of tank company; deputy commander of regiment; commander of airborne regiment; commander of airborne division, Commander-in-Chief of the Army; Chief of Staff of the Leningrad Military District; Commander-in-Chief of the Airborne Forces. *Principal awards and medals*: Order for Service to the Homeland in the USSR Armed Forces, Third Class (1975), Second Class (1981), First Class (1990). Six medals. Married, 16 July 1974, Larisa Pavlovna Gudzi; son, Pavel (1975), daughter, Larisa (1982).

ARKHIPOV, Army General Vladimir Mikhailovich Born 1 June 1933, Chelkar Railway Station, Aktiubinsk oblast; Russian; son of Mikhail Vasilievich, locomotive driver, and Valentina Afanasievna, housewife (brought up 7 children). *Education*: secondary school (graduated 1951, after ten years); Tashkent Military Tank College (graduated 1955). Command Faculty of the Armed Troops Academy (graduated 1966, with first-class honors and gold medal); Academy of the General Staff (graduated 1972). *Military career in brief*: leader of platoon; commander of company; deputy commander of battalion; deputy commander of regiment; commander of regiment; deputy commander of division; commander of division (1955–1970). After Academy of the General Staff appointed commander of tank division, then commander of corps, then commander of army. Then Chief of Staff, first deputy to the Commander-in-Chief of the Central Asian Military District (1979).

Commander of Transcaucasian Military District (1983), Commander of the Moscow Military District (1985); Deputy Minister of Defense, Chief of the Support Services of the Soviet Army (1988–). *Principal awards and medals*: Order of the October Revolution (1986); Order of the Red Banner (1969); Order of the Red Star (1981); Order for Service to the Homeland in the USSR Armed Forces, Third Class (1975). Married, 9 February 1958, Nina Troadievna Maksimkina (mathematics teacher, later housewife); sons, Yuri (1958), Major in the Soviet Army; Sergei (Captain in the Soviet Army) *Personal interests*: work and sport.

AUSHEV, Colonel Ruslan Sultanovich Born 29 October 1954, Volodarskoya village, Kazakhstan; son of Sultan Iosinpovich and Tamara Isultanovna. *Education*: Secondary School No. 11, Grozny; Higher Combined Arms College, Vladikavkas (graduated 1975); Frunze Academy (graduated 1985). *Military career in brief*: platoon leader (1 year), company commander (3 years), chief-of-staff of a battalion (1 year), battalion commander (2 years), chief-of-staff of regiment (2 years), regiment commander (2 years), deputy divisional commander. *Principal awards and medals*: Order of Lenin; Gold medal for the Hero of the Soviet Union (1982); Order of the Red Star (1987); 'Star' Order, First Class (Afghanistan 1982); Order of 'Glory' (Afghanistan 1987); Medal for Distinguished Services (First Class). Married, 1983, Aza Bamatiriyevna (housewife); daughter, Leika (1984); son, Ali (1988). *Personal interests*: football, karate, chess, satirical plays, cinema, and modern literature.

BASHKIROV, Colonel Mikhail Mikhailovich Born 1947, Kaliningrad; Russian; son of Mikhail Bashkirov, engineer, and Zoya Vasilievna, mineral-oil engineer. *Education*: Secondary School No. 211, Murmansk (graduated 1966); Flight College (graduated 1971); Gagarin Academy (graduated 1981); Academy of the General Staff (graduated 1989). *Military career in brief*: all posts from commander of aircraft to commander of division; *Principal awards and*

medals: Order of the Red Star. Married, 1969, to Ludmila Vasilievna; son, Dmitri (1970), college student. *Personal interests*: sport (automobiles); member of dog-breeding club.

DEINIKIN, Colonel General Petr Stepanovich Born 14 December 1937, Morotovsk, Rodovski district; Russian; son of Stepan Nikolaievich, pilot (died during World War II), and Zinaida Mikhailovna, teacher, now retired. *Education*: special secondary school, air force school, Balashovsk Military Aviation College (graduated 1957), Gagarin Military Academy (graduated 1969), Voroshilov Military Academy (graduated 1982 with gold medal). *Military career in brief*: commander of a crew (of an aircraft), of an aviation regiment, of a division, of the air force and of long-haul aviation. Now first deputy to the Commander-in-Chief of the Soviet Air Forces. *Principal awards and medals*: Honored military pilot of the USSR (1984) and two Orders for Service to the Homeland in the Air Force (1975 and 1990). Married, 1963, Nina Vasilievna (housewife); daughter, Elena (1964); daughter, Tatyana (1969); son Mikhail (1977). *Personal interests*: hand-to-hand fighting, boxing, unarmed combat, windsurfing, swimming, reading (Jack London, Conan Doyle, Sholokhov, Dumas, Simonov, war memoirs), theater, songs (folk).

GODUNOV, Captain Second Rank Andrei Vladimirovich Born 8 March 1952, Sevastopol; Russian; son of Vladimir Andreevich, naval officer, and Nina Ivanovna. *Education*: Secondary School No. 1, Krasnodar (graduated 1969); military school (graduated 1974); Naval Academy Named After Grechko (graduated 1986). *Military career in brief*: commander of hydroacoustic group (1974–1979); chief of radiotechnical service (1979–1984) senior research worker (1984–1990). *Principal awards and medals*: 2 Jubilee medals, Order for Perfect Service, Third, Second, and First Class. Married, 1976, Irina Vyacheslavna (research worker in biology); daughter, Daria (1976); son Nikita (1986). *Associations*: secretary of the primary (local) Party organization; member of the Comrades' Court of Honor; co-chairman of the Leningrad Communists' Association, 'Democratic Platform in the CPSU;' delegate to the 28th Party Congress. *Personal interests*: tennis. Address: Homeless.

GRACHEV, Major General Pavel Sergeivich Born 1 January 1948, Tula oblast; Russian; son of Sergei Sergeevich and Maria Ivanovna. *Education*: Kosogovsk Secondary School, Tula oblast (ten years); Ryazan Higher Airborne College (graduated 1969); Frunze Military Academy (graduated 1981); Academy of the General Staff (graduated 1990). *Military career in brief*: officer cadet of Airborne College (1965–69); platoon commander (1974–8); academy (1978–81); deputy commander of regiment (1981–2); commander of regiment (1982–3); chief staff of division (1983–5); commander of division (1985–8); Academy of the General Staff (1988–90); first deputy to the commander-in-chief of the airborne forces. *Principal awards and medals*: Badge of Honor (1974); Order of the Red Star (1982); Order of the Red Banner (1983); Order of Lenin (1986). Married, 1969, Liubov Alekseevna (technologist). Sons, Sergei (born 1970) and Valeri (born 1975). *Personal interests*: sport, books, light music, hunting.

GRISHKIN, Lieutenant Colonel Yuri Vladimirovich Born 1954, Vladimir; Russian; son of Vladimir Aleksandrovich, driver, and Maiya Mikhailovna, financial worker. *Education*: secondary school (graduated 1971), college (graduated 1975), Lenin Military Political Academy (graduated 1988). *Military career in brief*: Head of recreation club in the Far East (4 months); officer in political department of a division (1½ years); officer responsible for propaganda in a regiment in the Soviet Armed Forces in Germany; deputy commander of a battalion in the Urals; deputy commander of a motorized rifle regiment, Murmansk. *Principal awards and medals*: for distinguished service. Married, 1977, Yelena Evgenevna, engineer-mechanic; son Maksim (1978), school pupil. *Personal interests*: member of CPSU since 1974, sport, boxing, chess.

GROMOV, Colonel General Boris Vsevolodovich Born 7 November 1943, Saratov; Russian; son of Vsevolod Alekseevich, killed in the Great Patriotic War, and Marina Dmitrievna, employee (died 1964). *Education*: Suvorov schools in Saratov and Kalinin; Leningrad Higher Combined Arms Command College Named After S. M. Kirov (graduated 1965); Military Academy Named After M. V. Frunze (graduated 1972); Academy of the General Staff Named After

K. E. Voroshilov (graduated 1984). *Military career in brief*: all main command positions, from leader of a motorized rifle platoon to Commander-in-Chief of Kiev Military District; now Deputy Minister of the Interior. *Principal awards and medals*: Order for Service to the Homeland in the USSR Armed Forces, Third Class (1978); Order of the Red Star (1980); two Orders of the Red Banner (1982, 1985); Hero of the Soviet Union and Order of Lenin (1985); Married 17 October 1989 to Faina Aleksandrovna (second wife), engineer; sons, Maksim (1973), Andrei (1980); daughters (twins), Valya, Djenya (1985). Personal interests: tennis, acrobatics, gymnastics, football, handball, classical ballet, operetta, painting landscapes.

KHRONOPULO, Admiral Mikhail Nikolaievich Born May 1933, Dvuglinki village, Lukhovitski district of the Moscow oblast; Russian; son of Nikolai Pavlovich, biological researcher, and Varvara Evstafievna Chemyakina (Party and Soviet worker). *Education*, secondary school, Tyumeni (graduated 1951); Pacific Fleet Higher Naval Military College, Vladivostok (graduated 1956); Naval Academy, Leningrad (graduated 1972); higher courses attached to the Academy of the General Staff, Moscow (1984); and the Academy of the General Staff (graduated 1986). *Military career*: naval artilleryman on cruisers in the Pacific Ocean (8 years); senior assistant commander of ship, Pacific Ocean; commander of two ships, Pacific Ocean; chief of staff, then commander of large formation of surface ships, Kamchatka; chief of staff and commander of strategic formation, Indian Ocean; first deputy to the commander of the Red Banner Black Sea Fleet; Commander of the Black Sea Fleet. *Principal awards and medals*: Order of the Red Star (1970); Order for Service to the Homeland, Third Class (1975); Order of the Red Banner (1978), Order of the October Revolution (1985). Married, September 1958, Flora Nikolaevna (English language teacher); son, Sergei (1959) (naval officer). *Personal interests*: When younger, sailing, 1964, member of crew of yacht *Svetlana*; national champion long distance sailing. Now, working day of 12–14 hours. But I find time to read, especially history of the Fleet and of countries I have visited. Once in a blue moon, when I have the time, I play billiards and chess enthusiastically.

KVATOV, Admiral Gennadi Aleksandrovich Born 3 May 1934, Mishkino, Yaroslavskaya oblast; Russian; son of Aleksandr Vasilievich, serviceman killed in Great Patriotic War, and Aleksandra

Petrovna, worker. *Education*: Preparatory Naval Military School (graduated 1952); Higher Naval College (graduated 1956); Naval Academy (graduated 1973); Academy of the General Staff (graduated 1976). *Military career in brief*: all the posts in the chain of command, from commander of the navigation group on board a diesel submarine, up to Commander-in-Chief of the Pacific Fleet. *Principal awards and medals*: Order of the Red Banner, Order for Service to the Homeland in the USSR Armed Forces, Third and Second Classes; 13 medals. Married, January 2 1956, Taisia Ivanovna (textile technologist); son, Valeri, (1957); son, Vadim. *Personal interests*: work, tourism, reading.

KOSTENKO, Lieutenant General Anatoly Ivanovich Born 1940; Russian; *Education*: joined the armed forces in 1959, graduated from Odessa Higher Combined Arms Command College, Frunze Military Academy, Academy of the General Staff. *Military career in brief*: commanded a platoon, company, battalion; was a chief of staff, regiment commander; later occupied higher positions; was the first deputy of the commander of the forces of the Red Banner Byelorussian Military District; now Commander of the Forces of the Red Banner, Byelorussian Military District. *Principal awards and medals*: Order of the Red Star; Order for Service to the Homeland in the USSR Armed Forces, Second and Third Classes. Married with two sons.

LABUTKIN, Captain Oleg Veniaminovich Born 7 July 1962, Leipzig, GDR; Russian; son of Venianim Petrovich, soldier, and Mariya Ivanovna, employee of the state insurance company. *Education*: Kalinin Secondary School, Minsk (graduated after ten years); the Suvorov School, Minsk; the Suvorov School, Ussuriysk (graduated 1979); Higher Combined Arms College Named After Marshal Konev. *Military career in brief*: leader of machine-gun platoon in the Red Banner Far Eastern District; leader of platoon, Sakhalin; leader of a platoon, second motorized rifle company Petropavlovsk-Kamchatka; deputy to the commander of a motorized rifle battalion. *Military awards and medals*: Medal for Combat Merit (1987); Medal for Good Military Service (1989); Medal for the 70th Anniversary of the USSR Armed Forces; Medal for Perfect Service (1990). Married, 1 August 1986, Tatyana Igorevna, construction engineer; sons, Sergei (1987), Aleksandr and Aleksei (twins, 1989). *Personal interests*: shooting, sport, literature, music.

LEBYED, Major General Aleksandr Ivanovich Born 1950, Novocherkassk; Russian; son of Ivan Andreevich, electrician, and Ekaterina Grigorievna, supervisor of telegraph operators. *Education*: Secondary School No. 17, Novocherkassk (graduated 1967); Ryazan Higher Airborne College (graduated 1973); Frunze Military Academy (graduated 1985). *Military career in brief*: commander of platoon, Ryazan Higher Airborne College; commander of company, Ryazan College; battalion commander; commander of regiment (1985–1986); deputy commander of division (1988); commander of division (1988–) *Principal awards and medals*: Order of the Red Star; Order for Service to the Homeland in the USSR Armed Forces, Third and Second Classes; Medal for Heroism under Fire. Married, 1971, Inna Aleksandrovna; son, Aleksandr (1972); daughter Ekaterina (1973); son Ivan (1979). *Personal interests*: literature (classics and 'returned names'); physical training (so as not to get fat).

MAKSIMOV, Army General Yuri Pavlovich Born 1924, Michurinsk, Tambov oblast; Russian; son of Pavel Karpovich, peasant, then worker, and Olga Mikhailovna, housewife. *Education*: secondary school (graduated after ten years); First Moscow Machine-Gun Military School (graduated 1942); Frunze Military Academy (1950); Academy of the General Staff (graduated 1965). *Military career in brief*: leader of machine-gun platoon (1942–45); commander of machine-gun company at the southwest front and at the second, third, and fourth Ukranian fronts; military operations in the Alps; operations officer on the General Staff; battalion commander; chief of staff of division; commander of a motorized division; first deputy-in-chief of army; first deputy commander-in-chief of the Turkestan Military District (1973–84); senior official in the Ministry of Defense of the USSR; Commander-in-Chief of Strategic Rocket Forces; Deputy to the Minister of Defense of the USSR. *Principal awards and medals*: Order of the Red Star; two Orders of the Patriotic War; Order of the Red Banner; Hero of the Soviet Union; two Orders of Lenin; Order of the October Revolution; Order of the Red Banner; Order for Service to the Homeland in the USSR Armed Forces, Third Class. Married, 1950, Liudmila Mikhailovna (teacher); sons, Andrei (1953), Sergei (1955). *Personal interests*: history of the state, world history.

MANILOV, Major General Valeri Leonidovich Born 10 January 1939, Tulchin, Vinnitskaya oblast, Ukraine; Ukrainian; son of Leonid Yakovlich, serviceman, invalid of the Great Patriotic War, and Polina Andreevna, housewife. *Education*: secondary school (graduated 1956 after ten years); Higher Combined Arms Command College (graduated 1962); Military Political Academy (graduated 1976); Academy of the General Staff (1985). *Military career in brief*: leader of platoon; secretary of Komsomol Committee of the regiment; chief of department of military district newspaper; deputy editor, *Red Star* newspaper; deputy chief of the information department of the Ministry of Defense; chief of information department of the Ministry of Defense. *Principal awards and medals*: Order of the Red Star; Order for Service to the Homeland in the USSR Armed Forces, Third Class; 10 medals. Married, 1963, Lidia Aleksandrovna (hydrotechnical engineer); daughter, Elena (1964), lawyer. Associations and clubs: Member of Union of Journalists of the USSR. *Personal interests*: science, culture, vital political problems. *Note*: Candidate for doctor of philosophical sciences.

MIKHAILOV, Army General Vladlen Mikhailovich Born 24 January 1925, Smolensk region; Russian; son of Mikhail Mikhailovich, civil servant, and Olga Ivanovna, medical worker. *Education*: secondary school in Gorky, Frunze Military Academy (graduated 1954), Academy of the General Staff (graduated 1968). *Military career in brief*: commander of a platoon, company, battalion; chief of staff of a regiment; commander of a regiment; commander of a division; chief of staff of army; chief of staff of a military district; works now in General Headquarters of the USSR Armed Forces. *Principal awards and medals*: Orders of Lenin, October Revolution, Red Banner, For Service to the Homeland (all three classes), and some medals. Married, 1949, Ninel Valentinovna, medical worker; two daughters (1950 and 1956), both medical workers; two grandsons and one granddaughter. *Personal interests*: People's Deputy for the USSR, military science.

MOISEEV, Army General Mikhail Alekseeivich Born 22 January 1939, Amurskaya oblast; Russian; son of Aleksei Semyonovich, railway worker, retired, and Maria Yakovlevna, housewife, died 1988. *Education*: Secondary School No. 60, Svobodny (graduated 1957); Far East Tank College (graduated 1962); Frunze Academy (graduated 1972); Academy of the General Staff (graduated 1982). *Military career in brief*: leader of tank platoon; commander of tank company; commander of tank battalion; chief of staff of regiment; commander of regiment; deputy divisional commander; commander of division; deputy commander of army; commander of army; chief of staff of military district; commander-in-chief of military district; chief of the general staff. *Principal awards and medals*: 4 orders, 28 medals. Married, 1962, Galina Iosifovna (teacher); daughter, Viktoria, (1962) bibliographer; son, Vyacheslav (1969) officer. *Personal interests*: books, sport.

NOVIKOV, Lieutenant General Anatoly Ivanovich Born in 1941; Russian; member of the CPSU since 1962; in the armed forces since 1960. *Education*: graduated from the Moscow Higher Arms Command College Named After The Supreme Soviet of the RSFSR, the Lenin Military Political Academy and the Academy of the Social Sciences and the Central Committee of the CPSU. *Military career in brief*: 15 years of Komsomol work; later head of the political section of a tank division; member of the military council; head of the political section of a tank army; appointed first deputy and member of the military council; head of the political directorate of the Red Banner, Zakavkazsky Military District; Head of the Political Directorate of the Red Banner, Byelorussian Military District; delegate to the 27th Congress of the CPSU and 19th All-Union Party Conference; *Principal awards and medals*: Order of the Red Star; Order for Service to the Homeland in the USSR Armed Forces, Third Class. Married with two sons.

NOVOZHILOV, Colonel General Viktor Ivanovich Born 21 September 1939, Kalinin oblast; Russian; son of Ivan Yegorovich, peasant, and Matriona Andreevna, peasant. *Education*: Lukovnikovskaya Secondary School (graduated 1957); Military School (1962); Malinovski Armored Troops Academy (graduated 1973); Academy of the General Staff (graduated 1983). *Military career in brief*: leader of platoon; commander of company; chief of staff of battalion (then Academy); chief of staff of regiment; commander of regiment; chief of staff of division (then General Staff Academy); first deputy to commander-in-chief of army; first deputy to commander-in-chief of military district; commander-in-chief of Far Eastern Military District. *Principal awards and medals*: Order for Service to the Homeland in the USSR Armed Forces, Third Class, Second Class, and First Class; 9 Jubilee medals. Married, 1970, Larisa Nikolaevna (nurse); son, Vladislav (1972). *Personal interests*: sport.

OSTROVOSKY, Captain 2nd Rank Dmitri Dmitrievich Born 1952, Vladimir; Russian; son of Dmitri Fyodorovich, military man, and Taisiya Georgievna, bookkeeper. *Education*: secondary school (graduated 1969); Higher Naval College (graduated 1975); Naval Academy. *Military career in brief*: commander of combat compartment (1975–1978); deputy assistant to the commander of a ship of the third rank (1978–1979); commander of a ship of the third rank (1979–1980); senior assistant to the commander of a ship of the second rank (1980–1982); commander of a ship of the second rank (1982–1985); senior assistant to the commander of the *Novorossisk* (1985–1988); commander of the *Novorossisk* (1988–1990). *Principal awards and medals*: Order for Service to the Homeland in the USSR Armed Forces, Third Class. Married, 1979, Tatiana Vladimirovna (builder); daughters, Anna (1980) and Svetlana (1985). *Personal interests*: cultural interests, sport.

PAVLOV Major General Vitali Egorovich Born October 1944, Bryansk oblast; Russian; son of Egor Zakharovich and Anisya Ivanovna (peasants). *Education*: School for Young Workers, Sizrany; Military College for Pilots (Middle); Higher Military College for Pilots (correspondence course); Gagarin Academy; Academy of the General Staff. *Military career in brief*: senior pilot instructor; commander of *zveno*, deputy commander of *eskadrilya*; commander of *eskadrilya*; deputy commander of regiment; commander of regiment; commander-in-chief of aviation in army; deputy commander-in-chief of aviation of a military district; commander-in-chief of ground forces aviation. *Principal awards and medals*: Hero of the Soviet Union (1983). Married, 1965, Inessa Pavlova (paramedic); daughter, Larisa (1966); son, Aleksandr (1972). *Personal interests*: history, sport, parachuting.

PIMENOV, Colonel Vasili Vasilievich Born March 1954, Vitebsk; Russian. *Education*: secondary school No. 29, Vitebsk (graduated 1971); Ryazan Higher Airborne College (graduated 1987). *Military career in brief*: training platoon leader; commander of company; chief of staff of battalion; commander of battalion (1982–1984); commander of regiment. *Principal awards and medals*: Gold Star of the Hero of the Soviet Union; Order of the Red Star; Jubilee medals. Married, 1976, Antonina Ivanovna (economist); son, Andrei (1978). *Associations*: Chairman of the Officers' meeting, Member of the Party Committee of the Unit. *Personal interests*: sport, historical literature.

PLEKHANOV, Lieutenant General Valentin Filippovich Born 1 May 1933, Zemlyanski District, Voronezh oblast, RSFSR; Russian; son of Filipp Fyodorovich and Maria Sergeevna. *Education*: Secondary School No. 18, Voronezh (graduated 1950); military college (graduated 1953); Faculty of Philosophy, Leningrad State University (graduated 1962); Lenin Military Political Academy (graduated 1971). *Military career in brief*: leader of platoon (1953–1958); Komsomol worker (1958–1963); deputy commander of unit; chief of political department of large unit, large formation (1963–1980); first deputy to the chief of political administration, Odessa Military District (1980–1982); member of the military council and chief of political administration, Odessa Military District (1983–). *Principal awards and medals*: 3 orders, 12 medals. Married, 1957, Valentina Aleksandrovna (economist); daughters, Nadezhda (1957), teacher of mathematics; (1957); Svetlana, teacher of English, son, Aleksandr (1967), officer in the Soviet Army. *Associations*: member of the Central Committee of the Ukrainian Communist Party. *Personal interests*: cultural issues (Honored Culture Worker of the Ukrainian Soviet Socialists Republic).

RUTSKOI, Colonel Aleksandr Vladimirovich Born September 1947, Khmelnitsky; Russian; son of Vladimir Aleksandrovich, Lieutenant Colonel, and Zinaida Iosifovna. *Education*: secondary school (11 years); Barnaul Highest Military Aviation College (graduated 1971); Air Force Academy (graduated 1980); Academy of the General Staff (graduated 1990). *Military career in brief*: pilot; senior pilot; pilot-instructor; commander of *zveno*; commander of *eskadrilya*; chief of staff of air force regiment; commander of air force assault regiment; deputy to the commander of air force army. *Principal awards and medals*: Order of the Red Banner (1986); Order of Lenin (1988); Gold Star Medal of the Hero of the Soviet Union (1988); orders for service in Afghanistan. Married, 1971, Liudmila Aleksandrovna (economist-programmer); sons, Dmitri (1972), *kursant* at Barnaul Highest Military Aviation College; Aleksandr (1975). *Personal interests*: sport, visual arts.

SELIVANOV, Colonel Valery Petrovich Born 1941, Tambov; Russian; son of Pyotr Fedorovich, driver, and Serafina Semyonovna, teacher. *Education*: secondary school No. 1, Tambov (graduated 1958); Tambov Higher School for Pilots (graduated 1963); Gagarin Academy (graduated 1975).

Military career in brief: assistant aircraft commander, aircraft commander, *eskadrilya* commander; deputy commander of regiment; commander of regiment; deputy commander of division; commander of division; senior pilot-inspector of long-distance aviation. *Principal awards*: Order for Service to the Homeland in the USSR Armed Forces, Second and Third Class. Married, 1962, Nina Flavianovna (kindergarten teacher); daughter, Larisa, (1963), philologist; son Ivan (1976). *Personal interests*: physical culture, air clubs.

SHUSTKO, Colonel General Lev Sergeevich Born 1935, Perlovskaya settlement; near Moscow; Russian; son of Sergei Ilyich, peasant. *Education*: secondary school (ten years); Ulyánovsk Tank Military College; Malinovski Armored Troops Academy (graduated with gold medal); Academy of the General Staff. *Military career in brief*: after tank military college served in the Moscow Military District and elsewhere (including abroad). After the Academy of the General Staff occupied positions of commander of division, first deputy to the commander-in-chief of an army, commander-in-chief of an army, first deputy to the commander-in-chief of a military district. Now Commander-in-Chief of the Transcaucasian Military District. *Principal awards and medals*: Order for Service to the Homeland in the USSR Armed Forces, Second and Third Class; Order of the October Revolution, Order of the Red Banner; ten medals. Married; Zhanna Vasilievna; two daughters, Irina and Olga (graduate of medical institute). *Personal interests*: photography, sports.

SLYUSAR, Lieutenant General Albert Evdokimovich Born November 1939, Amurskaya oblast, Ivanovski; Russian; son of Evdokim Gavrilovich and Anastasia Ivanovna (workers). *Education*: ten years at secondary school (graduated 1958); Far East Combined Arms Command College (graduated 1962); Frunze Military Academy (graduated 1972). *Military career in brief*: parachute-landing platoon leader; deputy company commander; commander of parachute-landing company at Frunze ($3\frac{1}{2}$ years); commander of parachute-landing battalion (6 months); commander of parachute-landing regiment ($1\frac{1}{2}$ years); deputy commander of airborne division (3 years); commander of airborne division ($4\frac{1}{2}$ years); chief of Ryazan Higher Airborne College (7 years to date). *Principal awards and medals*: Order of Lenin (1982), Order of Red Star (1965), Order for Service to the Homeland in the USSR Armed Forces (1976 and 1990), 11 medals. Married, 1969, Idea

Nikiforovna (kindergarten teacher); daughters, Marina (1962), Oksana (1969); son, Oleg (1969). *Personal interests*: sport and history.

SOLYUYANOV, Colonel Aleksandr Petrovich Born 1953, Orenburg Oblast; Russian; son of Pyotr Yakovlevich, mechanic, and Raisa Petrovna, controller. *Education*: Kazan Suvorov School (graduated 1971); Ryazan Higher Airborne College (graduated 1976); Frunze Military Academy (graduated 1987). *Military career in brief*: leader of platoon (1975–1977); commander of company (1977–1980); chief of staff of airborne battalion (1980–1981); commander of airborne battalion (1981–1984); two-and-a-half years served in Afghanistan; commander of airborne regiment (1987–) *Principal awards and medals*: Order of Lenin; Order of the Red Banner; Gold Star medal of the Hero of the Soviet Union. Married, 1981, Larisa Vladimirovna; sons, Sergei (1982) and Aleksandr (1987). *Associations*: Hunters' Union. *Personal interests*: books, theater, sport.

STEFANOVSKI, Colonel General Gennadi Aleksandrovich Born 15 March 1936, Monastirishe village, Chernigov district, Primorski Krai; Byelorussian; son of Aleksandr Pavlovich, serviceman and Vera Ivanovna. *Education*: village secondary school (graduated 1954); Moscow Aviation Radio-technical School (1954–57); Lenin Military Political Academy (external student, 1962–65); Academy of the General Staff (1973–75). *Military career in brief*: student platoon leader; secretary of primary Komsomol organization; chief of Komsomol work department of the Moscow Military District; chief of Komsomol work department of the ground forces; chief of political department of large unit; member of military council; chief of political department of military district; deputy chief of the Main Political Directorate; First Deputy Chief of the Main Political Directorate. *Principal awards and medals*: Order of the Red Banner; Order of the Red Banner of Labor; two Orders of the Red Star; Order for Service to the Homeland in the USSR Armed Forces Third Class; 15 Soviet medals, 3 foreign orders, and 7 foreign medals. Married, 21 July 1960, Galina Yakovlevna Poyarkova (engineer in the meat and milk industry); daughter, Oksana (1971). *Personal interests*: skiing, science, history.

STOLYAROV, Colonel Nikolai Sergeevich Born 3 January 1947, Aleksandrovka village, Kalinkovinski district, Gomel oblast; Byelorussian. *Education*:

School for Young Workers No. 2, Rechitsa (graduated 1964); Yeisk Higher Military Aviation College for Pilots (graduated 1969); Gagarin Academy (graduated 1977). *Military career in brief*: combat control officer; chief of operations of division; deputy chief of staff of regiment; teacher and senior instructor, now senior instructor at the Academy. *Principal awards and medals*: 7 Gagarin medals. Married, 1970, Yelena Nikolaevna (engineer-programmer); daughter, Yelena (1970), son Vyacheslav (1973). *Associations*: USSR Philosophical Society; All-Union Knowledge Society. *Personal interests*: Philosophy, history of political thought, literature, poetry. *Note*: nominated for the post of General Secretary of the CPSU at the 28th Party Congress, withdrew and was elected to the Central Committee of the CPSU.

SUKHORUKHOV, Army General Dmitri Semyonovich Born November 1922, Kursk Oblast; Russian; son of Semyon Ivanovich, peasant, and Fedora Yakovlevna, peasant. *Education*: secondary school (graduated 1939); military college; Leningrad Military Engineering College (graduated 1941); Frunze Military Academy (graduated 1958); Academy of the General Staff (1968 and 1980). *Military career in brief*: leader of platoon; combatant in the Great Patriotic War, until wounded, holding the rank of Captain. After the war, commander of regiment, division, commander-in-chief of corps, of army, of central group of forces in Czechoslovakia, of airborne forces. Deputy Minister of Defense for Personnel (1987–1990). *Principal awards and medals*: 7 orders and 9 medals. Order of the Patriotic War presented during the war. Married, 1947, Nadezhda Nikolaevna Andreeva (medical worker, later housewife); son, former soldier, works at the Ministry of Agriculture. *Personal interests*: history, especially military history.

VISOTSKI, Lieutenant General Evgeni Vasilievich Born 4 April 1947, Belev, Tula oblast; Russian; son of Vassili Petrovich, serviceman, and Elena Alekseevna, secretary. *Education*: Secondary School No. 3, named after Karl Marx, in Termez (graduated June 1965), Tashkent Higher Tank Command College (graduated 1970); Frunze Academy (graduated 1978); Academy of the General Staff (graduated 1988). *Military career in brief*: reconnaissance platoon leader (2 years); reconnaissance company commander (1½ years); chief of staff of tank battalion (1½ years); chief of staff of regiment (1 year, 7 months); commander of regiment (2½ years); chief of staff of division (8 months);

commander of division (2 years and 6 months); chief of staff of large formation (8 months); commander-in-chief of corps, Sakhalin. *Principal awards and medals*: Gold Medal 'Hero of the Soviet Union'; Order of Lenin; Order of the Red Banner; Order for Services to the Homeland in the USSR Armed Forces, Third Class; Order for Distinguished Services, First Class; 7 medals. Married, 1 August 1969, Inessa Mikhailovna (medical attendant-obstetrician); son, Aleksander (1971). *Associations*: Chairman of Regional Soviet Deputy. *Personal interests*: culture, sport.

VOSTROTIN, Major General Valeri Aleksandrovich Born 20 November 1952, Kasli, Chelyabinskaya Oblast; Russian; son of Aleksandr Vasilyevich (commander of the Russian army). *Education*: secondary school (graduated after 8 years); Suvorov Military School (graduated 1971); Ryazan Higher Airborne Command College (graduated 1975); Frunze Military Academy (graduated 1985 with a gold medal). *Military career in brief*: commander of a parachute landing platoon (2 years), commander of a parachute landing company (3 years), chief of staff of a battalion (1 year), commander of a parachute landing battalion (1 year), student of the military academy (3 years), commander of a parachute landing regiment (4 years), commander of an airborne division (1 year). *Principal awards and medals*: Order of the Red Banner (1980); Order of the Red Star (1982); Order of the Red Star (1987); Order of Lenin (1988); Gold Star Medal (1988). Married, 1974, Irina Victorovna (kindergarten teacher); daughter, Yolia (1977). *Personal interests*: volley-ball, pistol shooting, chess, and photography.

YAKUNOV, Colonel Viktor Anatolievich Born 6 September 1951, Varnavino, Gorky oblast; Russian; son of Anatoli Pavlovich, agricultural worker, and Nina Vasilievna, agricultural worker. *Education*: special professional secondary school (graduated 1969); Tambov Higher Military Aviation College (graduated 1973); Gagarin Academy (graduated 1984). *Military career in brief*: commander of aircraft, commander of detachment, commander of aviation *escadrilya*, regimental commander, divisional commander (all positions served in the garrisons of Bobruisk, Machulishchi, Baranovichi, and Zebrovka). *Principal awards and medals*: several medals and one order. Married, 1973, Valentina Georgievna (teacher); son, Anatoli (1975); daughter, Elena (1980). *Associations*: People's Deputy. *Personal interests*: chess and historical literature.

YEPISHIN, Major General Sergei Petrovich Born 29 September 1951, Lyubertsi, Moscow oblast; Russian; son of Pyotr Aleksandrovich, motor mechanic, and Tamara Alekseyevna, toolmaker. *Education*: Secondary School No. 37, Litkarino (graduated 1968), Moscow Higher Combined Arms College Named After Supreme Soviet of the RSFSR (graduated 1972), Frunze Military Academy (graduated 1980). *Military career in brief*: platoon commander (2 years), company commander (1 year), chief of staff of battalion (1 year), battalion commander (1 year), chief of staff of a regiment (2 years), regiment commander (2 years), deputy of divisional commander (3 years), division commander (since 1987). *Principal awards and medals*: Order for Service to the Homeland in the USSR Armed Forces, Third Class. Married, 1972, Tatyana Andreyevna (engineer); daughter, Vera (1977). *Personal interests*: music.

ZAKHAROV, Lieutenant General Aleksander Imametdinovich Born 13 April 1938, Kuibishev; Tartar; son of Imametdin Belyalovich, trade union worker, and Polina Ivanovna, economist. *Education*: secondary school (graduated 1955); military school (1958); Lenin Military Political Academy (graduated 1970). *Military career in brief*: missile guidance station specialist; Komsomol worker; chief of political department of brigade; chief of political department of division and of army, including the 40th Army in Afghanistan; chief of political department of Turkestan Military District. *Principal awards and medals*: Order of the Red Banner; Badge of Honor; Order for Service to the Homeland in the USSR Armed Forces, Third and Second Classes; Order for Labor Heroism; Order of the Red Star, Third Class and Second Class, and others. Married February 23 1963, Ernessa Viktorovna (historian); daughter, Irina (1964). *Personal interests*: sport, science.

ZAPOROZHAN, Major Igor Vladimirovich Born 24 November 1959, Altai region; Russian; son of Vladimir Ilych, engineer-geologist and Zinaida Sergeevna, mechanic-geologist. *Education*: Suvorov School, Ussirisk (graduated 1976), the Far Eastern Higher Command College (graduated 1980), Frunze Military Academy (graduated 1990). *Military career in brief*: leader of platoon (1980–1982); deputy commander of airborne assault company; commander of airborne assault company; commander of battalion; academy (1987–1990); commander of a motorized rifle battalion, Murmansk. *Principal awards and medals*. Order of Lenin and Hero of the Soviet Union; Order of the Red Star. Married, 1984, Aleksandra Mikhailovna, typist; son, Dmitri

(1989). *Personal interests*: books, chess, sport.

ZUBKO, Colonel Ivan Vassilievich Born 1 September 1951, Selovichina, Brest Oblast; Byelorussian; son of Vassili Mikhailovich, worker, and Ekaterina Frantsevna, collective farmer. *Education*: Pervomaiskaya School (graduated 1958); Tashkent Higher Combined Arms Command College Named After Lenin (graduated 1972); Frunze Academy (graduated 1980). *Military career in brief*: leader of motorized rifle platoon (Sept–Dec 1972); company commander (Dec 1972–April 1974); chief of staff of motorized rifle battalion (April 1974–April 1975); senior assistant to chief of operational department of division (April 1975–May 1976); commander of motorized rifle battalion (May 1976–August 1977); deputy regimental commander (1980–81); commander of regiment (1981–1984); commander of mountain motorized rifle brigade (1984–1990). *Principal awards and medals*: Order of the Red Banner; Afghan Red Banner Order. 9 medals. Married, 1 April 1973, Larisa Pavlovna (pharmacist); son, Sergei (1974), Suvorov School pupil; daughter Ilona (1982). *Personal interests*: culture and sport. *Associations and clubs*: deputy to the Supreme Soviet of Kirghizia. *Note*: 23 February 1990: Honored Specialist of the Armed Forces of the USSR.

Short Reading List

Donnelly, Christopher, *Red Banner: The Soviet Military System in Peace and War*, Jane's Information Group, Croydon, UK, 1988.
International Institute for Strategic Studies, *The Military Balance*, Brasseys (published annually).
Isby, David, *Weapons and Tactics of the Soviet Army*, Jane's Publishing Company, Croydon, UK, 1988.
Scott, H. F. and W. F., *The Armed Forces of the USSR*, Westview Press, Boulder, Colorado, USA, 1981.
US Department of Defense, *Soviet Military Balance* (published annually).
Williams, Air Commodore E. S., *Soviet Air Power: Prospects for the Future*, Triservice Press, London, 1990.
Zaloga, Steven J., *Inside the Soviet Army*, Osprey Publishing, London, UK.

Periodicals

International Defense Review, Intervia, Geneva.
Jane's Soviet Intelligence Review, Jane's Information Group, Croydon, UK.
Journal of the Royal United Services Institute for Defense Studies, London, UK.

Aviatsiya i Kosmonavtika
Kommunist Vooruzhennykh Sil
Krasnaya Zvezda
Voyenno-Istoricheski Zhurnal

I should also like to recommend highly anything written by Jake Kipp, Steven Dalziel, David Glantz, or Henry Plater-Zyberk.

Table 1 Military ranks of officers of the Armed Forces of the USSR

GENERAL SERVICE	NAVY	AIR FORCE	MEDICAL SERVICE	JURIST SERVICE
JUNIOR OFFICERS				
Junior lieutenant	Junior lieutenant	Junior lieutenant	Junior lieutenant of medical service	Junior lieutenant of jurisdiction
Lieutenant	Lieutenant	Lieutenant	Lieutenant of medical service	Lieutenant of jurisdiction
Senior lieutenant	Senior lieutenant	Senior lieutenant	Senior lieutenant of medical service	Senior lieutenant of jurisdiction
Captain	Lieutenant Captain	Captain	Captain of medical service	Captain of jurisdiction
SENIOR OFFICERS				
Major	Captain 3rd rank	Major	Major of medical service	Major of jurisdiction
Lieutenant Colonel	Captain 2nd rank	Lieutenant Colonel	Lieutenant Colonel of medical service	Lieutenant Colonel of jurisdiction
Colonel	Captain 1st rank	Colonel	Colonel of medical service	Colonel of jurisdiction
HIGHER OFFICERS				
Major General	Rear Admiral	Major General of aviation	Major General of medical service	Major General of jurisdiction
Lieutenant General	Vice Admiral	Lieutenant General of aviation	Lieutenant General of medical service	Lieutenant General of jurisdiction
Colonel General	Admiral	Colonel General of aviation	Colonel General of medical service	Colonel General of jurisdiction
Marshal of artillery, Marshal of engineer troops, Marshal of communications troops; Army General	Admiral of the fleet	Marshal of aviation	—	—
Chief Marshal of artillery	—	Chief Marshal of aviation	—	—
Marshal of the Soviet Union	Admiral of the fleet of the Soviet Union	—	—	—
Generalissimo of the Soviet Union	—	—	—	—

Notes

1 The rank of Colonel General is the highest rank for officers of the chemical, railroad, automobile and highway, military topography services, as well as for officers of the logistics and financial services.
2 Officers of the military veterinary service are given the ranks of the medical service.
3 Aviation engineering personnel with the relevant education are given the military rank. Ship's staff of the interior troops have the same military rank as the ship's staff of the navy.
4 For officers in the reserve, the word 'reserve' is added to the military rank: Captain of the reserve, Lieutenant Captain of the reserve, Captain of medical service of the reserve, etc. For officers in retirement, the word retired is added to the military rank: Retired Major, Retired Captain 3rd rank, Retired Major of medical service, etc.

Table 2 Upper age limits for officers of the Armed Forces of the USSR on active military service, according to the Law of the USSR. 'On General Military Service.'

Junior lieutenants, lieutenants, senior lieutenants, and captains	40 years	Major Generals and Lieutenant Generals	50 years
Majors and Lieutenant Colonels	45 years	Colonel Generals	60 years

All officers who have reached the age limit are transferred to the reserve of the Armed Forces of the USSR. If necessary, some of them can remain on active military service for another five years.

Officers below the age limit can be discharged from active military service on the following grounds: ill-health, certified by the military health commission; reduction of the officer's staff; family circumstances, in the case of women officers; incompetence; acts discrediting the status of a Soviet officer; court conviction for a committed offense.

Table 3 Minimum periods of active military service for officers before promotion to the next rank

		For flying personnel and officers serving on submarines:	
Junior lieutenant	2 years	Junior lieutenant	1 year
Lieutenant	2 years	Lieutenant	2 years
Senior lieutenant	3 years	Senior lieutenant	2 years
Captain	3 years	Captain	3 years
Major	4 years	Major	3 years
Lieutenant Colonel	5 years	Lieutenant Colonel	4 years

For colonels and above there is no minimum period of service for promotion to the next rank.

Appendix II

Round-up list

Before any officer leaves a unit for another posting this list must be signed by each of the people named below. They must all verify that he has no equipment belonging to their department, no outstanding duties, and no debts. Finding all these people is, in itself, a time-consuming task.

1 Commander of the unit
2 Deputy to the commander for political work
3 Deputy to the commander for rear supplies
4 Deputy to the commander for armaments
5 Chief of staff of the unit
6 Chief of the engineering service
7 Chief of the missile and rocket service (RAV)
8 Chief of the chemical service
9 Chief of supplies
10 Chief of the armored vehicles (BTS)
11 Chief of the auto service
12 Chief of food services
13 Chief of fuel services (GSM)
14 Chief of reconnaissance
15 Chief of the financial service
16 Secretary of the Party committee
17 Chief of communications
18 Chief of the secret department
19 Chief of the non-secret file department
20 Library of the unit
21 Library of the officers club
22 Housing department
23 Chief of the club
24 Commander of the sub-unit
25 Senior assistant to the chief of staff for personnel
26 Chief of the apartment maintenance service
27 Rental point

Return to the senior assistant to the chief of staff for personnel.

Appendix III

Memo No. 3

To the conscript called up for active military service included in

Group No _____ ___ for dispatch to the forces

Before presenting yourself at the military commissariat for dispatch to the forces, obtain leave from your place of work and deregister at your place of residence. Party and Komsomol members should have their names removed from Party and Komsomol lists.

Present yourself at the military commissariat for dispatch to the forces in respectable clothes and shoes, appropriate to the time of year, and have with you:

> a set of underwear, a towel, spoon, mug, toiletries, suitcase, or bag to hold your personal effects;
> your internal passport, with a note of deregistration from your place of residence, your conscription-district registration certificate, certificates or attestations of fulfillment of Ready for Labor and Defense norms, sports ratings, specializations attained in DOSAAF training organizations or at establishments of professional technical education;
> drivers should bring their driving license;
> Party/Komsomol members should bring Party/Komsomol card.

Appendix IV

Character reference of conscript

1. General information

Surname, name, patronymic. Date, month, and year of birth. Nationality. Party membership. Education. Specialization. Degree of proficiency in Russian. Family members. Information on relatives (education, function, psychiatric illness, chronic alcoholism). Family relationships.

2. Political maturity, involvement in public life, moral qualities, and military professional specialization

Knowledge and understanding of internal and foreign politics of the CPSU and the Soviet government. Familiarity with the history and sociology of the USSR. Work in the Pioneer and Komsomol organization. Attitude toward fulfilling social duties. Moral qualities, and interests connected with military life. Preferred branch of the forces.

3. Relationship with comrades and behavior within the collective

Authority within the collective (independent, capable of leadership, easily influenced by others, communicative or reserved). Relationship with comrades. Behavior (tact, politeness, slackness, crudeness). Reaction to criticism by comrades and superiors (indifference, aggression, adequate).

4. Individual psychological qualities

Powers of observation, concentration, distraction. Memory. Reflexes, reliability. Purposefulness, decisiveness, and other characteristics associated with strength of will. Self-assurance. Predominant mood. Behavior in complex and conflict situations. Loudness and clarity of speech. Handwriting characteristics. Coordination and dexterity. Resistance to seasickness.

5. Harmful habits and behavioral deviancy

Smoking, use of alcohol (or narcotics). Tendencies towards illegal, antisocial behavior (encounters with the militia, participation in punch-ups) and inclinations. Dishonesty and lying.

6. Conclusions

General character – positive and negative qualities – and personality traits. Dominant abilities and talents, character traits, mood. Social maturity, preparedness for military service.

Director (chief) _____ _____

Military instructor (chief at place of study) _____

Class leader (master, brigadier) _____

_____ th _____ 19 _____ .

Appendix V

Conscript's family details

_____
(surname, name, patronymic)

Born _____ th _____ 19 _____

_____
(indicate place of birth)

Internal passport (birth cert.) series _____

Nationality _____

Resident at _____
(indicate address)

Conscript's parents

a) FATHER _____

_____ 19 _____ year of birth _____

Party membership _____ Nationality _____

Occupation and place of work _____

Income (av. pay, pension) _____ State of health _____

Place of birth _____

Currently resident at _____

b) MOTHER _____

19 _____ year of birth. Maiden name _____ Nationality _____

State of health _____ Party membership _____

Occupation and place of work _____

Income (av. pay, pension) _____

Place of birth _____

Currently resident at _____

c) Other relatives living with the parents

Rel.	Surname, name, and patronymic	Year of birth work place and function	Employment

	Surname, name, and patronymic	Year of birth	Residence and place of work	No. of children in employment

Additional Information

Do any of these relatives or the conscript himself have any criminal record, and for what? Are they members of a religious sect? Do any relatives live abroad? _____

_____

Property status of the conscript's family (indicate domestic economic situation): home, garden allotment, condition of building, domestic animals, main source of family income. Conscript's contribution. Apartment area and furnishings _____

Brief character assessment of the conscript

From domestic details, village soviet and from discussion with the parents

_____

Behavior in public and at home, work attitude, participation in social life and in the Komsomol organization, physical and general development, conscript's talents, illnesses as a child and now (fits, dislocation, trauma, hemorrhage, headaches, sleepwalking, other illnesses)

_____
_____
_____
_____
_____
_____
_____

Information certified _____
(signature of father and mother)

INFORMATION CERTIFIED
House manager (Head of Housing Office) _____

Internal passport officer (secretary) _____

Appendix VI

Timetable of military unit for the summer training period, 1989*

Activity	Start	Stop
Reveille for assistant platoon commanders and company *starshinas*	5:50	—
General reveille	6:00	—
Morning physical exercise	6:10	7:00
Cleaning barracks and surrounding area, making beds and washing	7:00	7:20
Morning check	7:20	7:30
Breakfast	7:30	8:00
Collective listening to latest radio news broadcast	8:00	8:15
Political information or exercise	8:20	8:50
Preparation for lessons	8:50	9:00
Training periods: 1st period	9:00	9:50
2nd period	10:00	10:50
3rd period	11:00	11:50
4th period	12:00	12:50
5th period	13:00	13:50
6th period	14:00	14:50
Lunch	15:00	15:30
Time for conscripts' personal needs	15:30	16:00
Maintenance of weapons and machinery	16:00	17:30
Individual preparation: 1st period	17:30	18:20
2nd period	18:30	19:20
Political-educational work (Monday, Wednesday, Thursday)	19:20	20:00
Group sports (Tuesday, Friday, Saturday)	19:20	20:00
Dinner	20:05	20:25
'Vremya' (Time) news program	20:30	21.00
Time for conscripts' personal needs	21:00	21:30
Evening walk	21:30	21:40
Evening roll call	21:40	21:50
Taps	22:00	—

*NOTE There are small variations in the timings of the day's activities in different units, often due to local conditions. But the routine is always broadly similar.

Appendix VII

Form No. 6   Supply of clothing for conscript soldiers and NCOs in the Soviet Army

Name of item	Quantity	Length of wear	Cost (rubles)
1 Clothing			
Service cap (parade uniform)	1	2 years	4.74
Field service cap (cotton)	1	1 year	1.44
Winter cap with earflaps	1	2 years	7.00
Overcoat	1	2 years	37.80
Work clothes	1 set	1 year	36.80
Parade uniform	1 set	2 years	51.45
Parade jacket	1 set	2 years	44.65
Parade jacket (cotton)	2 sets	1 year	17.25
Rain cape (cotton)	1	6 years	10.00
2 Footwear			
Shoes (parade uniform)	1 pair	2 years	12.00
Boots (imitation leather)	1 pair	8 months	15.20
3 Linen & underwear			
Shirt	2	2 years	6.00
Tie	1	2 years	0.80
Underwear	3 sets	1 year	4.75
T-shirt (cotton)	1	1 year	1.54
Shorts (cotton)	1	1 year	1.36
Towel (cotton)	3	1 year	1.81
Handkerchiefs	3	1 year	0.18
Undercollar	12	1 year	0.09
Footcloths (summer)	3 pairs	1 year	0.79
Socks (cotton)	3 pairs	1 year	0.43
Gloves (parade uniform)	1 set	2 years	1.40
Warm underwear	1 set	1 year	5.70
Footcloths	2 sets	1 year	1.82
Footcloths (flannelette)	1 set	1 year	1.24
Socks	1 set	2 years	2.89
Gloves (winter)	1 set	1 year	1.75
4 Accessories			
Waist belt (leather)	1 set	2 years	1.24
Waist belt (white)	1 set	4 years	0.85
Trouser belt	1 set	2 years	0.23

Standard No. 6   Submarine crew ration for 24 hours (grams per man), according to the resolution of the USSR Council of Ministers No. 301–86, signed 9 April 1982

Rye or wheat bread	300	Noodles	5	Bay leaf	0.2	onion	40
Wheat bread from high-grade flour	400[1]	Butter	60	Ground black pepper	0.5	tomatoes and cucumbers	70
Biscuits	20	Oil	10	Mustard powder	1	Canned food 'green peas'	10
High-grade wheat cereals	20	Milk	200[3]	Vinegar	2	Fresh fruit	80
Rice	30	Sour cream	20	Tomato paste	10	Canned fruit	20
Macaroni	40	Curds	25	Bakers yeast, dry or pressed	1	Canned fruits and berries compote	125
Meat	250	Unskimmed sweetened condensed milk	40	Potatoes and vegetables, total,	780	Fruit and berry juice	100
Poultry	50	Rennet cheese	20	to include:		Tomato juice	50
Liver	50	Eggs	1	potatoes	500[4]	Lemons	15
Liver pâté/canned meat	30[2]	Sugar	80	fresh or pickled		or edible citric acid	1
Smoked sausage/smoked meat	30	Salt	20	cabbage	100	Fruit or berry extracts	5
Fish/filleted fish	100/70	Tea	2	beet	30		
Herring	20	Natural coffee or cocoa powder	5	carrot	40		

Standard No. 6 (at sea)

The additional submarine crew ration for 24 hours when at sea (grams per man)

Mutton	20	Honey	10	Piquant delicatessen sauce	5	
Dried fish	40	Jam	15	Dry wine	50	
Salmon caviar	5	Prunes	25	Chocolate	15	
Dried whole milk	15	Garlic	2			
Dried yogurt	15	Canned vegetables	30			

Notes
1. When at sea, only 300 grams of wheaten bread from high-grade flour.
2. Liver or canned meat is only for crews of nuclear-propelled submarines.
3. Fresh milk only when at sea.
4. When at sea, 400 grams of potatoes.

Source: Chief General Food Supply Department, Ministry of Defense, Colonel-General I. Isayenko

Appendix IX

Soviet airlift capability

Type of aircraft	Troops maximum/normal	Payload (kg) maximum/normal	Range (km) maximum/empty payload
AN-12	96/60	200,000/105,000	1240/3600
AN-22	295/155	60,000	5000/2400
AN-26	44/30	4000/2500	700/2000
IL-14	18/18	3300/1700	1300/2800
IL-76	225/115	40,000	3200/6700
AN-2	10/10	1500/1000	1300/550
AN-8	60/40	8000/5000	3500/1100
Mi-1	2/1	200/180	590/275
Mi-2	6/4	800/700	600/230
Mi-4	12/10	1800/1200	600/270
Mi-6	60/50	1200/800	1200/550
Mi-8	24/16	3000/2000	900/460

Appendix X

Regimental Commander: Personal work plan for September 1989

Work content	1	2	3	4	5	6	7	8	9	10	11	12	13	14	15	16	17	18	19	20	21	22	23	24	25	26	27	28	29	30
I Participation in activities planned by superior commanders																														
II Activities to improve combat readiness																														
1 Plans, specifications, detailed personnel plans	•	•																												
2 Alert																		•	•	•	•	•	•							
3 Classes for operations planning groups																			•											
4 Briefing the officer of the day																							•							
III Political and combat training																														
1 Command training				•	•																									
2 Mobilization training for officers of the regiment																														
3 Parachute jumps from AN-2, AN-12 aircraft	•	•	•	•	•	•	•	•	•	•	•	•	•	•	•	•	•	•	•	•	•	•	•	•	•	•	•	•	•	•
4 Officers' and praporshchiks' conference	•							•							•							•							•	
5 Approval of Regimental HQs' monthly plans																														•
6 Assignment of monthly tasks to units																														•
7 Supervision of and assistance in combat and political training, military discipline, and service standards																														
8 Assessment of combat and political training, socialist competition, military discipline, and service standards																													•	
IV Service activities																														
1 Daily routine, internal and external inspection		•							•							•							•							•
2 Inspection of regimental medical post, analysis of injury and sickness rates							•							•						•								•		
3 Inspection of officers' and praporshchiks' quarters													•											•						
4 Inspection of inside guard duty																•												•		
5 Evening inspection of regiment																														
V Inspection of armaments and equipment																														
1 Inspection of combat and other equipment											•	•	•	•	•															
2 Control of work planning and maintenance days	•							•								•						•							•	
3 Organizing building improvements and construction work											CONTINUOUSLY																			
VI Organization of Party political work																														
1 Political information for officers and units				•															•											
2 Participation in Komsomol and Party Bureau meetings																														
3 Lectures and talks for personnel																														
VII Headquarters' work																														
1 Personal training (preparation)				•	•	•					•	•	•						•	•	•				•	•	•			
2 Counselling servicemen and family members on personal matters										ONCE A WEEK ON FRIDAY, 18:30–19:00																				
3 Analysis of combat training performance, studying guideline documents, issuing orders, signing references and reports, solving personal matters										ONCE A WEEK 16:00–20:00																				
4 Financial inspection of cash and deposit accounts										AS REQUIRED																				
5 Approval of six-monthly plans for deputies, commanding officers of arms and services, and of the weekly plans of unit leaders	•	•						•	•						•	•						•	•						•	•
– Best-kept barracks competition																										•				
– Tidiest assembly area competition																													•	

Note: Colonel Solyuyanov's workload was especially heavy because he was not only the commander of an independent regiment, but also the commander of the Fergana garrison.

Map of the Soviet Union, showing the military districts of the Soviet Armed Forces

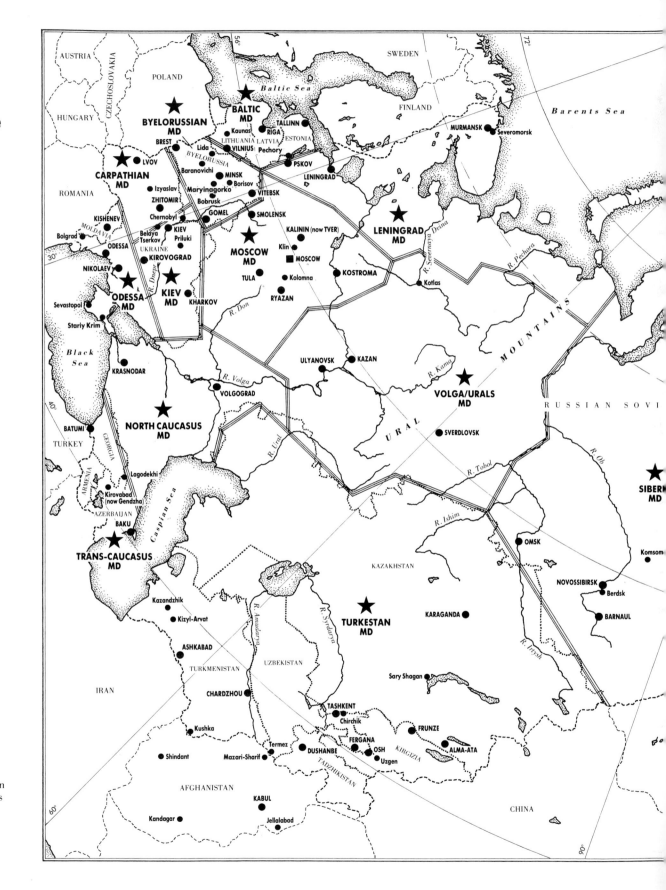

KEY

■ Capital cities

● Principal cities

• Cities/towns

---- Boundary of the Soviet Union

- - - - Boundaries between neighbouring states

.... Boundaries of Soviet Republics

══════ Boundaries of Military Districts

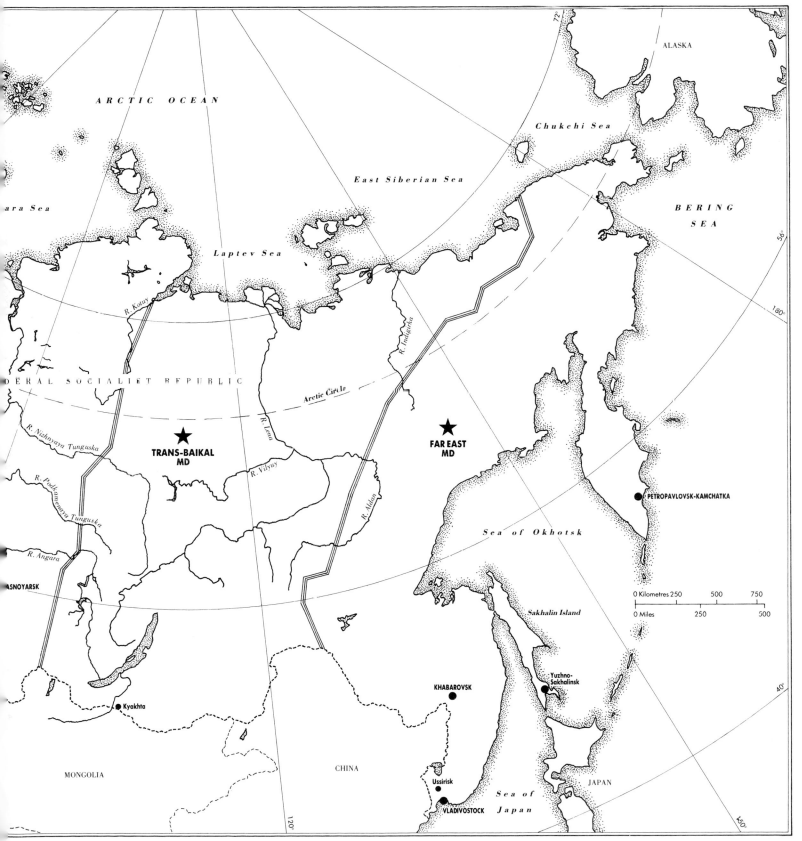

ALASKA

ARCTIC OCEAN

Chukchi Sea

East Siberian Sea

72°

B E R I N G

S E A

56°

Laptev Sea

R. Kotuy

180°

R. Indigirka

ara Sea

DERAL SOCIALIST REPUBLIC

Arctic Circle

R. Lena

R. Nizhnyaya Tunguska

★

**TRANS-BAIKAL
MD**

★

**FAR EAST
MD**

● **PETROPAVLOVSK-KAMCHATKA**

R. Podkamennaya Tunguska

R. Vilyuy

R. Aldan

Sea of Okhotsk

R. Angara

ASNOYARSK

| 0 Kilometres | 250 | 500 | 750 |

| 0 Miles | | 250 | 500 |

Sakhalin Island

Yuzhno-
Sakhalinsk
●

40°

● Kyakhta

KHABAROVSK
●

MONGOLIA

CHINA

Ussirisk
●

JAPAN

VLADIVOSTOCK
●

*Sea of
Japan*

120°

150°

INDEX